Journal of the Alamire Foundation

■

Journal of the Alamire Foundation

∎

Volume 5 - Number 1, Spring 2013

∎

General editors:
David Burn
Katelijne Schiltz

Journal of the Alamire Foundation

■

Volume 5 - Number 1, Spring 2013

BREPOLS

The *Journal of the Alamire Foundation* is published twice a year (spring and autumn)

- **General editors:**
  David Burn
  Katelijne Schiltz
- **Editorial board:**
  Barbara Haggh
  Christian Thomas Leitmeir
  Pedro Memelsdorff
  Klaus Pietschmann
  Dorit Tanay
  Giovanni Zanovello
- **Advisory board:**
  Bonnie J. Blackburn
  M. Jennifer Bloxam
  Anna Maria Busse-Berger
  Fabrice Fitch
  Sean Gallagher
  David Hiley
  Andrew Kirkman
  Karl Kügle
  John Milsom
  Emilio Ros-Fabregas
  Rudolf Rasch
  Thomas Schmidt-Beste
  Eugeen Schreurs
  Reinhard Strohm
  Philippe Vendrix
  Rob Wegman

- **Coordinator:**
  Stratton Bull
- **Music examples:**
  Vincent Besson
- **Music font:**
  Theodor Dumitrescu (CMME)

- **Subscriptions:**
  Brepols Publishers
  Begijnhof 67
  B-2300 Turnhout (Belgium)
  Tel.: +32 14448020
  Fax: +32 14428919
  periodicals@brepols.net

- **Submissions:**
  Journal of the Alamire Foundation
  c/o Prof. Dr. David Burn
  KU Leuven – Onderzoekseenheid
  Musicologie
  Mgr. Ladeuzeplein 21, bus 5591
  B-3000 Leuven (Belgium)
  jaf@alamirefoundation.be

  Submissions to the Journal can be sent at any time to the address listed above. For further information, including the Journal's style-sheet, see: http://www.alamirefoundation.org/en/publications/journal-alamire-foundation.

The Alamire Foundation was founded in 1991 as a collaborative venture between the Musicology Research Unit of the University of Leuven and Musica, Impulse Centre for Music. The organization is named after Petrus Alamire, one of the most important sixteenth-century music calligraphers. The Foundation aims to create an international platform for promoting research on music in or connected to the Low Countries from the earliest documents to the end of the Ancien Regime. The Foundation hopes especially to promote dialogue between the worlds of scholarship and performance. For more information, see: http://www.alamirefoundation.org/.

ISBN: 978-2-503-54679-7
ISSN: 2032-5371
D/2013/0095/47

Table of contents

■

Theme

■

Johannes Tinctoris I

Guest Editor: Ronald Woodley

Introduction

■

RONALD WOODLEY

To celebrate the 500th anniversary of the death of Johannes Tinctoris, two sessions of papers devoted to the work and career of this seminal figure of fifteenth-century music theory were held at the 2011 Medieval and Renaissance Music Conference in Barcelona. Interweaving compositional and notational theory with issues of performance, biography, music education, and Tinctoris's wider intellectual grounding, these sessions became the springboard for the present issue of this Journal, which presents more fully worked versions of some of these papers and picks up other threads of current Tinctoris research.

Although the significance of Tinctoris's writings has been, to a greater or lesser extent, appreciated for a long time—in the modern age, at least since the late eighteenth century—the scholarly and musical manifestations of that appreciation have, frankly, often been fairly superficial, using his life and texts either for purposes of dubious historical self-justification, for the riding of various musico-political hobby-horses, or for simplistic, under-contextualized or box-ticking referencing of individual theoretical and notational points. Recently, though, especially through the work of scholars such as Margaret Bent and Bonnie J. Blackburn, a much more nuanced and fine-grained approach is being achieved, especially with regard to the relationship between the detail of the theory and the creative, compositional or performative processes which that theory is—for all its problematics of language, history, and genre—attempting to articulate. Of course, Tinctoris was himself no mediocre composer, and Jeffrey Dean's reappraisal of the notational and compositional detail of the theorist's excellent four-voice *L'homme armé* mass shows how structural music analysis and a forensic examination of the work's unique source, Cappella Sistina Ms. 35, combined with close reading of Tinctoris's own Latin writings, can help reveal the major flaws in the surviving text of the mass. The Tenor part in two sections of the work is here shown to be an unsatisfactory rewriting by an unknown hand of the apparently lost original, and the groundwork is set by Dean for a potential new reconstruction of the work which accords more accurately with the mensural framework of the cantus firmus envisaged by the composer.

Tinctoris spent a good twenty years—in terms of his surviving written output, by far the most productive period of his life—working at the Aragonese court of King Ferrante (Ferdinand I) in Naples from perhaps the early 1470s to the early 1490s. In making this move from his familial and educational roots in Brabant, and from his university and early teaching career in the Loire Valley, he threw himself into a radically different cultural and intellectual environment. Exactly *how* radically different, though, is still the subject for ongoing debate, as is the level of genuine commitment to the ideals of Italian humanism that Tinctoris may or may not be overtly demonstrating in his writings. Nevertheless, it is indisputable—even if hard evidence is still tantalizingly sparse—that in Naples, as on his likely travels around other centres of Italian culture at this time, he would have rubbed up against many influential proponents of the new thinking and the new artistic principles. Evan MacCarthy is at the forefront of current research exploring how Tinctoris may have been involved in these complex social, intellectual, and institutional dynamics, including the still rather shadowy Studio or University of Naples, whose reputation in legal studies may have contributed to Tinctoris's decision to join Ferrante's court. In his work MacCarthy is managing to unpeel complex layers of relationship between individuals, groups, written works, and formal and informally constituted bodies of thinkers, in ways that some of us have long suspected were worth probing more deeply, but have never quite managed before to pull together. His article here is a fine demonstration that Tinctoris research, and humanistic musicology in a broader sense, is in safe hands with the upcoming younger generation of scholars.

By contrast, I have busied myself for perhaps too long, over the years, with aspects of Tinctoris's biography that may never reveal themselves adequately. That said, unexpected successes do occasionally emerge: I have tried here to make some sense of a repository of new archival documents rediscovered in Tinctoris's home town of Braine-l'Alleud, to piece together a provisional outline of his family background, and how this may have shaped the trajectory of the parallel musical and legal careers that seem to have run through a large part of his professional life.

Fundamentally, though, it is the treatises themselves that matter. The history of their publication in modern times has been somewhat chequered, and the story of their dissemination and readership in earlier times is still largely to be written. But one hopefully significant step in the direction of a proper, comprehensive evaluation of Tinctoris's work is a new online project, funded from 2011 to 2014 by the Arts and Humanities Research Council of the United Kingdom, which will establish new texts and translations of all the treatises, along with multi-layered technical, historical, and critical commentary material. Shortly to be released in its first stage of development as a freely accessible resource on the Early Music Theory website (http://www.earlymusictheory.org), the project is under the editorial leadership of Ronald Woodley and Jeffrey Dean; the technical development is being steered by David Lewis, who gives here, in the Forum section of this issue, an overview of some of the main technological decisions involved in the initial planning and implementation of the project. But the world of digital humanities is a fast-moving one, and by the time this issue appears, it is highly likely that some aspects of the user interface, and the linked technical/editorial decisions underpinning the presentation of the new edition, will have been further modified and improved. This is a positive symptom, though, of the fact that we are just at the right moment—a mere 500 years after the man's death—to catch the rising wave of both the musicological and technological advances in how Tinctoris's work can be explored to something closer to its full potential. Of such advances we hope that this special quincentenary issue can offer a first snapshot.

Towards a Restoration of Tinctoris's *L'homme armé* Mass: Coherence, Mensuration, *Varietas*

■

Johannes Tinctoris was not only a great theorist of music, he was an outstanding composer, responsible for at least six mass ordinary settings and an important early set of Lamentations as well as a host of small-scale pieces. The most impressive of these compositions is his *L'homme armé* mass.[1] A just appreciation and understanding of the composer's achievement in this work has been hindered, however, by a failure to realize that the music we have is not entirely by Tinctoris. His mass was damaged early on, and it was repaired by a musician who did not know what the composer had written and did not grasp what he had intended. It is my purpose here to demonstrate the damage by displaying Tinctoris's intention, and to lay the foundations for a more satisfactory restoration of the mass and for future study of it.

It is universally acknowledged that Tinctoris's *L'homme armé* mass must exemplify *varietas*, a rhetorical and ethical concept that the composer extolled towards the end of his treatise on counterpoint, citing Horace, Cicero, and Aristotle in support.[2] Some have judged the effort favourably: Gustave Reese wrote, 'Tinctoris treats the *cantus firmus* with considerable liberty and applies successfully, throughout the Mass and in all voices, his own rule regarding the desirability of variety.'[3] More recently, Reinhard Strohm has written, 'An ambitious masterpiece is the "L'homme armé" Mass…by Johannes Tinctoris, in which all the artifices of the tradition are put together: canons, transpositions, augmentations…In a word, Tinctoris tries to carry out as a composer what he advocates as a theorist: variety'.[4]

Others have been less generous: Manfred Bukofzer called Tinctoris's mass 'a bewildering work, full of absorbing and subtle detail, but lacking a broad line in its

---

[1] Unique source: Vatican City, Biblioteca Apostolica Vaticana, Ms. Cappella Sistina 35 (hereafter C.S. 35), fols. lxiij^v-lxxxij^r (85v-104v). Edited in Johannes Tinctoris, *Missa super L'homme armé*, ed. Laurence Feininger, Monumenta Polyphoniae Liturgicae Sanctae Ecclesiae Romanae, ser. 1, vol. 1, fasc. 9 (Rome, 1948); *Johanni [sic] Tinctoris Opera omnia*, ed. William Melin, Corpus Mensurabilis Musicae 18 (n.p., 1976), 74-114.

[2] *Liber de arte contrapuncti* (hereafter *De arte contr.*), book 3, ch. 8 (hereafter in the form III.viii): Edmond de Coussemaker (ed.), *Scriptores de musica medii aevi: nova series a Gerbertina altera*, 4 vols. (Paris, 1864-76; repr., Hildesheim et al., 1987), vol. 4, 152 (hereafter CS IV); *Johannis Tinctoris Opera theoretica*, ed. Albert Seay, 2 vols. in 3, Corpus scriptorum de musica 22 (n.p., 1975), vol. 2, 155-56 (hereafter Seay II). Quotations below correspond exactly to neither edition, having been collated with the manuscript sources and adopting their usage of 'e' to represent the classical 'ae' used by both Coussemaker and Seay. On *varietas*, see particularly Sean Thomas Patrick Gallagher, 'Models of *Varietas*: Studies in Style and Attribution in the Motets of Johannes Regis and his Contemporaries' (Ph.D. diss., Harvard University, 1998), esp. ch. 2, 'Tinctoris and the Concept of *Varietas* in the Fifteenth Century', 39-78; Alexis Luko, 'Tinctoris on *Varietas*', in *Early Music History* 27 (2008), 99-136.

[3] Gustave Reese, *Music in the Renaissance*, rev. ed. (New York, 1959), 149.

[4] Reinhard Strohm, *The Rise of European Music, 1380-1500* (Cambridge, 1993), 469. Maria Caraci, 'Fortuna del tenor "L'homme armé" nel primo Rinascimento', in *Nuova rivista musicale italiana* 9 (1975), 171-204, also with a positive view, is quoted below.

10.1484/J.JAF.1.103261   *JOURNAL OF THE ALAMIRE FOUNDATION* 5 (2013) ■ 11

formal design'.[5] Two scholars have elaborated on this observation in ways that are worth quoting at length; with a couple of important exceptions to which I shall come later, they are the fullest and most insightful treatments of this mass that have been published. Edgar Sparks wrote,

> two opposing tendencies coëxist in the 'Northern' style. Ockeghem is the chief representative of the irrational, or fanciful tendency, Busnois of the rational, or formalistic...A thorough mixture of the characteristic traits of the two tendencies is presented by the *Missa L'homme armé* of Tinctoris. The famous theorist, connoisseur, and admirer of Ockeghem, Busnois, and Regis creates a work in which there is a wilderness of effects...In the lack of a simple plan, of a dominant structural voice, or of any regular method of c[antus-]f[irmus] treatment, the Mass belongs to the irrational school of thought as surely as do any of Ockeghem. Yet, it goes beyond Faugues or Busnois in the use of devices which are especially favoured by the rationalists...Tinctoris, without doubt, is following his own recommendation that a composer make use of all artifices in a large composition such as a Mass, but the effect, on the whole, is rather jumbled. Even at this distance in time it is possible to detect in this Mass the work of an eclectic, of a man who is aware of all the current developments and who is making a conscious attempt to combine them in his writing. The contrasting elements which are brought together in this work are found also in the works of Josquin, but there they are combined much more successfully and on a much higher musical plane.[6]

Judith Cohen writes,

> There is no central device in this mass and no general plan; even motto openings are absent. Although the c.f. is divided up into natural parts...its treatment varies from strict c.f. techniques to free ones. His favourite device is to start conventionally and then switch over to the most unexpected techniques, such as juxtaposition, paraphrasing and eventually even a gradual or complete disappearance of the c.f. No attempt is made at planning on a large scale: no canon scaffolding, no piling-up towards the end (increase of voices, c.f.-inversion, etc.). Unlike Ockeghem's masses, which use similar procedures, the abundance of varying techniques creates no sense of intensification or an impression of the composer's brilliant command of his means. This mass applies the rule of *varietas* to its own detriment...[A] glance at the three *sine nomine* masses by Tinctoris suffices to show that in these compositions he is less of an eclectic, though he shows no less originality in handling his material.[7]

I hope what I have to show here may temper some of the harshness of these appraisals.[8]

5   Manfred Bukofzer, review of *Monumenta Polyphoniae Liturgicae*, ser. i, vol. 1, fasc. 4-10, ed. Laurence Feininger (Rome, 1948), in *The Musical Quarterly* 36 (1950), 307-9 at 309.
6   Edgar H. Sparks, *Cantus Firmus in Mass and Motet, 1420-1520* (Berkeley and Los Angeles, 1963), 239-41.
7   Judith Cohen, 'Munus ab ignoto', in *Studia Musicologica Academiae Scientiarum Hungaricae* 22 (1980), 187-204 at 197-98.
8   A note on terminology: I prefer to use the word 'tenor' to refer to a pre-existing melody used as the basis for a polyphonic composition. The more familiar 'cantus firmus' employed by the writers quoted was not yet in use in Tinctoris's time, and it strictly denotes plainchant, not a secular tune like 'L'homme armé'; and 'cantus prius factus' as a technical term is even more anachronistic. I capitalize 'Tenor' along with all the other names of voice-parts (normally 'Discantus', 'Contratenor', and 'Bassus', except as distinctively named in a source), using 'tenor' in lowercase for the pre-existing melody. Tinctoris's preferred designation for the highest part of a polyphonic complex, which most other musicians of the time called 'Discantus', was 'Supremum'; it is so indicated in the instruction for a canonic Contratenor in his

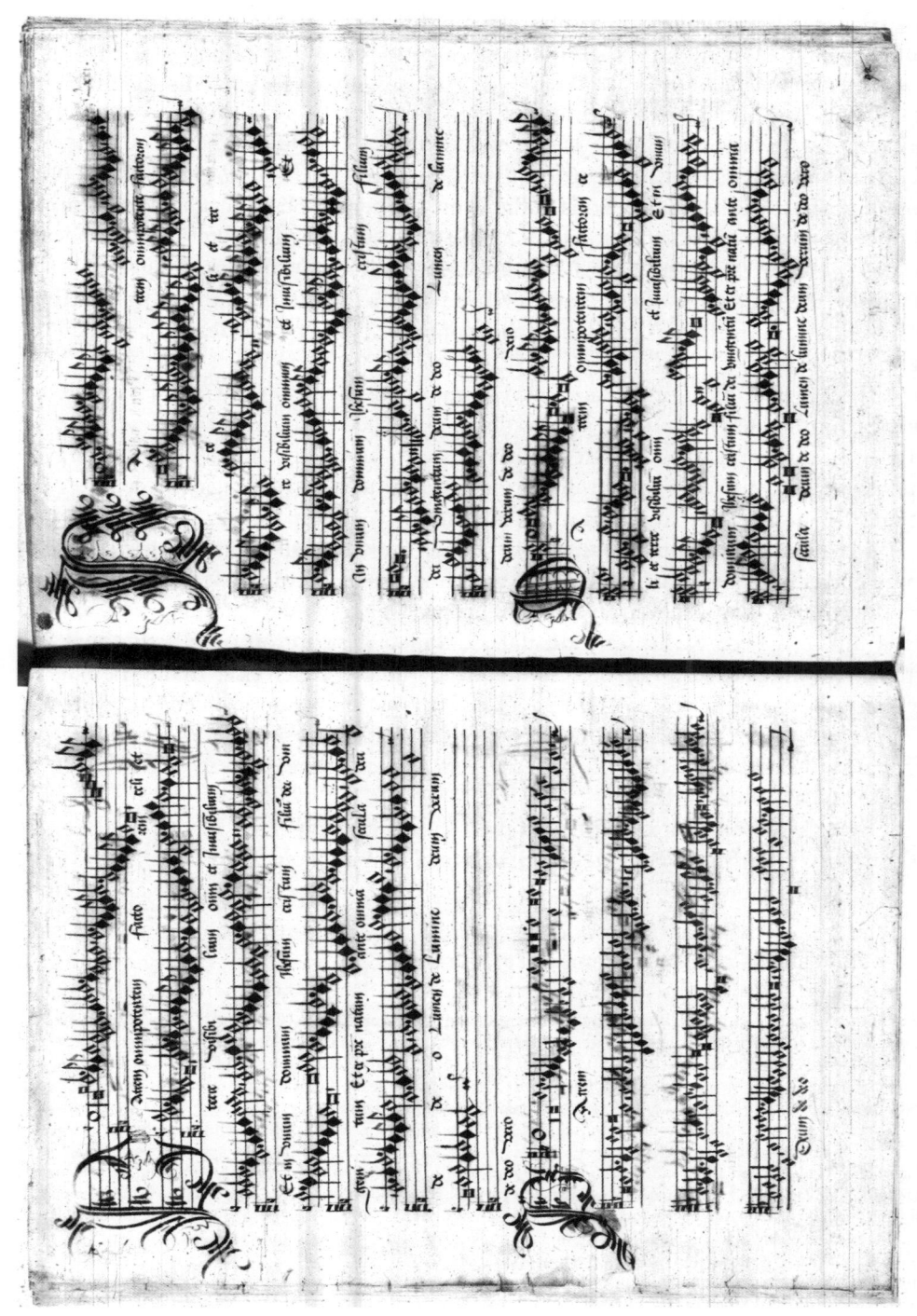

Figure 1. C.S 35, fols. lxxii^v–lxxii^r (92v–93r). Tinctoris, mass *L'homme armé*, beginning of 'Patrem', showing hands of Scribe 35 and the Tenor Scribe.

Photo copyright 2012, Biblioteca Apostolica Vaticana

Tinctoris's *L'homme armé* mass has come down to us in a single source, the manuscript C.S. 35. The core of this choirbook was a collection of settings of the ordinary of the mass (to which some other pieces were soon added), copied for the singers of the papal chapel by a single scribe (whom I designate as 'Scribe 35') during the year 1489.[9] The exemplar from which Scribe 35 copied Tinctoris's *L'homme armé* into C.S. 35 was defective: it was missing the Tenor part in the 'Et in terra' and 'Patrem' subsections (though not in the other subsections of the Gloria in between). I infer that the exemplar must have been in separate parts on loose leaves, a couple of which were lost.[10] The lack was made good by a different copyist (whom I call 'the Tenor Scribe') not long afterwards, probably at the beginning of the 1490s. Figure 1 shows the first opening of the 'Patrem': the Tenor part, in the lower-left-hand quadrant, was copied by the Tenor Scribe, all the rest by Scribe 35.

There is no indication in Laurence Feininger's 1948 edition of Tinctoris's *L'homme armé*, the ninth of ten *L'homme armé* masses he published in separate fascicles that year,[11] that the Tenor part in two subsections had been added by a different scribe; the annotations give only canonic inscriptions and manuscript readings corrected in the edition. It is more surprising to find no mention in William Melin's 'Critical notes' to his 1976 edition in Tinctoris's *Opera omnia*, since he does call attention to a couple of minute corrections by a third hand in 'Kyrie' I and 'Benedictus'.[12] Melin ought to have paid attention to an observation in Franz Xaver Haberl's 1888 catalogue of Cappella Sistina music, where within an unusually detailed description of C.S. 35 there is a particularly minute description of Tinctoris's mass: among much else, 'In the "Et in terra" and "Patrem" the third voice is textless'.[13] Feininger actually had noticed the change of hand: he had earlier transcribed this mass (along with thousands of other pieces) for personal study, and at the beginning of the Tenor voice in the 'Patrem' stands the note, 'III added by another hand'.[14]

The first definite notice in print of the Tenor Scribe appeared in 1988, in the entry on C.S. 35 in the *Census-Catalogue of Manuscript Sources of Polyphonic Music, 1400-1550*: 'Six additional scribes, as follows: ...(2) added individual voices to several Mass sections

---

L'homme armé mass, C.S. 35, fol. lxxiii[r] (95r): 'Et incarnatus ut suppremum Iuxta Canonem' ('"Et incarnatus" like the Supremum, according to the canon'), and frequently in the voice labels of examples for more than two parts in *De arte contr.* I.v, x, xv, II.xxiii: CS IV, 85, 97, 111, [135]; Seay II, 27, 49, 74, 122 (all other top voices are unlabelled). See also Joannes Tinctoris, *Terminorum musicae diffinitorium* ([Treviso]: [Gerardus de Lisa], 1495; repr., Monuments of Music and Music Literature in Facsimile 2/26 New York, 1966), entry 'Supremum'.

9   For a detailed inventory of C.S. 35 and discussion of its preparation, see Adalbert Roth, 'Die Entstehung des ältesten Chorbuches mit polyphoner Musik der päpstlichen Kapelle: Città del Vaticano, Biblioteca Apostolica Vaticana, Fondo Cappella Sistina, Ms. 35', in *Gestalt und Entstehung musikalischer Quellen im 15. und 16. Jahrhundert*, ed. Martin Staehelin, Quellenstudien zur Musik der Renaissance 3 (Wiesbaden, 1998), 43-63. I am preparing an article, provisionally entitled 'Music Copying at the Papal Chapel before 1497, part 1: The 1480s', in which I reassess the conclusions Roth has drawn about C.S. 35, including his longer span (1487-91) for the production of the *Hauptkorpus*.

10   I shall elaborate the argument in 'Music Copying: The 1480s'.

11   Tinctoris, *Missa super L'homme armé*; the other masses were those of Dufay, Busnois, Caron, Faugues, Regis, Okeghem, De Orto, Basiron, and Vaqueras.

12   Tinctoris, *Opera omnia*, xii.

13   Franz X. Haberl, *Bibliographischer und thematischer Musikkatalog des päpstlichen Kapellarchives im Vatikan zu Rom*, Bausteine für Musikgeschichte 2 (Leipzig, 1888; repr. Hildesheim etc., 1971), 15: 'Im "Et in terra" und "Patrem" ist die dritte Stimme ohne Text'.

14   Laurence Feininger, transcr., *Missarum liber IV* (Rome, Ponticio Instituto di Musica Sacra, Ms. 4799.4), fol. 145v: 'III nachträglich von anderer Hand'. There is no corresponding note in the 'Et in terra', however.

copied by main scribe, on ff. 88', 89', 92', 93', and 121' '.[15] That information was cited from Adalbert Roth's 1982 doctoral dissertation, which was focused on the earlier two-volume choirbook C.S. 14/51; most of Roth's findings on C.S. 35 did not appear in the published version of his dissertation (1991), but rather in 1998 as a separate, most valuable article in a volume of conference proceedings.[16] Here Roth made explicit the presence of the additions as being in Tinctoris's *L'homme armé*, though only very briefly, in a tabular appendix. Finally, in 2005, Jennifer Bernard (now Merkowitz), then a composition student at the University of Cincinnati, published a very intelligent and imaginative article (the single fullest treatment referred to above) in which for the first time a researcher came to grips with the implications of these Tenor parts' having been added to a copy of Tinctoris's mass that lacked them.[17]

Bernard did not question the authenticity of the added Tenor parts. Why should she? They had passed the scrutiny of two careful editors and a good many knowledgeable and perceptive investigators, besides those quoted above.[18] It had never occurred to anyone that the Tenor parts were not by the composer, and Bernard was brave enough to suggest, 'Could Tinctoris...have been that "additional scribe", adding missing parts...?', on the occasion of his inferred contact with the papal chapel in December 1492.[19]

My own research became focused on Tinctoris's *L'homme armé* with a reason to wonder about the authenticity of the added Tenor parts. I had been transcribing Philippe Basiron's *L'homme armé* mass, also uniquely preserved in C.S. 35, and had discovered for myself that a different hand had entered the Tenor voice of 'Agnus' III, on the last opening of the mass. Roth had identified this as the only occurrence outside Tinctoris's *L'homme armé* of the Tenor Scribe (whose hand has not been recognized in any other manuscript), and indeed here too Feininger had annotated his personal transcription, 'Added by another hand', although there is no hint in his published edition.[20] I was able

[15] Charles Hamm and Herbert Kellman (eds.), *Census-Catalogue of Manuscript Sources of Polyphonic Music, 1400-1550*, 5 vols., Renaissance Manuscript Studies 1 (Neuhausen-Stuttgart, 1979-88), vol. 4, 41-42.

[16] Adalbert Roth, 'Studien zum frühen Repertoire der päpstlichen Kapelle unter dem Pontifikat Sixtus' IV. (1471-84): Die Chorbücher 14 und 51 des Fondo Cappella Sistina der Bibliotheca Apostolica Vaticana' (Ph.D. diss., J.-W. Goethe-Universität, 1982); Adalbert Roth, *Studien zum frühen Repertoire der päpstlichen Kapelle unter dem Pontifikat Sixtus' IV. (1471-84): Die Chorbücher 14 und 51 des Fondo Cappella Sistina der Bibliotheca Apostolica Vaticana*, Capellae Apostolicae Sixtinaeque Collectanea, Acta, Monumenta 1 (Vatican City, 1991); Roth, 'Die Entstehung', esp. p. 56, 'Kopist CS 35 H'. The note '93v, Syst. ? (CTA), Korrektur?' should read '94v, Syst. 1 (CTA), Korrektur' ('staff 1 [contratenor altus], correction').

[17] Jennifer Bernard, 'Tinctoris's Missa L'homme armé: Music and Context', in *Music Research Forum* 20 (2005), 1-22, esp. 15-19. I am grateful to Stephanie Schlagel for making a copy of this article (hard to obtain in Britain) available to me.

[18] Three further studies worth signalling are Caraci, 'Fortuna del tenor "L'homme armé"'; Walter Haaß, *Studien zu den 'L'homme armé'-Messen des 15. und 16. Jahrhunderts*, Kölner Beiträge zur Musikforschung 136 (Regensburg, 1984), 53-141 passim; Theodor Dumitrescu, 'Leading Tones in *Cantus Firmi* and the Early *L'homme armé* Tradition', in *Studi musicali* 31 (2002), 17-55.

[19] Bernard, 'Tinctoris's Missa L'homme armé', 15. Unbeknownst to her, Richard Sherr had made the same suggestion (while being more cautious about the date) in 1989: 'Diskussion' following John Bergsagel, 'Tinctoris and the Vatican manuscripts Cappella Sistina 14, 51 and 35', in *Studien zur Geschichte der päpstlichen Kapelle: Tagungsbericht Heidelberg 1989*, ed. Bernhard Janz, Capellae Apostolicae Sixtinaeque Collectanea, Acta, Monumenta 4; Collectanea 2 (Vatican City, 1994), 497-527 at 523. The notice in *Johannis Burckardi Liber notarum ab anno MCCCCLXXIII usque ad annum MDVI*, ed. Enrico Celani, 2 vols., Rerum italicarum scriptores 32 (Città di Castello, 1906-13), vol. 1, 376, of a motet, *Gaude Roma vetus*, intended to be sung by the papal singers (at the instigation of Cardinal Ascanio Sforza) on 9 December 1492, actually states only that Tinctoris wrote the words ('Epigramma Joannis Tinctoris, legum doctoris atque musici'); it does not explicitly say that he composed the music or that he was present.

[20] Roth, 'Die Entstehung', 56 (I am grateful to Richard Sherr for bringing this to my attention); Laurence Feininger, transcr., *Missarum liber III* (Rome, Pontificio Instituto di Musica Sacra, Ms. 4799.3), fol. 180v: 'Nachträglich von anderer Hand'; Philippe Basiron, *Missa super L'homme armé*, ed. Laurence Feininger, Monumenta Polyphoniae Liturgicae

Table 1. Tinctoris, *L'homme armé*: tenor layout, mensurations, and proportions

Kyrie I

```
  O ————————————   ————III————
† C  IIII   223333  ²₁5555881112333
  O ————22————————   ————————
  O IIII22————————   ————————
```

Christe

```
  C          223333——     666666      IIIII333——
  C          223333333666666    ————————   II——
  C IIIIIIII              ————————   22——3—333
  C ————————         ————————  88888——
```

Kyrie II

```
  C  IIII22————————   ————III————
  C  IIII—22333   55555555888————————   ——
  C  IIII   223333   ————————  IIII   223333
  C  ————————   ————1122333————
```

Et in terra

```
  O IIII22333   ————————————————————————————————————
  O IIII2—33333————————————————————————————   666   6668888
  O            IIIII   2233333   555  22 ————   1122333223333 *
  O            ————————————————————————
```

Qui tollis

```
  C 5555555       888888   IIIIIII   ————————————————————55555——
  C      5555555——   ————   ————————————————  5555555——
  C  ————   ————————————   2233333  IIIIIIII  222333333——————————  8888888
  C  ————————————————   22—————   ————————————  55555——  ——
```

Cum sancto spiritu

```
  C ————————22——C²₃——   ————————————————
  C IIII      22333C²₃3——   ——   ————————
  C ————————  22—C²₃————   ————————
  C IIII  ————222——C²₃————————————————
```

Patrem

```
  O    IIIII————————   ————————   ————————————————
  O ————————   ————————   ————————————
  O ——2223333————————   ————————————   IIIII 2223333 *
  O ————————————   ————————   ————————————
```

Et incarnatus est

```
  C IIIII222233336666666688811111223333
  C IIIII222233336666666688811111223333 (fuga)
  C ————————————————————————
  C ————————————————————————
```

Et resurrexit

```
  C ————————————   666666   ————————————————
  C ————————————————6666688888————————   ————————
  C ————   ————   ————————IIIIII222333333333——————
  C IIIIII 22223333333   ————————   222————————  ——  ——
```

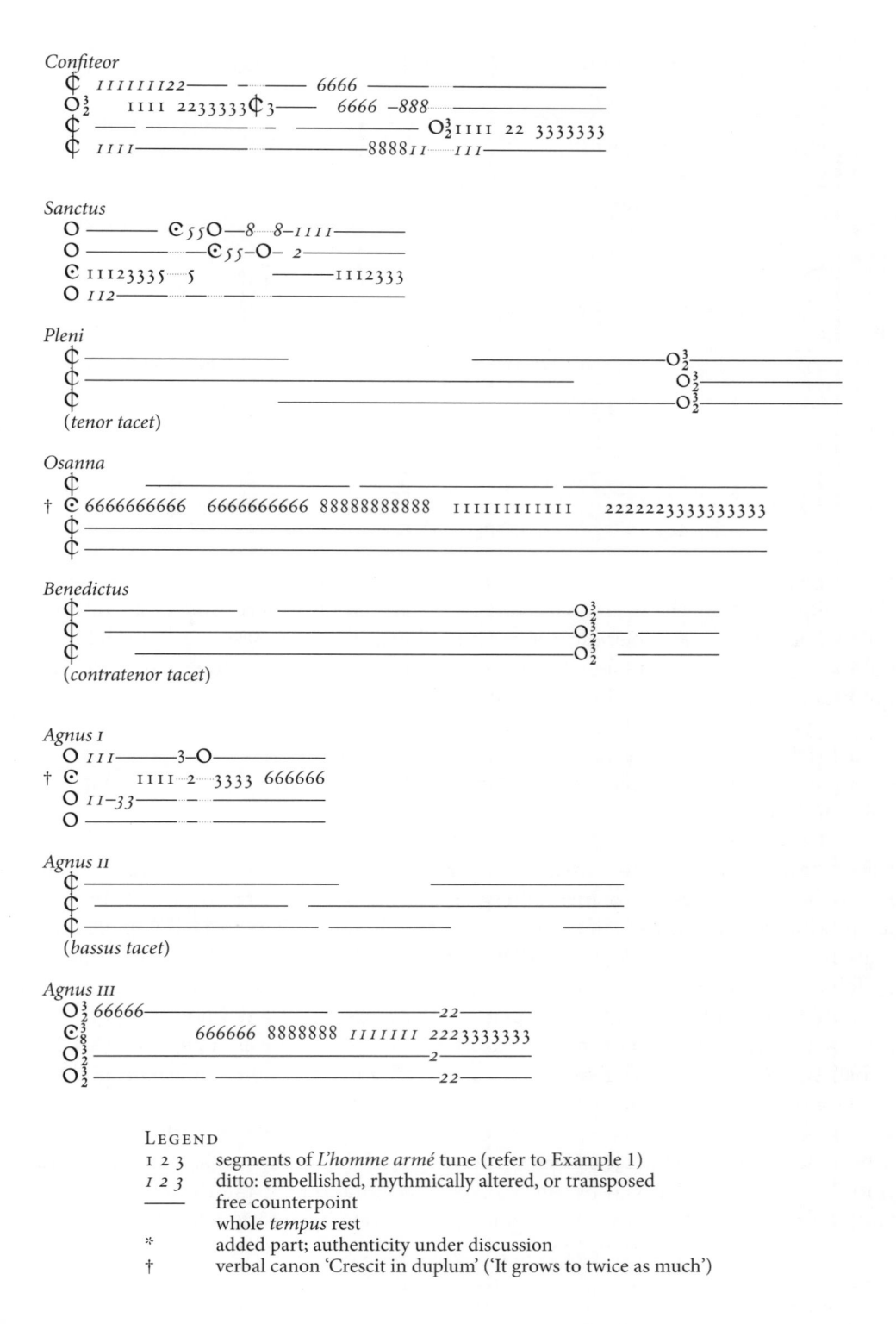

LEGEND

1 2 3	segments of *L'homme armé* tune (refer to Example 1)
1 2 3	ditto: embellished, rhythmically altered, or transposed
——	free counterpoint
	whole *tempus* rest
*	added part; authenticity under discussion
†	verbal canon 'Crescit in duplum' ('It grows to twice as much')

Example 1. Key to melodic segments of 'L'homme armé'

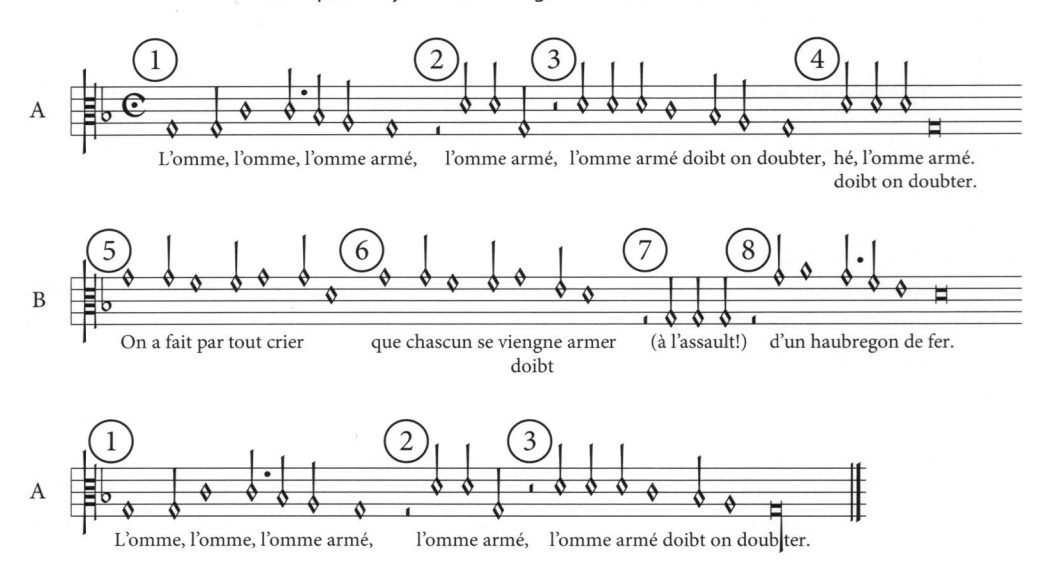

L'omme, l'omme, l'omme armé,   l'omme armé, l'omme armé doibt on doubter, hé, l'omme armé.
doibt on doubter.

On a fait par tout crier   que chascun se viengne armer   (à l'assault!)   d'un haubregon de fer.
doibt

L'omme, l'omme, l'omme armé,   l'omme armé,   l'omme armé doibt on doub|ter.

to demonstrate that the added Tenor in Basiron's mass could not have been written by the composer: there is an uncharacteristic contrapuntal progression in an internal cadence, and the overall melodic design varies drastically from Basiron's style, failing to outline the modal fifth and fourth and implying an F-*ut* tonality rather than G-*re*. This predisposed me to be cautious about accepting the added Tenors in Tinctoris's mass as the composer's own. I could detect no obvious faults of counterpoint or melodic style (which I hope might have raised the suspicions of my predecessors), so I chose to examine whether the manner of employment of the 'L'homme armé' tenor might shed light on the question.

Tinctoris's usage of the 'L'homme armé' tenor turned out to be a highly effective test of the authenticity of the added Tenor parts in his 'Et in terra' and 'Patrem'. In Table 1 I have charted the presence of melodic segments from the 'L'homme armé' tune in every *tempus* (breve-unit or 'bar') of each part in every section of Tinctoris's *L'homme armé* mass as it is preserved in C.S. 35. Example 1 is a musical key to the numbering of segments in Table 1; it deserves a little comment of its own. The melody shown in Example 1 is a construct, showing every melodic segment that appears in any known polyphonic setting as well as the overall melodic form. It does not occur as such in any setting (whether mass or any other genre), and I do *not* offer it as any kind of ideal or model of the monophonic 'L'homme armé' tune; it is a key to the analysis of the tune in all its surviving versions but is not equivalent to any of them. I believe the earlier settings of 'L'homme armé', up to the 1480s, demonstrate a variability of form characteristic of oral tradition (a view reinforced by alternative representations of the rhythm as perfect tempus or major prolation, and by the variability of tonality in early settings), which has

Sanctae Ecclesiae Romanae, ser. 1, vol. 1, fasc. 8 (Rome, 1948). I am preparing an article on Basiron's *L'homme armé*, mass and its consequences. Jeffrey J. Dean, 'Two Wounded Soldiers: *L'homme armé*, Basiron, Tinctoris—and Laurence Feininger', in *I codici musicali trentini del Quattrocento: Nuove scoperte, nuove edizioni e nuovi strumenti informatici*, ed. Danilo Curti-Feininger and Marco Gozzi (Trent, 2013), 89-100 at 91-92 offers a condensed account of this; pp. 92-95 are abridged from the present article, pp. 11-25.

not been adequately addressed in research on the 'L'homme armé' tradition up to now.[21] In particular, the tune as represented in the tenor of the sixth 'Naples' mass, 1 2 3 4 / 5 5 8 / 1 2 3,[22] has no more authority than other versions. For example, Johannes Regis's very early *L'homme armé* mass 'Dum sacrum mysterium' implies a longer version of the tune, 1 2 2 3 4 / 5 6 7 8 / 1 2 2 3, and the tune as used by Frémin le Caron had a much more abbreviated return, 1 2 2 3 / 5 5 8 / 2 3.[23] Tinctoris's mass is based on a version of 'L'homme armé' that was more symmetrical than Caron's, and provides the earliest instance of what became the normal form in the sixteenth century: 1 2 3 / 6 6 8 / 1 2 3, often giving the B section as 5 5 8 instead.

To be confident we are considering what Tinctoris intended, we must disregard for the moment the two suspect subsections, 'Et in terra' and 'Patrem', and examine the fifteen remaining subsections. The diagram of tenor usage in Table 1 clearly shows one striking pattern. The 'L'homme armé' tune is almost constantly present to the ears. Sometimes it is plain, sometimes embellished, sometimes rhythmically altered, sometimes transposed; sometimes it lies chiefly in one voice, sometimes in another, sometimes simultaneously in two or three.[24] But there are only two kinds of places where 'L'homme armé' cannot be heard for more than more than a few tempora.[25] One of these is in the subsections that are conventionally composed for fewer voices without the tenor: 'Pleni', 'Benedictus', and 'Agnus' II (in Tinctoris's mass these are all for three voices, and it is respectively the Tenor, Contratenor, and Bassus that are silent). The

[21] See, for instance, one of the more recent treatments of the subject: Alejandro Enrique Planchart, 'The Origins and Early History of "L'homme armé"', in *The Journal of Musicology* 20 (2003), 305-57. Richard Taruskin, 'Antoine Busnoys and the *L'homme armé* Tradition', in *Journal of the American Musicological Society* 39 (1986), 255-93, remains extremely influential. I hope to elaborate on this matter in a future publication.

[22] Given as the reference melody by Bernard, 'Tinctoris's Missa L'homme armé', 2, and by many other scholars. The first five *L'homme armé* masses in Naples, Biblioteca Nazionale Vittorio Emanuelle III, Ms. VI E 40 (copied in Burgundy, c. 1470) are based on verbal subdivisions (not melodic segments) of the 'L'homme armé' tune, used in its entirety as tenor of the sixth mass; the whole cycle is edited in Auctor ignotus, *Missa I[-VI] super L'homme armé*, ed. Laurence Feininger, 6 fascs., Monumenta Polyphoniae Liturgicae Sanctae Ecclesiae Romanae, ser. 1, vol. 3, fascs. 1-6 (Rome, 1957-74); *Six anonymous 'L'homme armé' masses in Naples, Biblioteca Nazionale, MS VI E 40*, ed. Judith Cohen, Corpus Mensurabilis Musicae 85 (Neuhausen-Stuttgart, 1981). Some have even treated this Tenor part as if it were a notation of the monophonic song: Reinhard Strohm, *Music in Late Medieval Bruges*, rev. edn. (Oxford, 1990), 129; Strohm, *The Rise of European Music*, 468; Michael Long, '*Arma virumque cano*: Echoes of a Golden Age', in *Antoine Busnoys: Method, Meaning, and Context in Late Medieval Music*, ed. Paula Higgins (Oxford, 1999), 133-54 at 151; Planchart, 'The Origins and Early History', 306-7.

[23] Johannes Regis, *Missa super L'homme armé*, ed. Laurence Feininger, Monumenta Polyphoniae Liturgicae Sanctae Ecclesiae Romanae, ser. 1, vol. 1, fasc. 5 (Rome, 1948); *Johannis Regis Opera omnia*, ed. Cornelis Lindenburg, 2 vols., Corpus Mensurabilis Musicae 9 (Rome, 1956), 1-24. Firminus Caron, *Missa super L'homme armé*, ed. Laurence Feininger, Monumenta Polyphoniae Liturgicae Sanctae Ecclesiae Romanae, ser. 1, vol. 1, fasc. 3 (Rome, 1948); *Les œuvres complètes de Philippe(?) Caron*, ed. James Thomson, 2 vols. (Brooklyn, 1971), vol. 2, 100-37. On the form of Caron's name, see Rob C. Wegman, 'Fremin le Caron at Amiens: New documents', in *Essays on Renaissance Music in Honour of David Fallows: Bon jour, bon mois et bon estrenne*, ed. Fabrice Fitch and Jacobijn Kiel, Studies in Medieval and Renaissance Music 11 (Woodbridge, 2011), 10-32.

[24] I wrote this sentence as spontaneous description, but noticed before I had finished it how strongly it resembles a famous sentence in Tinctoris's encomium of *varietas* in *De arte contr.* III.viii (CS IV, 152; Seay II, 155), 'Hanc autem diversitatem optimi quisque ingenii compositor aut concentor efficiet, si nunc per unam quantitatem, nunc per aliam, nunc per unam perfectionem, nunc per aliam, nunc per unam proporcionem, nunc per aliam, nunc per unam coniunctionem, nunc per aliam, nunc cum syncopis, nunc sine syncopis, nunc cum fugis, nunc sine fugis, nunc cum pausis, nunc sine pausis, nunc diminutive, nunc plane, aut componat aut concinat' ('Any really clever composer or improviser [upon a tenor] will bring about this diversity if he composes or improvises now by one mensuration, now by another, now by one kind of cadence, now by another, now by one proportion, now by another, now by one kind of melodic interval, now by another, now with syncopations, now without syncopations, now with *fugae*, now without *fugae*, now with rests, now without rests, now melodically embellished, now plain.')

[25] The longest tenor silence is 'Et resurrexit', tempora 19-24, a span comparable to three tempora in O, the mensuration of 'Et in terra' and 'Patrem'.

other is at the end of 'Cum sancto spiritu' and 'Et resurrexit', where Tinctoris has cast the ending music as a tenor-free coda (in the former case to the Gloria as a whole, hence its greater length).

This alone is sufficient to show that Tinctoris could not have composed the added Tenor of the 'Patrem'. As it stands, the subsection presents the music of the A section of 'L'homme armé' at the very beginning and the very end, but none at all of the tune in between. In the light of all the music copied by Scribe 35, I am positive this is not what Tinctoris intended. The 'Et in terra' has been better repaired (perhaps by a different composer than the 'Patrem'), and in particular the witty procedure at the end, where the B section of the tune in the Contratenor is presented simultaneously with the A section in the added Tenor,[26] probably represents Tinctoris's intention very accurately if fortuitously. But the 'Et in terra' is still defective: the tenor-free interlude in the third quarter of the subsection is without parallel in the unquestioned subsections of the mass,[27] and I cannot accept the tenor usage in tempora 27-32. In no other subsection of the mass did Tinctoris employ both melodic segments 5 (tempora 27-29 in the added Tenor) and 6 (tempora 50-57 in the Contratenor), but always used one or the other (see below). Segment 5 here is intervallically inaccurate, ending with a leap of a downward fifth when it ought to be a fourth (and is so everywhere else it appears), and otherwise it is never subject to the sort of rhythmic alteration and melodic embellishment it receives here. The insertion, out of sequence (and transposed), of segment 2 immediately after segment 5 is also unparalleled. This passage is 'jumbled' (to use Sparks's word) in a way that does not occur anywhere else in the mass. I also wonder whether the tenor entry may be a few tempora too late; it would strengthen the parallels Bernard observes with Du Faÿ's *L'homme armé* (see in the last section below) if, after the long opening duo for Supremum and Contratenor, Tenor and Bassus entered together.

The way the 'L'homme armé' tune has been laid out throughout the mass helps to show how Tinctoris must have presented it in the Tenor parts of 'Et in terra' and 'Patrem'. Each of the three subsections of the Kyrie presents the tune once straight through; in 'Kyrie' I the Contratenor has the whole tenor, but in the 'Christe' and 'Kyrie' II all the parts contribute to the exposition. In the Agnus Dei, the opening A section of the tune and the first segment of the B section are given in 'Agnus' I, while 'Agnus' III presents the rest of the B section and the concluding A section.[28] It is apparent that only the Contratenor 'counts' in this part of the mass, so that the music of segment 6 in the Supremum at the beginning of 'Agnus' III is not the first phrase of the B section (heard in the Contratenor at the end of 'Agnus' I) but a prefiguration of the second phrase (heard

[26] Sparks, *Cantus firmus*, 241, called attention to this.

[27] Jesse Rodin has suggested to me that the animated texture of the Supremum and Contratenor in tempora 41-48 is characteristic of duos, pointing to tempora 1-7 and observing that 'Et in terra' and 'Patrem', as the longest subsections of most mass settings, tend to be places where patterns observed elsewhere find exceptions. Similar textures and procedures can be found in trio passages within four-voice sections elsewhere in the mass, however, and even more strikingly in several three-part examples in *De arte contr.* II.xxv, xxvii, xxxii, III.iv (Ex. 2), v (Ex. 2), CS IV, 138-39, 142, 145, 149, 150; Seay II, 128-30, 135-36, 141-42, 149, 151. Part of 'Et in terra' tempora 41-48 may well be an actual duo, especially since tempora 40-42 in the Supremum may be interpreted as an embellishment of tenor segment 1 (though I am not sufficiently certain of this to incorporate it in Table 1); the issue is the absence not of the Tenor but of the tenor. Possibly Tinctoris treated the tenor in 'Et in terra' and 'Patrem' by inversion or cancrizans, procedures employed in earlier *L'homme armé* masses (see below) but not elsewhere in this mass.

[28] A division imitated from Busnoys, as noted by Cohen, 'Munus ab ignoto', 190; Bernard, 'Tinctoris's Missa L'homme armé', 12.

in the Contratenor at its entrance). The Sanctus has an interesting repetition scheme, owing to the composer's evident wish for the layout of the 'L'homme armé' tune to make sense in the Sanctus as whole, including the repetition of the 'Osanna' (for Tinctoris composed only one 'Osanna', to be repeated after the 'Benedictus'). The tune is given all the way through in the 'Sanctus' proper, but the initial A section is omitted from the 'Osanna', so the layout in the whole Sanctus becomes A–B–A—B–A—B–A.

If we turn now to the Credo, we can see that each of the subsections other than the 'Patrem' ('Et incarnatus', 'Et resurrexit', and 'Confiteor') presents the 'L'homme armé' tune once entire. That must therefore have been Tinctoris's intention in the 'Patrem'. In all the other subsections in which one voice gives one or more segments of the tune once at the beginning but has no more reference to the tune after that, as the Supremum does here,[29] the segments in question are also covered by another voice, so I should be confident that the Tenor in Tinctoris's 'Patrem' included *all* the segments of the 'L'homme armé' tune, exactly once and in order—but I would not pronounce on whether they might have been melodically embellished, rhythmically varied, or transposed.

Tinctoris's Gloria seems to have been designed similarly to his Sanctus, but with a more complicated plan: 'Qui tollis' begins and ends with the middle of the tune (with its ending and beginning in the middle of the subsection), and 'Cum sancto spiritu' gives only the concluding A section. The result is [?]—B–A–A–B—A. I see two possible restorations of the 'Et in terra': either the A section was presented alone, so the whole Gloria would have two complete instances of the tenor, or more likely the whole tune was given complete and then begun again, resulting in three instances, [A–B–A–A]—B–A–A–B—A. But it is just possible that in this case, since the opening A section of the tune had been set forth in Supremum and Contratenor, the Tenor might have entered with the B section, allowing more room for all the music needed.

Tinctoris had a somewhat unusual approach to the selection of melodic segments 5 and 6 in the B section of the 'L'homme armé' tune: he would use either, but only in such a way that the two successive phrases were the same. In 'Kyrie' I, 'Kyrie' II, 'Qui tollis', and 'Sanctus' he chose 5-5, while in 'Christe', 'Et in terra' (Contratenor), 'Et incarnatus', 'Et resurrexit', 'Confiteor', 'Osanna', 'Agnus' I, and 'Agnus' III he chose 6-6. We may note that on the one hand he was willing to mix the two patterns between subsections within a section (Kyrie, Gloria, and Sanctus), but on the other he did not mix them within a single subsection ('Qui tollis', which begins and ends with the B section, involving all voices but the Tenor, is the best example of this). Since the pattern in the Contratenor of 'Et in terra' is 6-6, we can be certain that is what Tinctoris will have used in the Tenor. There is no such clear evidence about the 'Patrem', but it is notable that only 6-6 appears in the three other subsections of the Credo, so it is most likely that this was his intention in the 'Patrem' as well.

One final detail about the restoration of Tinctoris's Tenor parts in 'Et in terra' and 'Patrem' affects their notation rather than their musical content. All the other subsections of Tinctoris's *L'homme armé* mass for which the governing mensuration is O have one part in ₵: 'Kyrie' I, Contratenor; 'Sanctus', Tenor; 'Agnus' I, Contratenor. (For 'Agnus' III, in which the other three parts are in O_2^3, the Contratenor has $₵_8^3$; I shall examine these mensuration-plus-proportion signs below.) I conclude that the Tenors of 'Et in terra'

<hr />

[29] 'Kyrie' I, Bassus; ['Et in terra', Supremum]; 'Sanctus', Bassus; 'Agnus' I, Supremum and Tenor; 'Agnus' III, Supremum.

and 'Patrem' were also notated in major prolation, since that is what Tinctoris used in the first subsections of each of his other sections. It is important to keep in mind that, unlike most composers of his time, Tinctoris assumed minim equivalence, not augmentation, to govern the relationship between major and minor prolation;[30] on the other hand, he specified augmentation in 'Kyrie' I, 'Osanna', and 'Agnus' I with the canon 'Crescit in duplum' ('It grows to twice as much').

It is probably significant that 'Et in terra' is one of only two subsections of the entire mass in which Tinctoris wrote longa rests covering three spaces instead of the usual two ('Et in terra', Bassus, tempora 1-6, 43-48; 'Osanna', Supremum, tempora 1-6). This is indicative of perfect minor modus.[31] In 'Osanna' the relation of ₵ 'Crescit in duplum' to ₵ creates a 1:4 proportion (see below) so that major prolation in the Contratenor corresponds to perfect minor modus. This suggests that the mensuration of the original Tenor of 'Et in terra' was ⊙ 'Crescit in duplum': the major prolation of the Tenor would then correspond to the perfect tempus of the other parts in ○, and the perfect tempus of the Tenor to the perfect minor modus of the others. This relation between ⊙ in the Tenor and ○ with perfect minor modus in the other voices obtains in the first subsection of each section in Busnoys's *L'homme armé* mass; Okeghem's *L'homme armé* has ⊙ against ○ in the 'Patrem' without any indication of perfect minor modus, and both composers seem to have been inspired by the 'Patrem' of De Domarto's mass *Spiritus almus* (a frequent object of Tinctoris's ire on account of its apparently having introduced a number of proportional notations he abhorred, including the tacit augmentation of major prolation in all three masses), which has ⊙ against ○ with perfect minor modus.[32] The connection to Okeghem's and Busnoys's *L'homme armé* masses suggests to me the possibility that Tinctoris may have applied in either 'Et in terra' or 'Patrem' the canonic transposition of the tenor down a fifth (as in Okeghem's 'Patrem') or down a fourth (as in Busnoys's); either transposition would fit within the normal *C-e* compass of Tinctoris's Tenor.

Like most other composers, whenever Tinctoris notated the 'L'homme armé' tune in major prolation, he presented it in semibreve-minim motion, while he used breve-semibreve motion as the norm when notating the tune in perfect tempus (the beginning of the Kyrie provides a straightforward juxtaposition of the latter in the Bassus with the former in the Contratenor); a little after Tinctoris, Marbrianus de Orto uniquely used

---

[30] See esp. *Proportionale musices* (hereafter *Prop. mus.*) III.iii: CS IV, 172; Seay IIa, 48-50.

[31] Tinctoris wrote divided pairs of breve rests instead of single longa rests in 'Kyrie' II, Tenor, tempora 6-7, 32-33, showing imperfect minor modus to be operative and not merely incidental, at least in this section. Most sections of *L'homme armé* have an even number of tempora before their final longa; besides 'Et in terra' (60 tempora before final longa) and 'Osanna' (66), 'Agnus' III (42) is the only section in which the number is also divisible by 3, but here the proportional Contratenor means that a perfect semibreve of major prolation corresponds to a longa of imperfect minor modus. In the sections divisible by neither 2 nor 3—'Patrem' (65), 'Sanctus' (25) 'Pleni' (71), 'Benedictus' (59)—imperfect minor modus (indicated by two-space longa rests) must be merely incidental.

[32] Antonius Busnois, *Missa super L'homme armé*, ed. Laurence Feininger, Monumenta Polyphoniae Liturgicae Sanctae Ecclesiae Romanae, ser. 1, vol. 1, fasc. 2 (Rome, 1948); Antoine Busnoys, *Collected works*, parts 2-3: *The Latin-texted works*, ed. Richard Taruskin, 2 vols., Masters and Monuments of the Renaissance 5 (New York, 1990), part 2, 11-48; Johannes Ockeghen, *Missa super L'homme armé*, ed. Laurence Feininger, Monumenta Polyphoniae Liturgicae Sanctae Ecclesiae Romanae, ser. 1, vol. 1, fasc. 6 (Rome, 1948); Johannes Ockeghem, *Collected works*, I, ed. Dragan Plamenac, 2nd edn. (n.p., 1959), 99-116; Johannes Ockeghem, *Masses and Mass Sections*, ed. Jaap van Benthem, fasc. II,2 (Utrecht, 1999); Petrus de Domarto, *Complete works*, ed. David Kidger, 2 vols., Renaissance Church Music 127 (Newton Abbot, 1994-2005), vol. 2, *Missa Spiritus almus*. On Tinctoris's criticism of *Spiritus almus*, see Rob C. Wegman, 'Petrus de Domarto's *Missa Spiritus almus* and the Early History of the Four-Voice Mass in the Fifteenth Century', in *Early Music History* 10 (1991), 235-303, esp. 238-40.

breve-semibreve motion regardless of whether his mensuration was perfect tempus or major prolation.[33] Tinctoris allowed more elaboration of the tenor melody in major prolation than Busnoys or the 'Naples' composer, but not as much as Okeghem; like Du Faÿ, Regis, and all others who gave 'L'homme armé' in perfect tempus, he was much freer in his treatment of the melody in this mensuration.[34]

I have demonstrated several consistent patterns of tenor usage, independent of one another, that govern all sections of Tinctoris's *L'homme armé* mass apart from the two whose Tenor parts were at first omitted by Scribe 35 and afterwards added by the Tenor Scribe. If this evidence does not constitute proof, it allows us to draw a strong inference that the added Tenor parts are faulty, and that the composer intended the 'Et in terra' and 'Patrem' subsections to participate in the patterning that governs the rest of the mass. Any defence of the authenticity of the added Tenors must be based upon counter-arguments of comparable force, showing *why* Tinctoris would have broken those patterns in just the two subsections where the Tenor parts were missing and had to be added, perhaps demonstrating other patterns in which the added Tenors share but that are broken in other subsections. I do not wish to remove the added Tenor parts in the 'Et in terra' and 'Patrem' from consideration in any future study of Tinctoris's *L'homme armé*, but rather to insist that they must be recognized as a faulty repair job, adequate to make the mass performable by the singers of the papal chapel, but not to represent the composer's purposes.

Late in my investigation of Tinctoris's 'Et in terra' and 'Patrem', I discovered one more puzzling detail that may be pertinent. At three points in the 'Et in terra' (the beginnings of tempora 22, 24, and 26) and two points in the 'Patrem' (the beginnings of tempora 36 and 54; see Figure 1 at 'deum de deo' for the first of these), and in no other subsection, an early singer wrote *signa congruentiae* (𝕊) with a finer pen in all parts *except* the added Tenor. Such signs normally indicate a tenor entrance after a long silence or some striking occurrence in another part, but nothing of the sort is apparent in the added Tenor; only the last coincides with an entrance, after only three tempora of rest.

---

[33] [Marbrianus] De Orto, *Missa super L'homme armé*, ed. Laurence Feininger, Monumenta Polyphoniae Liturgicae Sanctae Ecclesiae Romanae, ser. 1, vol. 1, fasc. 7 (Rome, 1948); see also Jesse Rodin, "'When in Rome . . .': What Josquin Learned in the Sistine Chapel', in *Journal of the American Musicological Society* 61 (2008), 307-72 at 322 n. 38. See further n. 63 below.

[34] Besides masses in editions cited above and below, see Gulielmus Dufay, *Missa super L'homme armé*, ed. Laurence Feininger, Monumenta Polyphoniae Liturgicae Sanctae Ecclesiae Romanae, ser. 1, vol. 1, fasc. 1 (Rome, 1948); *Guglielmi Dufay Opera omnia*, ed. Heinrich Besseler, 6 vols., Corpus Mensurabilis Musicae 1 (Rome, 1951-66), vol. 3, 33-65.

I am unpersuaded of the position that the major-prolation, semibreve-minim version of the notation ('prolation' for short) should take precedence over perfect-tempus, breve-semibreve ('tempus') notation; I would urge a neutral interpretation of the evidence. The 'primacy' of prolation notation for 'L'homme armé' has been strenuously asserted, but Emily Carolyn Zazulia, 'Verbal Canons and Notational Complexity in Fifteenth-century Music' (Ph.D. diss., University of Pennsylvania, 2012), ch. 4, 'Notational Reference in the Armed Man Masses', 204-82, offers the first thoroughgoing argument I have encountered. In my opinion, her very imaginative reasoning about the treatment of 'L'homme armé' would gain in cogency and rigor if it were framed neutrally and consistently in terms of the 'sounding length' (her own term) of tenor rhythm relative to the other parts of the polyphonic texture rather than in terms of notational appearance (valid though that is in other parts of her dissertation).

The noticeably greater tendency of presentation in prolation notation towards what Zazulia calls 'notational consistency' can be explained historically by reference to De Domarto's mass *Spiritus almus*, which Tinctoris identified as the origin of the practice of notating a tenor in major prolation with implicit augmentation (*Prop. mus.* III.iii: CS IV, 172; Seay IIa, 48-49); the tenor of *Spiritus almus* is notationally invariant and varies in rhythm according to its mensuration (see Wegman, 'Domarto's *Missa Spiritus almus*'), and the use of implicitly augmented major prolation and notational consistency are only two of a number of ways in which Okeghem's, the earliest *L'homme armé* mass to employ this notation, was inspired by *Spiritus almus*.

The absence of the *signa congruentiae* from the Tenor itself, together with the lack of correlation with notable Tenor events, suggests that they may have been written before the Tenor parts were added to 'Et in terra' and 'Patrem', and may therefore reflect some structural aspect or other of an alternative Tenor part, sung from another copy, which may or may not have been Tinctoris's original but must have been unsatisfactory to the papal singers. Bonnie Blackburn has suggested to me the possibility that Scribe 35's exemplar may have given one (or less likely both) the missing Tenor parts with an enigmatic canonic inscription that the scribe and singers were unable to work out.[35] After discussion, though, we agreed that this is improbable: all the canons and other explanatory matter in the mass are entirely clear and straightforward (if verbally elegant), as is the only other one I know of in all Tinctoris's works, 'Crescit in triplo' ('It grows to treble') in one example in *De arte contrapuncti*; despite his definition, '*Canon* is a rule showing the composer's wish beneath a certain obscurity', it is evident that Tinctoris thought verbal canons ought *not* to be obscure in practice.[36]

I lack the skill to compose a more convincing replacement for the missing Tenor parts, a better representation of Tinctoris's purposes. I hope what I have shown will inspire someone with more pertinent talent to attempt a better repair.[37] But I trust it is already apparent that this *L'homme armé* mass is more coherent than it seemed to be, and that the strictures quoted above from Bukofzer, Sparks, and Cohen about the absence of a general plan are misplaced. It should now be easier to appreciate the justice of the assessment in the other full and insightful treatment mentioned above, that by Maria Caraci (Vela):

> The counterpoint is notable for its richness and flexibility, interwoven with imitations in which often one and the same melodic fragment is presented in two separate voices, adopting different duration values and slight variations, and it is constructed in large part out of the material provided by the cantus prius factus with a standard of constructive logic and architectonic balance that makes this work one of the most effective and interesting anticipations of the style of Josquin.[38]

---

[35] For an instance of the kind of enigma envisioned, see Bonnie J. Blackburn, 'Obrecht's *Missa Je ne demande* and Busnoys's Chanson: An Essay in Reconstructing Lost Canons', in *Tijdschrift van de Koninklijke Vereniging voor Nederlandse Muziekgeschiedenis* 45 (1995), 18-32.

[36] See n. 8 and p. 22 above, pp. 25 and 31 below; *De arte contr.* II.xxvii, Ex. 1, *Katerina sponsa Dei*: CS IV, 142; Seay II, 135-36; Tinctoris, *Diffinitorium*, entry 'Canon': 'Canon est regula voluntatem compositoris sub obscuritate quadam ostendens.'

[37] A convincing restoration will need to satisfy all the patterning identified above, and also the patterns of contrapuntal usage identified in Dumitrescu, 'Leading Tones in *Cantus Firmi*'. A thorough comprehension of Tinctoris's melodic and contrapuntal style goes without saying. For example, Ronald Woodley has pointed out to me that, although the Tenor part as copied by Scribe 35 descends to low *C* not infrequently, there is only one instance of this note that is longer than a semibreve (a dotted longa at a cadence in 'Agnus' II, tempus 35), significantly in a section in which the Bassus is entirely silent. The breve low Cs in the Tenor of 'Et in terra' (tempora 29, 32) and 'Patrem' (tempora 27, 42) are out of keeping with Tinctoris's usage in *L'homme armé*. Tinctoris's Tenor also never approaches the last note before a rest by direct leap of a descending fifth, as in all these instances, except when it embodies segment 2 of the 'L'homme armé' tenor. A word of caution to would-be restorers: both Jesse Rodin and Emily Zazulia, for whose opinions I have great respect, have expressed themselves as unconvinced by my argument (e-mail messages of 5 September and 12 September 2012 respectively); they do not see how the missing Tenor parts can be restored to fit the patterns I have described, and they regard the added Tenor parts (especially in 'Et in terra') as effective and convincing.

[38] Caraci, 'Fortuna del tenor "L'homme armé"', 192: 'Il contrappunto è notevole per ricchezza e duttilità, intessuto di imitazioni in cui spesso un medesimo frammento melodico si presenta in due diverse voci adottando differenti valori di durata e lievi variazioni e si costruisce in gran parte sul materiale offerto dal cantus prius factus con un criterio di logica costruttiva e di equilibrio architettonico che fa di quest'opera una delle anticipazioni più valide ed interessanti dello stile di Josquin.'

There is much more that could be said about Tinctoris's *L'homme armé* mass than I can touch upon here. In the space that remains, I shall return to a point I touched upon a few paragraphs above and examine the notation of proportions in the mass. I shall conclude with a discussion of the relationship of Tinctoris's mass to earlier *L'homme armé* masses in terms of the rhetorical categories of *imitatio* and *varietas*.

∗

In a recent conference paper, Emily Zazulia called attention to the notation of a *sesquialtera* proportion (3:2) at the beginning of the 'Confiteor' of Tinctoris's *L'homme armé*: ¢ in three parts against O_2^3 in the Contratenor. There was some discussion as to whether this notation correctly represents what Tinctoris would have written: would he not have wished Φ_2^3 in the Contratenor to normalize the basic relationship of the four parts before the proportion is applied? Might we therefore need to be cautious about the accuracy of the readings in Scribe 35's own text of Tinctoris's mass, not just the Tenor Scribe's additions?[39] I am convinced that C.S. 35 reproduces Tinctoris's proportional notation very exactly (with one exception at a different point, to be discussed below), and that these misgivings are the result of a misunderstanding. We must consider all instances of proportional notation in the *L'homme armé* mass, and we must consider them in the light of two separate aspects of Tinctoris's proportional doctrine: the relation of proportions to mensurations, and the relation of the stroke through ¢ and Φ to both.

Tinctoris notated the 'L'homme armé' tune in major prolation and semibreve-minim motion in five subsections (see Table 1). In two of these, 'Kyrie' I and 'Agnus' I, he gave the verbal canon 'Crescit in duplum' ('It grows to twice as much') to effect what we should call 'augmentation'[40] relative to the other voices in perfect tempus and minor prolation: ¢ ↓ = O ♪ (I shall return below to the effect of the same canon in the 'Osanna'). In the first instance, in the 'Kyrie' I, the augmentation is revoked midway through the subsection by the proportional fraction $\frac{2}{1}$, returning the relation to Tinctoris's norm, ¢ ↓ = O ↓. All instances of proportions are shown in Table 1, the verbal canon keyed by †, the others represented as they appear in C.S. 35.

The situation at the beginning of the 'Confiteor' is only the first of eleven instances in five events where O_2^3 occurs: in the Contratenor and then in the Tenor of the 'Confiteor', in all three voices towards the end of both the 'Pleni' and the 'Benedictus', and in all but the Contratenor of 'Agnus' III. Earlier, C_3^2 appears in all parts together of 'Cum sancto spiritu'. In only four cases (twice each in 'Confiteor' and 'Pleni') does O_2^3 stand simultaneously with ¢, but without exception these two unstroked mensuration-plus-proportion signs follow after a stroked mensuration sign: C_3^2 after Φ, O_2^3 in every case after ¢. This is at least a consistent practice—is it consistently wrong?

Both the expression of the proportional relationship as what we may call a 'fraction' (placing the figure designating the succeeding quantity above that for the

[39] E-mail message, Ronald Woodley to Jeffrey J. Dean, 10 July 2011, with reference to discussion after Emily Zazulia, 'Tinctoris and Busnoys's *L'homme armé*', presented at the Medieval and Renaissance Music Conference, Barcelona, 7 July 2011. I was not able to be present at the conference.

[40] Tinctoris did not use the words 'augmentation' or 'diminution' in this kind of context, although Gaforus did. See e.g. Tinctoris, *Diffinitorium*, entries 'Augmentatio', 'Diminutio'; Franchinus Gaforus, *Practica musice* (Milan, 1496); repr. Monuments of Music and Music Literature in Facsimile 2/99 (New York, 1979), II.xiv, sig. cc iiij^r.

preceding quantity)[41] and the placement of a mensuration sign before it are propounded in Tinctoris's *Proportionale musices*. He insisted on fractions and deprecated the common usage of single figures or mensural signs to represent the relation of two values, 2 standing for 2:1, 3 for 3:2, ꟻ for 4:3, ¢ for 1:2, and so on.[42] The use of fractions to denote proportions was long established in practical music,[43] but by no means frequent in the 1470s. In the Roman choirbook San Pietro B80, for instance, copied for St Peter's Basilica in 1474-75, not long after Tinctoris had written the *Proportionale*, 3 for sesquialtera is found innumerable times (it was far and away the most commonly used proportion in the late fifteenth century), but fractions appear on just two openings out of 250. They are worth examining, for they show that fractional proportion signs were not only scarcer than we might suppose, they could be stranger than we might suppose. The 'Christe' of the Kyrie ascribed to 'Egidius cervelli' (possibly an autograph if the unknown Cervelli is the same as the singer Egidius Crispini or Gile Crépin, who copied this piece in 1475) shows ¢ succeeded in all three voices by Φ_2^3.[44] This coincides with Tinctoris's advice to use the mensuration sign as well as both figures, when most contemporaries would have found 3 entirely satisfactory; it probably does not imply that the composer was acquainted with Tinctoris's *Proportionale*, but rather that Tinctoris's doctrine was a development of an established practice.[45]

The end of 'Agnus' II of the anonymous mass *D'ung aultre amer* in San Pietro B80 (also preserved in two other manuscripts) is even more interesting, as it shows two different ways of notating proportions with two figures, neither of them the one taught by Tinctoris. His method was apparently more familiar, though: all three scribes seem to have been confused by what they saw in their common exemplar, whose notation can be deduced from the pattern of mistakes they made.[46] The exemplar's figure 4 was

[41] The word *fractura* for 'fraction' was used in this sense already by Prosdocimus de Beldemandis, *Tractatus practice de musica mensurabili* (1408), CS III, 200-228 at 218-19.

[42] *Prop. mus.* III.ii: CS IV, 169-72; Seay IIa, 42-48.

[43] Proportional fractions appear, for example, in a good few pieces in Oxford Bodleian Library, Ms. Canon. misc. 213 (c. 1428-34); facs., ed. David Fallows, *Oxford, Bodleian Library, Ms. Canon. misc. 213, Late Medieval and Early Renaissance Music in Facsimile* 1 (Chicago, 1995). $\frac{3}{2}$: [Binchois], Credo 19 'a versi', fol. 3v staff 2 (cited with an altered context by Tinctoris, *Prop. mus.* III.ii: CS IV, 170; Seay IIa, 45); Cordier, *Pour le deffault*, fol. 108v staff 1; Cordier, *Dame excellent*, fol. 116r staves 6, 8; Cesaris, *A virtutis ignicio / Ergo beata nascio / Benedicta filia tua*, fols. 116v-117r staves 1-5 (12 times). $\frac{6}{4}$: anon. (Malbecque?), *Ma doulce amour*, fol. 123v staves 9, 11. Single figures—2, 3, 4, 6 in descending order of frequency—are found about four times as often as fractions; verbal canons for proportion are very common; and the use of coloration for sesquialtera and ꟻ for sesquitertia (4:3) with imperfect tempus is ubiquitous (as are other implicit proportions arising from the simultaneous or successive combination of different mensurations in ways Tinctoris would have condemned). The early history of proportional notation in general is especially well covered in Jason Stoessel, 'The Captive Scribe: The Context and Culture of Scribal and Notational Process in the Music of the *Ars Subtilior*', 2 vols. (Ph.D. diss., University of New England, 2002), ch. 5.5, 'Proportional Uses of Mensuration Signs in the *Ars Subtilior*', and ch. 6, 'Algorism, Proportionality and the Notation of the *Ars Subtilior*', vol. 1, 273-81 and 284-316; see esp. 295-300 on fractions.

[44] Vatican City, Biblioteca Apostolica Vaticana, Ms. San Pietro B80, fols. 143v-144r; facs. ed. Christopher A. Reynolds, *Vatican City, Bibilioteca Apostolica Vaticana, San Pietro B 80*, Renaissance Music in Facsimile 23 (New York, 1986). See Christopher A. Reynolds, *Papal Patronage and the Music of St. Peter's, 1380-1513* (Berkeley, etc., 1995), 94-97.

[45] There are a couple of mensuration-plus-proportion combinations used as initial signatures in Canon. misc. 213: $\frac{9}{3}$ over O: Johannes de Sarto, *Verbum patris*, fol. 12v staff 6 (with a verbal explanation); ¢$\frac{2}{3}$: anon., *Toute biaulté*, fol. 122v staff 9 (see Robert D. Reynolds, '*Toute biaulte et toute honneur*, a Neglected Chanson of the Fifteenth Century', in *Musica disciplina* 39 [1985], 45-51). The Contratenor of Cordier, *Amans amés*, fol. 123r staff 11, has the sequence (*ab initio*) O3 - ¢ - C - O3 - O - O3 - ¢.

[46] San Pietro B80 (**A** in the collation below), fols. 60v-61r; Vatican City, Biblioteca Apostolica Vaticana, Cappella Sistina 51 (**B**), fols. 120v-121r; Verona, Biblioteca Capitolare, Ms. DCCLV (**C**), fols. 51v-52r; edited in Rex Eakins (ed.), *An Editorial Transnotation of the Manuscript Capella Sistina 51, Biblioteca Apostolica Vaticana, Città del Vaticano: Liber missarum*, Collected works 17 (Ottawa, 2001), vol. 3, 235-315 at 311-12. See Rob C. Wegman, 'The Anonymous Mass

evidently written in such a way that it could be confused with either ¢ or ⊘, something like ⵀ or ⵜ, and the fraction ⅔ was written so strangely that two scribes transcribed it as ⅗, although the other seems to have copied its peculiar shape faithfully. All three voices of 'Agnus' II (the Tenor is silent here) begin with ¢, and the Bassus remains there throughout. About three-quarters of the way through, the Contratenor has first 3, then, a few tempora from the end, 42. As far as I am aware, this way of notating the relation 4:2 (normally with a point between the figures, 4.2, but sometimes without) is otherwise found only in sixteenth-century English sources. The Eton choirbook, from the beginning of the century, shows many instances of 3.2 for sesquialtera written by the original scribe,[47] and there are examples of this notation for many different proportions in a group of proportional compositions in John Baldwin's commonplace book. Although this is a very late source (from the 1590s), a sub-group of seven pieces occurring early in the much larger sequence originated in the mid fifteenth century, and three of these are ascribed to John Bedyngham—but their original notation may have been modernized.[48] The mass *D'ung aultre amer* is the only case I know of to display this notation either on the continent or before 1500.

The Discantus of this mass has a longer sequence of proportions: 3 - ²⁄₄ - ⅔ - 42, the second sign occurring simultaneously with 3 in the Contratenor and the last with 42. The fractions are inverted with respect to the way they are normally expressed (something I have never encountered in any other piece), and the duple proportions refer not to the sesquialtera (with implied perfect mensuration) that immediately precedes each, but to the imperfect mensuration before that (the actual relations are easy to determine from the counterpoint). Tinctoris would have been aghast at the illogicality; setting aside the need for mensural signs (see below), he would have demanded the sequence be written as ³⁄₂ - ⁴⁄₃ - ³⁄₂ - ⁴⁄₃. The result (possibly expressing the sense of the sung words 'miserere nobis', 'have mercy upon us') is that in the three tempora before the end, an identical rhythm is expressed in the Bassus as semibreves and a breve, in the Contratenor as breves and a longa, and in the Discantus as longas and a maxima.[49]

Musicians throughout the fifteenth century regularly understood proportions as affecting the mensuration at the same time, so that 3, ³⁄₂, ⁶⁄₄, or the like entailed triple

---

D'ung aultre amer: A Late Fifteenth-Century Experiment', in *The Musical Quarterly* 74 (1990), 566-94 at 589; n. 12 is corrected here. The actual notation in the sources is as follows: *Contratenor*: 3 **ABC** | 42 **A** : ¢2 **BC**. *Discantus*: 3 **AC** : coloration **B** | 2 over ¢ **A** : 2 over ⊘ (stroke extending through 2) **BC** | ⅔ **B** : ³⁄₉ **AC** | 42 **C** : ¢2 **B** : ²⁄₄ **A**.

[47] Windsor, Eton College Library, Ms. 178, passim; facs. ed. Magnus Williamson, *The Eton Choirbook*, DIAMM Facsimiles 1 (Oxford, 2010).

[48] London, British Library, Ms. R. M. 24.d.2, Nos. 80-114, fols. 100v-120r; facs. ed. Jessie Ann Owens, *London, British Library, R.M. 24.d.2*, Renaissance Music in Facsimile 8 (New York, 1987). On the date of Nos. 84-90, fols. 103v-107r, see David Fallows, *A Catalogue of Polyphonic Songs, 1415-1480* (Oxford, 1999), 24.

[49] I have included the mass *D'ung aultre amer* in a body of anonymous compositions I believe to be the work of a single musician whom I call 'the *Incomprehensibilia* composer'; see Jeffrey J. Dean, 'Verona 755 and the *Incomprehensibilia* Composer', in *Manoscritti di polifonia nel Quattrocento europeo*, ed. Marco Gozzi (Trent, 2004), 93-108; Jeffrey Dean, 'Some Observations on *Motetti C*: C for Confusion, Chronology, and *Concede nobis*', in *Venezia 1501: Petrucci e la stampa musicale / Venice 1501: Petrucci, Music, Print and Publishing*, ed. Giulio Cattin and Patrizia Dalla Vecchia (Venice, 2005), 375-89. For reasons of contrapuntal style and compositional planning, I would also assign to the *Incomprehensibilia* composer the anonymous mass *L'ardant desir* (C.S. 51, fols. 90v-104r; edited in Eakins [ed.], *An Editorial Transnotation of Capella Sistina 51*, 65-167); on the distinctive use in this mass of mensural signs (not fractions) for proportions, see Jason Stoessel, 'Looking Back over the "Missa L'ardant desir": Double Signatures and Unusual Signs in Sources of Fifteenth-Century Music', in *Music & Letters* 91 (2010), 311-42. The imaginative and radically non-Tinctorian approach to proportional notation apparent in both masses may be further evidence of common authorship.

subdivision at some level, 2, $\frac{2}{1}$, $\frac{4}{3}$ etc. duple subdivision. By Tinctoris's time the most common such relations were 3 after ₵, signifying perfect tempus (♮ = ♦♦♦), and 3 after C, signifying major prolation (◊ = ♩♩♩) without augmentation.[50] Tinctoris and Franchinus Gaforus, who was deeply influenced by his contact with Tinctoris in Naples in 1478-80, considered this usage illogical and incorrect. Tinctoris's language may be less limpid than we might like, but his meaning is unequivocal:

> notes must always be reckoned according to their perfection or imperfection with respect to the sign of mode, tempus, and prolation under which they stand...[examples of De Domarto and Cousin using the same sign, C3, in different senses] One of them must have gone wrong. And in fact each is deficient: De Domarto in the sign of prolation, Cousin in that of tempus, and both in that of proportion. For De Domarto ought to have signed ₵$\frac{3}{2}$, seeing that [in his case] it is major prolation, but Cousin O$\frac{3}{2}$ because it is perfect tempus. I advise, all the same, that for any proportion, if not mediately, a mensuration [*quantitas*] rather similar to it should be signed immediately before: for example, for a binary one [i.e., a proportion whose upper figure is divisible by two] imperfect mode, imperfect tempus, and minor prolation, for a ternary one perfect mode, perfect tempus, and major prolation...[51]

Gaforus was more explicit and more generous with his examples of bad practice; he dealt with the matter in his manuscript *Tractatus practicabilium proportionum*, written about 1482 and largely revised as Book IV of his *Practica musice*, printed in 1496, and returned to it more briefly in his Italian *Angelicum ac divinum opus musice* of 1508. On the last occasion, he made a rather endearing remark: 'Many years ago now [it must have been in 1489], I warned the most worthy composers Josquin des Prez and Gaspar [van Weerbeke] about these inappropriate [practices]; they welcomed my opinion, but it was difficult to make them give up their nasty habit.'[52]

[50] C3 is the signature of *Il sera pour vous conbatu / L'homme armé*, as preserved in Yale University, Beinecke Rare Book and Manuscript Library, Ms. 91, fols. 44v-45r; facs. and ed. in Leeman L. Perkins and Howard Garey (eds.), *The Mellon Chansonnier*, 2 vols. (New Haven and London, 1979), vol. 1, 124-25. Planchart, 'The Origins and Early History', 314-27, has advanced a strong argument in support of the conjecture in Ruth Hannas, 'Concerning Deletions in the Polyphonic Mass Credo', in *Journal of the American Musicological Society* 5 (1952), 155-86 at 168, that the chanson was composed by Du Faÿ; Planchart would date its composition about 1460. The manuscript uniquely preserving *Il sera pour vous / L'homme armé* was copied in Naples in the mid 1470s, probably under Tinctoris's supervision; see Perkins, Introduction to *The Mellon Chansonnier*, vol. 1, 9-32.

[51] Tinctoris, *Prop. mus.* III.v: CS IV, 174-76; Seay IIa, 53-56: 'semper note iuxta perfectionem aut imperfectionem earum per respectum signi modalis, temporalis et prolationalis sub quo consistunt computande sunt...Alterum errasse necessarium est. Et revera uterque deficit: de Domarto in signo prolationis, Cousin in temporis, et ambo in proportionis. Debebat enim de Domarto, quoniam ibi prolatio maior sit, taliter signare ₵$\frac{3}{2}$, Cousin vero quia tempus perfectum est sic: O$\frac{3}{2}$. Consulo tamen ut cuilibet proportioni, si non mediate, quantitas sibi similior immediate presignetur, ut puta binarie modus imperfectus, tempus imperfectum, et prolatio minor, ternarie modus perfectus, tempus perfectum, et prolatio maior, utrique vero et neutre indifferenter.' It would appear that 'mediate' is to be construed as the adverb parallel to 'immediate' and not as the adjective 'mediatae' (in classical spelling) qualifying 'proportioni'. Tinctoris used *mediatus* in just three other contexts, all of them parallel (*immediatus* alone, usually adverbial, is much more frequent), *Liber de natura et proprietate tonorum* viii: 'pro *immediato* aut *mediato* progressu...quamvis humana vox tritono *mediato* possibiliter utatur, eam tamen *immediato* uti aut est difficile aut impossibile'; *Liber imperfectionum notarum musicalium* II.viii: 'nec refert si ille precedant aut sequantur istas *mediate* vel *immediate*' [my italics]: CS IV, 23, 65; Seay I, 76, 166. I would interpret 'if not mediately' as referring to instances like the $\frac{3}{1}$ proportion in Tinctoris's 'Agnus' I (see below), governed by the 'mediately' preceding O at the beginning of the section, 'mediated' in Tinctoris's terminology by all the notes between the mensural sign and the proportional sign.

[52] Franchinus Gafurius, *Angelicum ac divinum opus musice* (Milan: Gotardo de Ponte, 1508), V.vi, sig. I ii^r: 'De questi inconvenienti ne advertite gia molti anni passati Jusquin despriet & Gaspar dignissimi compositori: qui quanquam acquieverunt sententie nostre tamen ab assueta eorum corruptela difficile diverti potuerunt.' See also Franchinus Gaforus, *Tractatus practicabilium proportionum*, ch. 5, Bologna, Museo Internazionale e Biblioteca della Musica, Ms.

The issue of the implicit relation among proportion, mensuration, and metre seems puzzling today.[53] The point that must be understood is that mensuration affects the metrical organization of rhythm only as a side effect; its real purpose is strictly notational, to govern the presence or absence of perfection and alteration at the different levels of note values. There is a particularly clear example of the distinction in the 'Crucifixus' of an untitled mass by Gaforus in Librone 2 of the Duomo of Milan, copied in the 1490s under the composer's supervision.[54] The initial mensuration is C (signed only in the Tenor); at 'Confiteor' the Discantus and Altus have $C\frac{3}{2}$, while one and a half tempora later at 'in remissionem' the Tenor and Contra Bassus have simply $\frac{3}{2}$. The rhythm is congruent in both pairs, with minims regularly grouped in threes. But there are altered minims before semibreves in the Altus, whereas the same rhythmic value (twice that of an unaltered minim) is expressed by semibreves in Tenor and Contra Bassus; this would be a solecism in major prolation, so it shows that the initial sign of minor prolation is still operative in these voices. The Altus also has dots of division, as needed in major prolation, but there are no perfect semibreves in the upper voices or dotted ones in the lower, and the rhythm of the Discantus is such that it would be notated identically in either mensuration.

In Tinctoris's *L'homme armé* mass, therefore, the reason for the C before $\frac{2}{3}$ and the O before $\frac{3}{2}$ is clear: the first mensuration sign ensures that after the proportion semibreves cannot be altered or breves perfected as they would have been under the preceding Φ, while the second ensures that they can be as they would not have under ₵; and, indeed, Tinctoris made both of those provisions count. But should Scribe 35 have written all those mensuration-plus-proportion signs with a stroke, as Crispini had done in the Cervelli 'Christe' in San Pietro B 80, mentioned above? I think not—I believe he copied faithfully what Tinctoris had written.

The interpretation of the stroke has received much attention, and I do not intend to revisit the larger question of what it meant for other musicians than Tinctoris himself.[55] Tinctoris treated the stroke as an 'accidental' or inessential sign. It is absent from his *Tractatus de regulari valore notarum*, which treats the signs of all the different mensurations and their 'species' or combinations.[56] In the *Proportionale* Tinctoris indicated two distinct uses of the stroke, one (positively) qualitative and the other (grudgingly) quantitative. Early in the treatise, he castigated Okeghem,

> who signed his *chanson rustique* 'L'aultre d'antan', composed in every part with equal numbers [that is, with no proportion between parts], not just with a sign of proportion [O3], but with that assigned (by itself [i.e., with a single figure rather than a fraction]

A 69, fols. 19v-22r; Gaforus, *Practica musice* IV.v, sig. gg iij^v-[gg v]^r. I am grateful to Bonnie Blackburn for making her transcription of the *Tractatus* available to me.

[53] It has tripped up even such well-grounded scholars as Anna Maria Busse Berger in her standard book *Mensuration and Proportion Signs: Origins and Evolution* (Oxford, 1993), 187-96, esp. 188, 190.

[54] Milan, Archivio Musicale del Duomo, Ms. 2 [2268], fols. 93v-100r at 97v-98r; facs. ed. Howard Mayer Brown, *Milan, Archivio della Veneranda Fabbrica del Duomo, Sezione musicale, Librone 2 (olim 2268)*, Renaissance Music in Facsimile 12b (New York, 1987). Edited in Franchino Gaffurio, *Messe*, ed. Amerigo Bortone, Archivium Musices Metropolitanum Mediolanense 1-3 (Milan, 1958-60), vol. 2, 111-37 at 128-29, but better consulted from the facsimile.

[55] Bonnie J. Blackburn, 'Did Ockeghem Listen to Tinctoris?', in *Johannes Ockeghem: actes du XLe Colloque international d'études humanistes*, ed. Philippe Vendrix, Collection 'Épitome musical' 1 ([Paris], 1998), 597-640 at 603-12, offers the best current discussion of Tinctoris's theory and practice of the stroke.

[56] CS IV, 46-53; Seay I, 121-38.

and badly) by some to tripla, by others to sesquialtera...Whenever, in fact, they hold the aforementioned song, 'L'aultre d'antan', or another similarly signed, the inexperienced say straight away, 'Let's sing; it's sesquialtera.' What childish ignorance, to call a proportion of equality one of inequality! Nor do I suppose that the composer, even though he may have so signed it according to some, wished it to be so spoken of, but rather that his song should be sung speeded up after the fashion of sesquialtera, to effect which, a stroke [*virgula*] drawn through the middle of the circle [*per medium circulum*] of each part would have sufficed; for it is proper to it to signify acceleration of the measure, be it either perfect or imperfect tempus...its form in both is such: Ⲫ ₵.[57]

I have quoted Tinctoris's statement of the fundamental problem, because understanding it will help clear up our own perplexity. Tinctoris's objection is that the apparent proportion is false because it compares something to nothing—nothing preceding, nothing in another voice. The assumption on which this hinges is that proportions do not refer to mensurations in the abstract or to their signatures but to actual notes, as Tinctoris said in so many words: 'This proportional relation...occurs in two ways, either when we immediately compare the following to the preceding notes in one and the same part of a piece...or when the notes of one part are directly compared to the notes of another against which they are composed'.[58] Tinctoris would not have accepted the argument that the missing comparand must be the 'natural' speed of O, even though he would have had to accept that such a natural speed must exist, or the stroke could not speed things up.

I differ in my interpretation of the latter part of this passage from Bonnie Blackburn, who has argued that the Latin needs to be construed so as to be translated 'sung like a speeded-up sesquialtera'; taking 'concite' as an adverb (as I have done) 'would not make sense in the context, because Tinctoris has just stated that he did not believe that Ockeghem wanted it to be performed as a sesquialtera'.[59] But saying one thing is *like* another is entirely consistent with saying it *is not* the other. My love is not a red, red rose—but she is like one. And we must remember that, because Tinctoris did not understand proportions as altering mensuration, the effect of sesquialtera would always be a speeding up, albeit in a definite proportion, whereas I entirely agree with Blackburn that, according to Tinctoris, the acceleration produced by the stroked mensuration is indefinite: she has shown this clearly in the way he alternated between O and Ⲫ in a section of one of his masses.[60]

[57] *Prop. mus.* I.iii: CS IV, 156; Seay IIa, 15: '...Okeghem, qui suum carmen bucolicum Lautredantan, ab omni parte numeris equalibus compositum, nedum signo proportionis, sed illo qui a quibusdam triple, ab aliis sesquialtere, per se et male attribuitur signavit...Dum vero carmen premissum scilicet Lautredantan aut aliud similiter signatum habent, imperiti dicunt repente, canamus, sesquialtera est. O puerilis ignorantia, equalitatis proportionem inequalitatis asserere! Nec existimo compositorem, quamvis ita secundum aliquos signaverit, ita dici voluisse, sed ut carmen suum concite instar sesquialtere cantaretur, ad quod efficiendum virgula per medium circuli cuiusque partis traducta sufficiebat; nam proprium est ei mensure accelerationem significare sive tempus perfectum sive imperfectum sit...cuius in utroque forma talis est: Ⲫ ₵.' I construe 'concite' as the adverb, not the adjective 'concitae' qualifying 'sesquialterae' (as given by both Coussemaker and Seay).
[58] See *Prop. mus.* I.ii: CS IV, 155; Seay IIa, 12-13: 'ista proportionalis habitudo...dupliciter contingit, vel quando notas sequentes ad precedentes in una et eadem parte cantus immediate referimus...Vel quando note unius partis ad notas alterius contra quas componuntur directe referuntur'.
[59] Blackburn, 'Did Ockeghem Listen to Tinctoris?', 605 with n. 10. We differ in other details of less consequence as well.
[60] Blackburn, 'Did Ockeghem Listen to Tinctoris?', 610-12 with Ex. 1.

Towards the end of the *Proportionale*, Tinctoris returned to the stroke:

> But others, for a sign of *dupla* [2:1], merely place the sign of imperfect tempus and minor prolation drawn with a stroke [*cum tractulo*], denoting acceleration of the measure as stated above, whence it is commonly called 'singing by half' [*cantus ad medium*]... Which...I consider tolerable on account of a sort of equivalence [*quandam equipollentiam*] between the former proportion and the latter prolation; for when something is sung by half [*ad medium canitur*] two notes are measured together with one as if by duple proportion.[61]

Tinctoris did not here equate the two effects of the stroke: his explanation of the tolerability of using the stroke for duple proportion is based on the 'sort of equivalence' between that proportion, 2:1, and the 'prolation', meaning imperfect tempus with minor prolation, in which all note values are divisible by two, whereas the acceleration he had spoken of earlier was indefinite. This suggests that the stroke as a modifier of an unstroked mensuration sign is analogous to the dot as a modifier of a note: the dot of division clarifies the application of alteration or imperfection and may or may not change any note values, whereas the dot of augmentation always adds one-half to a preceding imperfect note value, and the dot of perfection always prevents the subtraction of one-third from a perfect one;[62] one and the same sign is used for different purposes whose relation is only vaguely similar.

In practice, however, the distinction between two meanings of the stroke is not so clear. When Tinctoris placed ₵ in the Contratenor of the 'Osanna' of *L'homme armé*, against ₵ in all the other voices, he cannot have intended the notes under ₵ to be sung faster than they had been under ₵ in the 'Pleni' or than they would be under ₵ in the 'Benedictus'. But the Contratenor is superscribed 'Crescit in duplum' ('It grows to twice as much'), and the proportion between the parts is not 1:2 but 1:4, so Tinctoris must have regarded ₵ as representing a kind of duple proportion even when it really signified an indefinite acceleration.[63] So even though he explicitly applied the expression 'ad medium' only to the simultaneous proportional use of the stroke and not to acceleration, and even though he used the phrase only in reference to ₵, not to Φ or any other stroked mensuration, and even though his examples show ₵ only in combination with C,[64] and even though he never placed Φ simultaneously against O,[65] or any other combination of stroked and unstroked mensurations, he must nevertheless have intended all these to be equivalent, and in particular for his advice about the appropriate note values to

---

[61] *Prop. mus.* III.ii: CS IV, 171; Seay IIa, 45-46: 'Alii vero pro signo duple signum temporis imperfecti minorisque prolationis cum tractulo traducto accelerationem mensure ut premissum est denotante, quo cantus vulgariter ad medium dicitur, tantummodo ponunt...Quod...tolerabile censeo propter quandam equipollentiam illius proportionis ac istius prolationis; dum enim aliquid ad medium canitur, due note sicut per proportionem duplam uni commensurantur.'

[62] See Tinctoris, *Super punctis musicalibus*: CS IV, 70-76; Seay I, 181-98.

[63] It is very interesting in this context to observe that De Orto's usage in his *L'homme armé* mass (see n. 33 above) applies minim equivalence not only between ⊙/₵ and O (in 'Kyrie' I, 'Kyrie' II, 'Et in terra', 'Patrem', 'Et in spiritum', and 'Sanctus'), which is in accordance with Tinctoris's precept and practice, but between ₵ and ₵ (in 'Christe' and 'Osanna' I), which is not. It would appear that De Orto understood the acceleration implicit in the stroke to have no proportional implication whatever when applied to the primary mensuration of a polyphonic complex; he did give the stroke the sense 'ad medium' when placing Φ in the Tenor against O in all other parts ('Agnus' I).

[64] *Prop. mus.* III.ii, Ex. 5; *De arte contr.* II.xxiv, Ex. 1; III.vii, Ex. 1: CS IV, 171, 137-38, 152; Seay IIa, 46; II, 125-27, 154.

[65] Though he did achieve the result we might expect this to have by signing fractions against and after O: *De arte contr.* II.xix, Ex. 2 ($\frac{4}{2}$ followed by $\frac{4}{3}$); II.xxv, Ex. 1 ($\frac{2}{1}$); II.xxvii, Ex. 1 ($\frac{2}{1}$): CS IV, 128, 138-39, 142; Seay II, 106, 128-30, 135-36.

receive dissonance to apply to ₵ (or Φ̵) as an independent mensuration and not merely in simultaneous proportion with C.[66] The difference between ₵ in its proportional sense and $\frac{2}{1}$ is that ₵ is in a fixed proportion with respect to simultaneous C: in the example for the rule of dissonance just mentioned, beginning in C, ₵ follows immediately after $\frac{1}{2}$ in a 4:1 proportion, whereas $\frac{2}{1}$ in this position would simply cancel the previous proportion and, as the example goes on to show, must follow C in its own part in order to signify duple proportion against simultaneous C.

Tinctoris gave only a few examples of ₵ in proportional combination, but there are plenty of examples in which he used Φ and ₵ as non-proportional mensuration signs, not to mention his compositions outside his theoretical writings. When Φ succeeds ₵ in all parts, we may assume a relation of minim equality; when ₵ follows O in all parts, the relation must be one of acceleration rather than proportion.[67] Both unstroked and stroked mensurations are used to revoke previous proportions notated with fractions. Not one of Tinctoris's examples ever shows a mensuration-plus-proportion sign with a stroke. As for what relation a given proportion should be referred to, whether successively in a single part or simultaneously between one part and others, Tinctoris had explicitly stated,

> I would advise...that proportions should be signed according to the relation to another part, unless it stands in the way that in the other manner, namely through the relation to the preceding number in one and the same part, many proportions are singable that otherwise would not be.[68]

The examples in Tinctoris's treatises show consistently that he related proportions simultaneously whenever they are expressed at the very beginning of a piece, but whenever they occur during the course of a piece they must be construed successively within the single part. And these show further that (as we might expect from his objection to Okeghem's use of initial O3) mensuration-plus-proportion signs carry no implication of relation to the value of the mensuration sign on its own: the proportional fraction controls absolutely the proportion of the succeeding notes to the preceding ones, and the mensuration sign merely controls the mensural properties of what follows.[69]

The proportions employed in Tinctoris's *L'homme armé* mass show that he regarded each major section—Kyrie, Gloria, Credo, Sanctus, Agnus Dei—as a single

---

[66] *De arte contr.* II.xxiv: CS IV, 136-38; Seay II, 124-27: 'in singing by half or by duple proportion, which...is the same thing (in cantu ad medium vel per proportionem duplam quod...idem est)' with its example. See Blackburn, 'Did Ockeghem Listen to Tinctoris?', 608 with n. 19.

[67] E.g., *Prop. mus.* I.vi, Ex. 7; *De arte contr.* II.xxxii, Ex. 1: CS IV, 160-61, 145; Seay IIa, 24; II, 141-42.

[68] *Prop. mus.* I.ii: CS IV, 155; Seay IIa, 13: 'consulerem...quod secundum relationem ad alteram partem proportiones signarentur, nisi obstaret altero modo, scilicet per relationem ad numerum precedentem in una et eadem parte, multas proportiones esse cantabiles que alias non essent.'

[69] A particularly clear example is *De arte contr.* II.xxi, Ex. 1: CS IV, 130-31; Seay II, 110-12 (the Contrapunctus is mistranscribed in the first bar of the Tenor). Here the sequence in the Contrapunctus of O - $\frac{3}{1}$ - C$\frac{8}{3}$ - $\frac{1}{2}$ - O$\frac{3}{2}$ against O in the Tenor ends up creating a 6:1 proportion between minims in the two parts, and consequently also between O$\frac{3}{2}$ and the O that follows in both parts. Incidentally, *De arte contr.* II.xxviii, Ex. 1 (CS IV, 143; Seay II, 137-38), demonstrates that, contrary to the assertion in Bonnie J. Blackburn, 'A Lost Guide to Tinctoris's Teachings Recovered', in *Early Music History* 1 (1981), 29-116 at 42, by the time he wrote the treatise Tinctoris had *not* 'acquiesced in the practice of his contemporaries' so as to accept O and C as silently augmented: all three parts begin in O, but the Tenor moves to C after four tempora and remains in minim equivalence to the end. There is therefore no reason to consider 1477 (the date of completion of *De arte contr.*) as a *terminus ad quem* for the composition of the *L'homme armé* mass (or for that matter the composition of *Difficiles alios*, the didactic motet under consideration in Blackburn's article).

'piece' in this sense; the mensurations and proportions at the beginning of subsections after the first must be construed in relation to the preceding subsection, for Tinctoris would not have countenanced music that truly began with a proportion in all parts, as 'Agnus' III seems to do. ₵ after O ('Christe', 'Qui tollis', 'Et incarnatus', 'Pleni', 'Agnus' II) entails acceleration. But once that acceleration has been instituted, all the other relations of mensurations and proportions in the mass follow with the signs as they appear in C.S. 35. Φ follows ₵ ('Kyrie' II, 'Cum sancto spiritu') with minim equality; when C$\frac{2}{3}$ follows Φ in 'Cum sancto spiritu', the proportion puts two minims in the place of three and the mensuration changes the tempus to imperfect. No stroke is necessary, as it would add nothing to the performers' understanding of what they had to do; and Tinctoris's logic would not admit the notation of the unnecessary.[70] The same argument applies to O$\frac{3}{2}$ after ₵ ('Confiteor', 'Pleni', 'Benedictus', 'Agnus' III), *quod erat demonstrandum*: Tinctoris would never have written Φ$\frac{3}{2}$. The simultaneous proportions of 'Agnus' III are explainable in terms of their common relation to the preceding ₵, so that ₵ ≟ ≟ = ♩♩ ⌠⌠ ♩♩ ⌠⌠ = O$\frac{3}{2}$ ≟ ≟ = ♪♪ ♪♪ ♪♪ ♪♪ ♪♪ ♪♪ = ℭ$\frac{3}{8}$ ◊ = ♪♪♪.[71]

There is, however, as I mentioned above, one error in the notation of proportions in Scribe 35's copy of Tinctoris's *L'homme armé*. In the Supremum of the tenth tempus of 'Agnus' I, the sign 3 occurs after the first two minims; it must be interpreted as signifying a triple proportion, the value of six semibreves taking the place of the remaining two semibreves of the tempus before the original mensuration O is restored. This could never have been Tinctoris's notation, as we have seen above; although he admitted that some considered 3 to indicate tripla rather than the usual sesquialtera, he censured them for writing a single figure to stand for the comparison of two quantities. But it is not hard to see how the error came about. The figure 3 in 'Agnus' I is Scribe 35's normal 3, written with the bottom of its lower curve swinging back to the right as a sinuous hairline. But all the instances of the fraction $\frac{3}{2}$ are written in a distinctive way: the lower curve of 3 is quite large and does not swing right but rather left, while the figure 2 is written quite small *inside* the lower curve of 3, with its bottom stroke joining the bottom of 3, thus: ₃. If $\frac{3}{1}$ had appeared in the exemplar in a similar fashion, then the figure 1 within it, simply a vertical stroke appearing to stand on the end of the horizontal finish of 3, might well have seemed (to a scribe accustomed to seeing and writing 3 on its own) simply an accidental part of the 3 rather than a separate figure.

Incidentally, we may wonder why Tinctoris should have chosen to employ a triple proportion in this instance—it is merely a brief melodic embellishment without the structural implication present in other cases of fractionally notated proportion in his *L'homme armé*—and not the more usual sesquialtera (whether indicated by fraction or by coloration). Apart from the cases already discussed, in which proportions are specified verbally or by fraction, and all of which occur at structurally significant points (see Table 1), there are a small number of cases where Tinctoris dropped briefly into sesquialtera

---

[70] The *locus classicus* of this principle is his objection to Busnoys's simultaneous application of both coloration and the figure 3 to bring about sesquialtera, *Prop. mus.* III.iv: CS IV, 174; Seay IIa, 52. See also his censure of the unnecessary signing of B-flat to mitigate a melodic tritone (*Liber de natura et proprietate tonorum* viii) and of the redundant writing of dots of division or perfection (*Scriptum super punctis musicalibus* xv), both of which he called 'asinine': CS IV, 22, 75; Seay I, 74, 195.

[71] As recognized by Busse Berger, *Mensuration and Proportion Signs*, 130 and Ex. 5.6; see also Blackburn, 'Did Ockeghem Listen to Tinctoris?', 608 and n. 18.

as a melodic embellishment like the one in question. All the rest of these are notated by coloration, blackening the normally void note heads.[72] This would have been ambiguous in the present instance: the rhythm would have had to be written ♩.♪♪♪♩♩.♪, which singers would doubtless have interpreted as semiminims and fusae—or as Tinctoris would have preferred to say, minims in duple and quadruple proportion rather than the desired sesquialtera.[73] He had written exactly this rhythm in coloration in the Supremum of the 'Patrem', tempus 53, but there the interpretation is made unambiguous by a more extensive context beginning with filled semibreves, which can mean nothing other than sesquialtera. Since coloration was inappropriate and a fraction necessary, I can think of only three reasons for writing $\frac{3}{1}$◊.♩♩◊◊♩.◊ rather than $\frac{3}{2}$♩.♩♩♩♩♩.♩: (a) in order to be able to join the last two semibreves in a ligature; (b) in order to emphasize the metrical division into two proportional breves (corresponding to two semibreves) rather than into three proportional semibreves; (c) in order to produce a desired count of a particular note value. The first two are rather weak; the last seems entirely far-fetched to me, but I include it for the sake of completeness.

In the end, there is a single apparent departure in the notation of proportions in the copy of Tinctoris's *L'homme armé* in C.S. 35 from the notation demanded by Tinctoris's theoretical writings and the examples therein, and it is not difficult to account for this error as miscopying from an exemplar in which the faulty proportion was correctly notated. There may well be other minor errors in Scribe 35's copy of Tinctoris's mass—it is virtually impossible that there should not be—but in most cases it should be possible to infer what stood in the exemplar, just as in the case of '3'. I am confident in the overall accuracy of the work of Scribe 35, and I am confident that the only substantial defect in his exemplar of this mass was the missing Tenor parts of its 'Et in terra' and 'Patrem'.[74]

*

There is space here only to begin a discussion of how Tinctoris might have used his *L'homme armé* mass to exemplify his famous doctrine of *varietas*—the culmination of

---

[72] 'Qui tollis', Bassus, tempus 45; 'Patrem', Supremum and Contratenor, tempora 51-53; 'Osanna', Supremum, tempora 28-30, Tenor, 34-36; 'Agnus' I, Tenor, tempus 8. I omit all cases where coloration is used simply to imperfect larger values in perfect tempus. Coloration is also used much more extensively in the 'Confiteor' (tempora 13-15, 21-30, 40-46) to distinguish sesquialtera in the free voices from sesquialtera in the 'L'homme armé' tenor (Contratenor, tempora 1-15; Tenor, tempora 32-46), indicated by O$\frac{3}{2}$ as discussed above.

[73] On the impropriety of the term 'semiminim', see Tinctoris, *Tractatus de notis et pausis* I.vii: CS IV, 42; Seay I, 112; on the ambivalent effect of blackening to achieve both duple and sesquialtera proportion, see *Prop. mus.* I.vi: CS IV, 158-60; Seay IIa, 20-24. It has been claimed that the term *fusa* appears only in central-European sources of music theory, but the *Tractatus de musica* 'Quoniam per magis noti notitiam' ('Anonymus XII') says that a full, stemmed, and flagged note 'is called *fusa* in Latin, but in French it is called *fusiel* (*fusa* dicitur latine, sed gallice dicitur *fusiel*, ut hic: ♪)': CS III, 477; Anonymus, *Tractatus et compendium cantus figurati (Mss. London, British Libr., Add. 34200; Regensburg, Proskesche Musikbibl., 98 th. 4°)*, ed. Jill M. Palmer, Corpus Scriptorum de Musica 35 (s.l., 1990), 49 (in this edition the passage restates the Latin-French equivalency twice more, the latter time with *semifusa = semifusiel*).

[74] There is a faint possibility that a whole subsection of Tinctoris's Credo may have been lost: the words 'Et in spiritum sanctum...et apostolicam Ecclesiam' are lacking between the two last sections. But this portion of the Creed was often omitted in contemporaneous masses, including the *L'homme armé* masses of Busnoys and Josquin ('super voces musicales'). Hannas, 'Concerning Deletions', esp. 167-69, has accounted for this as a conciliatory gesture towards the Greek Orthodox Church in the context of the conflict with the Turks. (She mistakenly included Tinctoris among the composers of *L'homme armé* masses who 'present the unaltered Credo', p. 168.) See also Jesse Rodin, 'Finishing Josquin's "Unfinished" Mass: A Case of Stylistic Imitation in the *Cappella Sistina*', in *The Journal of Musicology* 22 (2005), 412-53 esp. 418 n. 26.

his eight rules of composing. Two particularly valuable models of how to go about such an investigation have been offered by Agostino Magro's treatment of Du Faÿ's *L'homme armé* mass (expressly cited by Tinctoris as a model of *varietas*) and Alexis Luko's of Okeghem's *Missa quinti toni*, which explore quite different approaches that seem to me equally applicable to Tinctoris's mass.[75] The aspects investigated by Magro (in a mass on the same tenor as Tinctoris's) are tenor usage, modality, and *fuga*, those by Luko (in a mass without pre-existing tenor) articulated and concealed imitation, 'motivic modules' and 'motto constellations', and strict and varied repetition.[76] The essential point grasped by both, though articulated in methodological terms only by Luko, is that Tinctoris's concept of *varietas* has two complementary components, which he called 'quantity' and 'quality'; in other aesthetic or rhetorical writings of antiquity or the Renaissance, these correspond approximately to *copia*, 'plenty', and *varietas*, 'variety' of treatment or 'variation', or to *res*, 'matter', and *verba*, 'language'. Tinctoris's *varietas* is neither one nor the other but the interaction of both: the application of varied techniques to plentiful material in a coherent manner.[77]

I should like to conclude this article by proposing another complementary mode of *varietas* that pervades the composition of Tinctoris's *L'homme armé*. In her classic study of Tinctoris's contemporary, the Florentine humanist Angelo Poliziano (1454-1494), Ida Maïer examined Poliziano's own self-criticism in terms of *docta varietas*, 'learned variety', drawing further on writings by Poliziano's older compatriot Leon Battista Alberti (1404-1472). Maïer showed an important aspect of the *varietas* expressed in Poliziano's writings to have been the selection of words, quotations, or allusions drawn from many classical authors, combined in ways they would not have done themselves (*contaminatio*) in order to bring about a beauty of style (*concinnitas*).[78] Precisely this procedure is a feature of Tinctoris's *L'homme armé* mass, which I shall attempt to outline here.

One of the virtues of the fine article by Jennifer Bernard cited above is to have drawn together and called attention to a number of references in Tinctoris's mass to *L'homme armé* masses by his predecessors, which she discusses in terms of the rhetorical concept of *imitatio*.[79] As she sets them out, the Kyrie is related to the anonymous 'Naples'

---

[75] Agostino Magro, 'Varietas et uniformité dans la messe *L'Homme armé* de Guillaume Dufay', in *Musurgia* 7 (2001), 7-28; Alexis Luko, 'Ockeghem's "Aesthetic of Concealment": *Varietas* and Repetition in the *Missa quinti toni*', in *Tijdschrift van de Koninklijke Vereniging voor Nederlandse Muziekgeschiedenis* 61 (2011), 3-24.

[76] My own article, Jeffrey Dean, 'Okeghem's Valediction? The Meaning of *Intemerata Dei mater*', in *Johannes Ockeghem*, ed. Vendrix, 521-70, may also suggest some useful analytical methods. I have in mind what in the light of Luko's work might be called 'concealed repetition' and 'varied quotation', though I did not coin names for the techniques: see esp. pp. 534-35, 537-47, 553-54.

[77] Luko, 'Tinctoris on *Varietas*', esp. 126-34. Although Luko asserts (p. 106), 'Tinctoris's conception of *varietas* is actually much more focused than previously thought, as in his *Liber* he applies the aesthetic of *varietas* exclusively to counterpoint', she also recognizes (p. 134) that 'Tinctoris's *Liber de arte contrapuncti* is, after all, a counterpoint treatise, and so it follows that his definitions of *varietas* are specific to the study of counterpoint.' Magro's analysis of tonality, and mine (below) of *imitatio*, would seem to demonstrate that Luko's approach can be extended from counterpoint to other dimensions of composition.

[78] Ida Maïer, *Ange Politien: la formation d'un poète humaniste (1469-1480)*, Travaux d'humanisme et Renaissance 81 (Geneva, 1966), ch. 5, 'Le goût de la "docta varietas"' (pp. 203-15). Cited in passing in Luko, 'Tinctoris on *Varietas*', 101 n. 11 (I am grateful for this stimulus to return to Maïer's work). Gallagher, 'Models of *Varietas*', 54-58, addresses Alberti's evidence with a different focus.

[79] Howard Mayer Brown, 'Emulation, Competition, and Homage: Imitation and Theories of Imitation in the Renaissance', in *Journal of the American Musicological Society* 35 (1982), 1-48, has given rise to a sizeable musicological literature in the three decades since. A particularly cogent contribution, though not cited by Bernard, is David Burn, '"Nam erit

cycle of six *L'homme armé* masses by the 'troped' text of all three subsections (better termed 'prosulae'), and Bernard calls attention to specific verbal parallels between Tinctoris's prosulae and those of 'Naples' masses I and VI.[80] Tinctoris's Sanctus refers to that of Regis's *L'homme armé* 'Dum sacrum mysterium' by underlaying the 'L'homme armé' melody in his 'Sanctus' and 'Osanna' subsections with Latin texts derived from the ritual: in Regis's case throughout his mass, texts directly taken from the Office of St. Michael the Archangel, in Tinctoris's, texts reworked from the *Te Deum* and the Palm Sunday Office. Further, Regis's 'Osanna' quotes the melody associated with the words 'Pueri Hebraeorum' in the two Palm Sunday antiphons whose words Tinctoris conflated and adapted for the 'L'homme armé' tenor in his own 'Osanna'. Bernard observes a 'structural correlation' between Tinctoris's Gloria and Du Faÿ's:

> Both Dufay and Tinctoris begin the 'Et in terra' with a duet between the superius and contratenor, and a melodic motive in the superius of a stepwise ascending fourth (Dufay uses this ascending fourth as the head motive for his Mass). Both composers set the word 'hominibus' to a paraphrase of the *L'homme armé* tune, and both come to a cadence after 'voluntatis' on G. In both masses, the tenor cantus firmus enters on 'Laudamus te'. Throughout the rest of his Gloria, Tinctoris seems to be using Dufay's scheme for the number of voices together in counterpoint, and both end with an extended, lively 'Amen' in four-voice polyphony.

She also notes that, despite his condemnation of the notation of major prolation with implied augmentation in Busnoys's *L'homme armé* mass, Tinctoris's own mass

> pays tribute to Busnoys's mensural and proportional games (with the proper notation, of course). For example, the mensural and proportional layout out of both composers' Credos is strikingly similar. Both begin in perfect time, minor prolation, and proceed to imperfect time in the 'Et incarnatus', as would be expected. However, both 'Confiteor' movements use proportional fireworks, setting a cantus firmus in imperfect time, major prolation in counterpoint with the other parts in minor prolation (a 3-against-2 proportion) [actually perfect/imperfect tempus, not major/minor prolation]. Both begin to switch this proportional relationship around the text 'et expecto resurrectionem', eventually leading to all voices ending in major prolation [i.e., perfect tempus].

And in his Agnus Dei Tinctoris also reflected Busnoys's peculiar articulation of the 'L'homme armé' tenor into two parts by dividing between the two repeated segments (always 5 5 for Busnoys, in this case 6 6 for Tinctoris) instead of before the first.[81]

Some (though by no means all) of Bernard's observations had been made earlier. Reese had noticed a connection between the Sanctus of Tinctoris's *L'homme armé* and Regis's *L'homme armé* 'Dum sacrum mysterium', but he buried it in a cross-reference to

---

haec quoque laus eorum": Imitation, Competition and the "L'homme armé" Tradition', in *Revue de musicologie* 87 (2001), 249-87.

[80] These parallels actually reflect the traditional language of Latin-texted Kyries: see e.g. Clemens Blume and Henry Marriott Bannister (eds.), *Tropi graduales: Tropen des Missale im Mittelalter*, vol. 1, *Tropen zum Ordinarium Missae*, Analecta Hymnica 47 (Leipzig, 1905), 43-216. The character of Tinctoris's Latin-texted Kyrie is more typical than those of the 'Naples' masses; the theological structure of both, in which the prosulae of 'Kyrie' I address God the Father, those of 'Christe' Christ the Son, and those of 'Kyrie' II the Holy Spirit, is frequent in the tradition.

[81] Bernard, 'Tinctoris's Missa L'homme armé', 7-12; quotations from 11, 12.

a footnote on a remote page (he also identified the *Te Deum* adaptation, which Bernard did not). Cohen had observed that in his Agnus Dei Tinctoris employed the same division of the 'L'homme armé' into two equal halves that Busnoys had used throughout his mass, but suggested no direct connection. Walter Haaß summed up Tinctoris's mass by saying that its composer 'uses the cantus firmus in a similar manner to' Du Faÿ.[82] Ronald Woodley had remarked that Tinctoris's 'use of trope texts in the Kyrie, "Sanctus" and "Osanna" suggests a possible influence from the anonymous Naples cycle of six "L'homme armé" masses'.[83] Bernard may not have been the first to discover these correspondences, but she is certainly the first to put all these references together. More recently, Sean Gallagher has expanded on the relation of Tinctoris's to Regis's Sanctus,[84] and Emily Zazulia has called attention to the correspondence between Busnoys's and Tinctoris's 'Confiteor' subsections. Neither was aware of Bernard's contribution.[85] Zazulia has further proposed that Tinctoris's entire mass was modelled on Busnoys's by means of a correspondence of 'sounding length' of the tenor; her argument will need refinement before it is altogether persuasive, but it is a stimulating suggestion.

I would point out two different ways in which Tinctoris's *L'homme armé* mass reflects that of Guillaume Faugues. On the larger scale, Faugues's is the only *L'homme armé* mass preceding Tinctoris's that gives the 'L'homme armé' tune in both alternative mensural notations and treatments: often in perfect tempus with breve-semibreve motion, quite freely embellished or rhythmically altered, sometimes more plainly in major prolation with semibreve-minim motion. A more specific allusion is in the sole *fuga* canon in Tinctoris's mass, that in 'Et incarnatus'. Tinctoris's verbal canon is the leonine hexameter 'Absque mora primum ruit in dyatessaron ymum' ('Except for the first rest, it drops down to the fourth below'), so the unwritten voice anticipates the written one rather than following it—a most uncommon procedure for the time.[86] Faugues's mass involves a *fuga* canon in every four-voice section; there is no verbal canon in the sources, but a *signum congruentiae* consistently stands on the rest *before* the notated voice enters, and the counterpoint makes it clear that the unwritten voice is a fifth above the written one.[87] Tinctoris's fourth below is the complement of this and has the same contrapuntal constraints.

[82] Reese, *Music in the Renaissance*, 149; Cohen, 'Munus ab ignoto', 190; Haaß, *Studien zu den "L'homme armé"-Messen*, 141.

[83] Ronald Woodley, 'Tinctoris, Johannes', in *The New Grove Dictionary of Music and Musicians*, ed. Stanley Sadie and John Tyrrell (London, ²2001), vol. 25, 500. Others who have explicitly made the connection to 'Naples' are Klaas van der Heide, 'New Claims for a Burgundian Origin of the *L'homme armé* Tradition, and a Different View on the Relative Positions of the Earliest Masses in the Tradition', in *Tijdschrift van de Koninklijke Vereniging voor Nederlandse Muziekgeschiedenis* 55 (2005), 3-33 at 31; Jeffrey Samuel Palenik, 'The Early Career of Johannes Tinctoris: An Examination of the Music Theorist's Northern Education and Development' (Ph.D. diss., Duke University, 2008), 198-200 (but see n. 80 above). I myself and many scholars I know were aware of the connection before 2001, and none of us thought we had made a discovery, but I have no idea who first noticed it.

[84] Sean Gallagher, *Johannes Regis*, Collection 'Épitome musical' (Turnhout, 2010), 78-79.

[85] I am grateful to Emily Zazulia for making available to me the script of her unpublished paper 'Tinctoris the Reader', read at the Annual Meeting of the American Musicological Society, San Francisco, 12 November 2011. This is a revision of the paper cited in n. 39 above, and has since been further revised as part of Zazulia, 'Verbal Canons and Notational Complexity', 223-45. Here (224 n. 21) she does cite Bernard's article.

[86] Of the pieces cited by Bonnie J. Blackburn, 'Canonic Conundrums: The Singer's Petrucci', in *Basler Jahrbuch für historische Musikpraxis* 25 (2001), 53-69 at 56-57 with n. 10, only the two chansons are possibly contemporaneous with Tinctoris's *L'homme armé*; there are no earlier pieces in her unpublished catalogue of 'precursor' canons, which I thank her for sharing with me.

[87] G. Faugues, *Missa super L'homme armé*, ed. Laurence Feininger, Monumenta Polyphoniae Sanctae Ecclesiae Romanae, ser. 1, vol. 1, fasc. 4 (Rome, 1948); *Collected Works of Faugues*, ed. George C. Schuetze jr, Collected Works 1 (Brooklyn,

This suggests a couple of further references. Faugues's anticipatory *fuga* was probably suggested by the written-out procedure in all sections but the Sanctus of Regis's *L'homme armé* 'Dum sacrum mysterium', in which much of the Contratenor is in anticipatory *fuga* at the upper fifth with the Tenor in varying time intervals, and Tinctoris copied Regis's procedure very nicely at the opening of his 'Kyrie' II (tempora 1-14, Contratenor and Tenor). Further, the procedure of *fuga* at the fifth or lower fourth necessarily involves the presentation of the 'L'homme armé' tenor at more than one pitch level, and not only Faugues but several earlier composers of *L'homme armé* masses had presented the tune at two levels. But only Regis had so far presented it at three: in his Kyrie, Gloria, Credo, and 'Agnus' III it is on D and A, but in his 'Sanctus' and 'Agnus' I it is on A and E. Tinctoris presented the tenor chiefly on G and often on D, but in the Supremum at tempora 25-30 of his 'Et resurrexit' it appears on C; this may be simultaneous homage to Regis's three pitch levels and to Okeghem's transposition of the tenor down a fifth to C in the Credo of his *L'homme armé* mass.

Tinctoris had actually cited in his theoretical writings three of the *L'homme armé* masses to which his mass makes reference: those by Busnoys, Du Faÿ, and Regis.[88] It is clear he was well acquainted with the music of the other named composers of *L'homme armé* masses earlier than his own, Caron, Faugues, and Okeghem, referring to them frequently even though he never cited their *L'homme armé* masses. The 'Naples' masses are an interesting case: they now survive in a single manuscript in the National Library in Naples, which bears an inscription presenting the manuscript as a gift to Beatrice of Aragon (1457-1508), daughter of King Ferrante of Naples, wife (1476-90) of King Mathias Corvinus of Hungary, and at one time Tinctoris's pupil. The manuscript had formerly belonged to Charles le Téméraire, duke of Burgundy, and probably came into Beatrice's possession after his death in 1477, when she was already in Hungary. It would therefore have arrived in Naples only at the time of Beatrice's return in 1501, and was never there when Tinctoris himself was.[89] Nevertheless, he could well have made acquaintance with the music before he ever came to Naples; he was a Burgundian subject by birth, and despite their unique preservation at present the masses seem to have been more widely known in the late fifteenth century. For instance, I suspect the method of the 'Naples' masses also inspired one aspect of the procedure in Josquin's mass *L'homme armé* 'super voces musicales', in which the notational form of the tenor is unaltered throughout the mass and rises by step from the beginning to the end.[90]

1960), 85-116; facsimiles of original manuscripts: *Opera Omnia Faugues*, ed. George C. Schuetze jr, Publications of Mediaeval Musical Manuscripts 7 (Brooklyn, 1959), 46-78.

[88] Busnoys, *Prop. mus.* III.iii, III.v; Du Faÿ, *De arte contr.* III.viii; Regis, *Prop. mus.* III.v: CS IV, 172, 175, 152, 175; Seay IIa, 49, 55; II, 156; IIa, 55. I would endorse the argument in Gallagher, *Johannes Regis*, 98-111, that Regis wrote only one *L'homme armé* mass, 'Dum sacrum mysterium', and that Tinctoris cited a differently notated copy of the mass that now survives uniquely in C.S. 14.

[89] See Judith Cohen, *The Six Anonymous L'homme armé Masses in Naples, Biblioteca Nazionale, MS VI E 40*, Musicological Studies and Documents 21 (s.l., 1968), 62-71; Cohen, 'Munus ab ignoto', 199-202. The actual origin of the manuscript at the Burgundian court c. 1470 has now been demonstrated by Heide, 'New Claims for a Burgundian Origin', 26-31; Heide believes the manuscript was presented to Beatrice before her departure from Naples to be married in Buda (she had first been married by proxy), allowing Tinctoris to have known the manuscript itself. Palenik, 'The Early Career of Johannes Tinctoris', 186-95, offers a good rebuttal of this notion.

[90] I see this view as complementing, by no means contradicting, the case for Josquin's dependence on De Orto made by Jesse Rodin, '"When in Rome . . .", 307-72 at 322-30. Burn, '"Nam erit haec quoque laus eorum"', 270, justly observes that *L'homme armé* 'super voces musicales' follows the unique precedent of Regis in using D-*re* as the governing tonality of the mass. I would also suggest that Josquin's conversion of a modally authentic tenor into a plagal one in his

Tinctoris's references to earlier *L'homme armé* masses are made in many different ways and on different scales. I would classify as *imitatio* only the more extensive of them, those that involve the whole of his mass (e.g., Zazulia's proposal about the 'sounding length' of the tenor in Busnoys's and Tinctoris's masses), of a major section (e.g., Bernard's observation of the structural modelling of Tinctoris's Gloria on Du Faÿ's and his Credo on Busnoys's), or of a subsection (e.g., my suggestion that Tinctoris imitated Faugues's anticipatory *fuga* in his 'Et incarnatus'). Such a fleeting reference as the allusion to Regis and Okeghem in the brief presentation of a segment of 'L'homme armé' on C in Tinctoris's 'Et resurrexit' is not enough to be *imitatio* in itself; but it hints that there may be more of Okeghem's mass in Tinctoris's than has so far been noticed (there is after all clear imitation of Regis's mass in Tinctoris's 'Kyrie' II and 'Sanctus'). What strikes me as significant is the variety of ways in which Tinctoris made reference to preceding *L'homme armé* masses and the ways in which he combined these references. For instance, his Credo as a whole is modelled on Busnoys's, but 'Et incarnatus' employs a variant of Faugues's *fuga* procedure and 'Et resurrexit' includes an allusion to Okeghem's tenor transposition. There are doubtless other instances and modes of reference that have not yet been recognized, here and elsewhere in Tinctoris's *L'homme armé*, and they all constitute a sphere within which *varietas* is at work.

Here is one sort of *varietas* in Tinctoris's *L'homme armé* mass that has a clear parallel in the literary work of his Florentine contemporary Poliziano. There may well be others: the objection common to the scholars quoted early in this article, that there is too much going on in Tinctoris's mass, that it 'applies the rule of *varietas* to its own detriment', cannot be dismissed simply because I have demonstrated a greater coherence to its tenor usage than had previously been apparent. There is precedent in Poliziano's writings:

> Sometimes from the juxtaposition of opposites and of colorful paintings springs a work that is harmonious, balanced, classical in spite of its architectural artifices, like, for example, the *Epicedion in Albieram*; sometimes the multiplicity of the descriptions, the variations of tone—corresponding to the simultaneous presence of different genres within a single poem—end up in the creation of a hybrid work like the *Sylva in Scabiem*, which, more than any other Latin poem of this period, seems conceived under the sign of the most bizarre variety.[91]

L'homme armé 'sexti toni' was prompted by Tinctoris's identical manipulation in the *fuga* of his 'Et incarnatus' and the Tenor of his 'Sanctus'. Building on a discovery by Peter Király, 'Un séjour de Josquin des Prés à la cour de Hongrie?', in *Revue de Musicologie* 78 (1992), 145-50, David Fallows, *Josquin*, Collection 'Épitome musical' (Turnhout, 2009), 112-15, declares (115) 'it is all but certain that Josquin was at the royal court of Hungary...between the summer of 1485 and the end of 1488'; if this is true (I remain doubtful), Josquin might have had access to the existing manuscript of the 'Naples' masses.

[91] Maïer, *Ange Politien*, 204: 'Parfois, de la juxtaposition des contraires, et des peintures multicolores, jaillit l'œuvre harmonieuse, équilibrée, classique en dépit des artifices d'architecture, comme, par exemple, l'Épicède pour Albiera; parfois la multiplicité des descriptions, les variations de ton—correspondant à la présence simultanée de genres divers à l'intérieur d'un même poème—, aboutissent à la création d'une pièce hybride, comme la *Sylva In Scabiem*, qui, plus que toutes les autres poésies latines de cette période, semble conçue sous le signe de la variété la plus bizarre'. Maïer discusses the *Epicedion in Albieram* more fully ibid., 171-79; an important portion of the poem is treated in Alessandro Perosa, 'Febris: A Poetic Myth Created by Poliziano', in *Journal of the Warburg and Courtauld Institutes* 9 (1946), 74-95. *Sylva in Scabiem* is dealt with in Maïer, *Ange Politien*, 191-200. It is edited with a useful introduction in *Angeli Politiani Sylva in Scabiem*, ed. Alessandro Perosa, Note e discussioni erudite 4 (Rome, 1954). The late-classical literary genre of the *silva*, with its emphasis on variety, miscellaneity, and spontaneity, provides a valuable context for Tinctoris's conception of *varietas* in general and for his purposes in composing the *L'homme armé* mass in particular, which I hope

Poliziano is a writer who demands serious attention even to the most problematic of his writings. Surely Tinctoris is a composer who demands the same attention to a challenging composition like his *L'homme armé* mass. We have scarcely begun to discover what its composer put into this work.[92]

Abstract

The *L'homme armé* mass by Johannes Tinctoris has been repeatedly criticized for lacking coherence, but it has scarcely been noticed that in its unique source the Tenor part in the two largest subsections of the mass, 'Et in terra' and 'Patrem', was added by a different scribe than the copyist of the other parts and the rest of the mass. If these two subsections are left aside, the remainder of the mass demonstrates several independent patterns of usage of the 'L'homme armé' tenor, so it is proposed that the composer's intention was for these patterns to obtain in 'Et in terra' and 'Patrem' as well, and that the added Tenor parts are not by Tinctoris. The notation of mensural proportions in the source is shown to be entirely consistent with Tinctoris's distinctive theory of proportions, except in one instance in which a copying error can be explained. Various scholars have noticed allusions to *L'homme armé* masses by other composers in Tinctoris's mass, but only one study so far has attempted to bring these together; further references are observed, and Tinctoris' references to the predecessors of his mass are accounted for as one dimension of *varietas*, a compositional principle Tinctoris had emphasized in his treatise on counterpoint.

to take further. See also Frans De Bruyn, 'The Classical Silva and the Generic Development of Scientific Writing in Seventeenth-Century England', in *New Literary History* 32 (2001), 347-73.

[92] I wish to thank Bonnie Blackburn, Alejandro Planchart, Jesse Rodin, Jason Stoessel, Ronald Woodley, and Emily Zazulia for helpful and stimulating comments on earlier drafts of this article.

Tinctoris and the Neapolitan *Eruditi*[*]

■

Evan A. MacCarthy

At five hundred years' distance from the death of the composer and music theorist Johannes Tinctoris (c. 1435-1511), we can claim today to know a reasonable amount about his biography and his accomplishments, both in music and music theory. With varying degrees of certainty and precision, we know of his birth, time spent in Cambrai, his education at Orléans, his employment in Chartres and Naples, as well as a more precise date for his death in February of 1511.[1] Even with these strong chronological markers of documents, there still remain stretches of time for which Tinctoris's activities and whereabouts remain unclear, including the last fifteen or twenty years of his life, possible travels to Hungary, or the precise date (or even year) of his arrival in Italy. When the archival documents become hazy, we have turned to Tinctoris's many treatises and their dedications to royal patrons and musical colleagues as well as their references to contemporaneous events and musical compositions. From them we have been able to discern finer details about the chronology of his scholarship and, in certain cases, begin to sketch a picture of his intellectual development.

A sole surviving letter penned by Tinctoris stands as another document that adds an interesting component to our understanding of his career.[2] The humanist Johannes Trithemius (1462-1516) praised Tinctoris for writing 'several most ornate letters', and yet this single letter is our only evidence to substantiate this acclaim.[3] In the letter, dating

[*] An earlier version of this article was delivered at the 2011 Medieval and Renaissance Music Conference in Barcelona. I would like to thank Margaret Bent, Bonnie J. Blackburn, Suzannah Clark, David Fallows, Sean Gallagher, James Hankins, Keith Polk, Leofranc Holford-Strevens, Lewis Lockwood, Stephen Milner, Joshua Rifkin, Ronald Woodley, and Emily Zazulia. Preliminary research for this study was made possible with a Reader in Renaissance Studies fellowship in 2007 at Villa I Tatti, The Harvard University Center for Italian Renaissance Studies.

[1] Ronald Woodley, 'Iohannes Tinctoris: A Review of the Documentary Biographical Evidence', in *Journal of the American Musicological Society* 34 (1981), 217-48; Richard Sherr, 'Notes on Some Papal Documents in Paris', in *Studi musicali* 12 (1983), 5-16; Ronald Woodley, 'The Printing and Scope of Tinctoris's Fragmentary Treatise *De inventione et usu musice*', in *Early Music History* 5 (1985), 239-68; Allan W. Atlas, *Music at the Aragonese Court* (Cambridge, 1985), 71-77; Richard Sherr, 'A Biographical Miscellany: Josquin, Tinctoris, Obrecht, Brumel', in *Musicologia Humana: Studies in Honor of Warren and Ursula Kirkendale*, ed. Siegfried Gmeinwieser, David Hiley, and Jorg Riedlbauer (Florence, 1994), 65-73; Gianluca D'Agostino, 'Note sulla carriera napoletana di Johannes Tinctoris', in *Studi musicali* 28 (1999), 327-62; Bonnie J. Blackburn, 'Music Theory and Musical Thinking after 1450', in *Music as Concept and Practice in the Late Middle Ages*, ed. Reinhard Strohm and Bonnie J. Blackburn, New Oxford History of Music, vol. 3, Part I (Oxford, 2001), 301-45 esp. 325-27; Ronald Woodley, 'Tinctoris and Nivelles: The Obit Evidence', in this Journal 1 (2009), 110-21. See also the useful online resource, <www.stoa.org/tinctoris>, currently being updated as part of the Early Music Theory online project, at <www.earlymusictheory.org>.

[2] Naples, Biblioteca Nazionale, Ms. XII. F. 50, fols. 11-14, ed. and trans., Ronald Woodley, 'Tinctoris's Italian Translation of the Golden Fleece Statutes: A Text and (Possible) Context', in *Early Music History* 8 (1988), 173-244 at 236-44. See also Atlas, *Music at the Aragonese Court*, 77; Rob C. Wegman, 'Tinctoris's *Magnum opus*', in *Uno gentile et subtile ingenio: Studies in Renaissance Music in Honour of Bonnie J. Blackburn*, ed. M. Jennifer Bloxam, Gioia Filocamo, and Leofranc Holford-Strevens (Turnhout, 2009), 771-82 esp. 782.

[3] The line is 'epistolas ornatissimas complures dedit ad diversos'. This is found among the biographical notices in Trithemius's *Catalogus illustrium virorum Germaniam...exornantium* ([Mainz], c. 1495). A full transcription of this entry is found in Woodley, 'Iohannes Tinctoris: A Review', 247; translated in Gustave Reese, *Music in the Renaissance* (New York, 1954; rev. edn., 1959), 138. Many of its details are accurate, confirmed by evidence surviving elsewhere. The opening of the printed version of *De inventione et usu musice* serves as our only other evidence of Tinctoris's epistolary

from about 1494/5, when apparently no longer employed by the Aragonese chapel in Naples, Tinctoris replied to a friend and former colleague at the Neapolitan court, Joanmarco Cinico (c. 1430-1503), with what could be considered a brief tract on various social issues that were under debate in Naples at the time.[4] Ronald Woodley and Rob C. Wegman have proposed that in this letter Tinctoris is bewailing the state of courtly life, possibly after his tenure at the Neapolitan court has ended.[5] I will propose another interpretation of this letter, in the context of intellectual endeavours in Naples in the late fifteenth century. In particular, the closing of this letter sheds light on how Tinctoris viewed himself in relation to the Neapolitan colleague whom he is addressing:

> Hec ad te scribere me tue ornatissime aptissimeque littere, postridie quam veni Putheolis mihi reddite, compulerunt…Hinc tibi pro littera syllabam, pro syllaba dictionem orationem remitto, supplicans ut hanc ipsam epistulam omni elegantiarum dignitate nudissimam non Athenis sed Putheolis, **non ab oratore sed musico**, conditam animadvertas. Sic enim pro Cynica discretione ac modestia mihi actuum qui fiunt secundum vitam humanam parumper experto ac minus in arte dicendi perito benignissime parces. Vale Cynicorum specimen peculiarissimum; utque verbo Nasonis concludam: Vive memor nostri.

> I have been constrained to write to you of these matters by your own most ornate and fitting letter, which reached me at Pozzuoli the day after I arrived…And so I return this to you: for every letter of yours a syllable, for every syllable a phrase, for every phrase a sentence, begging you to bear in mind that this missive, quite stripped as it is of any merits of refinement, was composed not at Athens but at Pozzuoli, **not by an orator but by a *musicus***. For in this way, as befits your Cynic discretion and propriety, you will of your abundant good nature pardon me, a man but briefly experienced in the ways of the world and still less skilled in eloquence. Farewell, then, most singular example of the Cynics; and if I may close with an expression from Ovid: Live with me in your memory.[6]

Cinico was a scribe and translator at the royal court in Naples for over twenty-five years, having arrived in 1469 and remaining until at least 1498.[7] Cinico regularly participated in meetings of the celebrated intellectual circle known as the *Accademia Pontaniana*, to which I shall return later. He also wrote a treatise on justice and punishment, citing classical and medieval authorities while providing historical examples of punishing traitors and other criminals.[8] Before Naples, Cinico had been in Florence in the 1450s, where he had been a student of Pietro Strozzi and in 1452 he was listed as a *familiare* of the later sainted Antoninus (1389-1459), archbishop of Florence, and was

---

writings. Tinctoris also apparently fashioned a table depicting all of the 'vetostissimos musicos'. On this, see Woodley, 'Tinctoris's Italian Translation', 194; Wegman, 'Tinctoris's *Magnum opus*', 782.

[4] On the dating of the letter, see Woodley, 'Tinctoris's Italian Translation', 198-200; Tinctoris, *Proportionale musices. Liber de arte contrapuncti*, ed. Gianluca D'Agostino (Florence, 2008), lvi-lvii. By the time of composing this letter, Tinctoris held the title of doctor of canon and civil law, and had likely spent time in Rome as well as, perhaps, Buda, in the service of Beatrice d'Aragona.

[5] Woodley, 'Tinctoris's Italian Translation', 200-1; Wegman, 'Tinctoris's *Magnum opus*', 782.

[6] Woodley, 'Tinctoris's Italian Translation', 243-44.

[7] On Cinico, see Tamaro De Marinis, *La biblioteca napoletana dei re d'Aragona*, 4 vols. (Milan, 1947-1952), vol. 1, 42-51; idem, *La biblioteca napoletana dei re d'Aragona. Supplemento*, 2 vols. (Verona, 1969), vol. 1, passim; Mauro De Nichilo, 'Giovan Marco Cinico', in *Dizionario biografico degli italiani* 25 (Rome, 1981), vol. 25, 634-36. See also Woodley, 'Tinctoris's Italian Translation', 175 n. 8.

[8] For a description of Cinico's treatise and its citation of recent Neapolitan events, see Jerry H. Bentley, *Politics and Culture in Renaissance Naples* (Princeton, 1987), 220.

involved in the copying of Antoninus's popular devotional text, his *Confessionale*.[9] Cinico's letter to Tinctoris that inspired this response does not survive. One must therefore imagine its contents, but it is likely that it also concerned the leading of a virtuous life.

The sensitivity, or more likely false humility, that Tinctoris conveys in this letter's closing about his abilities as a Latin writer deserves more attention from us. False humility is certainly not uncommon in his other writings or in the dedicatory introductions of treatises by many other fifteenth-century writers. In Tinctoris's surviving music treatises, one finds him eagerly introducing his technical writings with overwrought Latin prose, filled to the brim with references to classical and early Christian authors and texts. When it came to music, Tinctoris never shied away from highlighting his superior knowledge or skill. For example, in the *Terminorum musicae diffinitorium*, he wrote in his dedication to Princess Beatrice d'Aragona (1457-1508): 'Tamen, si in theoria musices pariter et praxi omnes nostri temporis cantores excedam aut excedar ab aliquo, tue ceterorumque in ipsa arte peritissimorum perspicientie discurrendum relinquo' ('I leave to the perspicacity of yourself and of others skilled in this art [of music] to determine whether in musical practice and likewise in musical theory I may surpass all musicians of our time or be surpassed by some').[10] Tinctoris also referenced his skill at teaching music, law, and other arts when giving himself the title of '[musice] artis professor minimus' and counting himself 'inter musice professores minimus' and 'inter legum artiumque mathematicarum professores minimus'.[11]

The phrase in his letter to Cinico, 'non ab oratore sed musico' ('not by an orator but by a *musicus*'), might be one more example of false humility. However, I propose that there could be the perception of vulnerability on Tinctoris's part with respect to his intellectual capabilities as a *musicus*. A document written by Tinctoris thirty years before the letter to Cinico, while he was procurator of the German nation at the University of Orléans, reveals an unabashed, haughty side that made him the subject of harsh castigation from later readers.[12] In an official university document, where a formulaic entry from Tinctoris regarding matriculation should have appeared, Tinctoris instead supplied a lengthy and supercilious passage filled with erroneous classical references. Leofranc Holford-Strevens has stated that 'the pomposity of Tinctoris' youthful folly is medieval in spirit, despite…false classicisms' and this 'provoked marginalia of humanistic allure.'[13] One marginal remark blasts that this prose came from 'clearly the brain of a

9 Albinia C. de la Mare, 'The Book Trade', in *Journal of the Warburg and Courtauld Institutes* 39 (1976), 239-45 esp. 242-44. De la Mare continues the accepted reading of this document as 1462, but it must be 1452 (even 1442) since Antonino Pierozzi died in 1459.

10 Iohannes Tinctoris, *Diffinitorium musice: Un dizionario di musica per Beatrice d'Aragona*, ed. Cecilia Panti (Florence, 2004), 4.

11 The prefaces to Tinctoris's *Liber imperfectionum notarum musicalium*, *Expositio manus*, and *Complexus effectuum musices* contain these references, respectively. All texts are found in Tinctoris, *Opera theoretica*, ed. Albert Seay, 2 vols. in 3, Corpus scriptorum de musica 22 ([Rome], 1975-78). See <www.stoa.org/tinctoris> for vastly improved editions of Tinctoris's *Liber imperfectionum* and *Expositio manus*, among other treatises. For the *Complexus effectuum musices*, see J. D. Cullington and Reinhard Strohm (eds.), *'That Liberal and Virtuous Art': Three Humanist Treatises on Music* (Newtownabbey, 2001).

12 Archives départmentales du Loiret, D 213 ('Liber procuratorum 1'), fol. 62r; see Cornelia Ridderikhoff and Hilde de Ridder-Symoens (eds.), *Les Livres de procurateurs de la nation germanique de l'ancienne université d'Orléans, 1444-1602* (Leiden, 1971), Part I, vol. 1, 29-30; Woodley, 'Iohannes Tinctoris: A Review', 243.

13 For a fuller evaluation of Tinctoris's Latin style, see Holford-Strevens, 'Humanism and the Language of Music Treatises', in *Renaissance Studies* 15 (2001), 415-49 esp. 424-28. See also Ronald Woodley, 'Renaissance Music Theory as Literature:

musician; that is, ignorant'.[14] While it seems unlikely that Tinctoris saw this vituperative commentary, one might expect that his grandiosity incurred similar remarks from his colleagues and students and thus we might understand a later sensitivity (even in the form of false humility) when it came to rhetorical strengths as a Latin writer.[15]

In fifteenth-century music studies today, Tinctoris has become a central figure for a number of reasons, which include his teachings on counterpoint, mensuration, and notation, his opinions regarding the compositional practices of several contemporaries, and his commentary on the history of music, musical performance, and musical style. In order to better understand these influential contributions, several treatises by Tinctoris have been scrupulously examined for traces of literary, rhetorical, and musical influence, both ancient and modern, especially his *Proportionale musices*, *Complexus effectuum musices*, *Liber de arte contrapuncti*, and *De inventione et usu musice*.[16] Recent work has shown us that the explosion of his treatises over the course of about five years in the mid-1470s was not necessarily the inspired fruit of his arrival at the royal court of Naples in or around 1472-73, but rather the result of several years of singing, instructing, reading, and even drafting treatises before his arrival in Naples.[17] I will argue here that, however much those years of training and experience in musical practice and theory before Naples might have shaped Tinctoris, it is only at Naples that

On Reading the *Proportionale Musices* of Iohannes Tinctoris', in *Renaissance Studies* 1 (1987), 209-20 esp. 212, where Woodley describes Tinctoris's writing here as 'pretentious doggerel'; also Jeffrey Palenik, 'The Early Career of Johannes Tinctoris: An Examination of the Music Theorist's Northern Education and Development' (Ph.D. diss., Duke University, 2008), 134, where Palenik argues that 'Tinctoris's early Neapolitan treatises display a marked literary development over both of his pre-Neapolitan writing examples, the Cambrai fragments of *De inventione*, and the German nation's log of the University of Orléans'.

[14] 'Musicum plane ingenium id est indoctum': see Woodley, 'Iohannes Tinctoris: A Review', 243.

[15] Tinctoris is also claiming his status as a *musicus* over that of a mere *cantor*, according to the then centuries-old Boethian distinction. On this distinction, see Christopher Page, 'Musicus and Cantor', in *Companion to Medieval and Renaissance Music*, ed. Tess Knighton and David Fallows (Oxford, 1997), 74-78.

[16] Tinctoris, *Proportionale musices. Liber de arte contrapuncti*, ed. D'Agostino; Tinctoris, *Complexus effectuum musices*, ed. in Cullington and Strohm, 'That Liberal and Virtuous Art'; Weinmann, *Johannes Tinctoris (1445-1511) und sein unbekannter Traktat 'De inventione et usu musicae'*; Woodley, 'The Printing and Scope'. Some of the main analytical readings of these texts include Margaret Bent, 'Resfacta and Cantare super librum', in *Journal of the American Musicological Society* 36 (1983), 371-91; Woodley, 'Renaissance Music Theory as Literature'; Jessie Ann Owens, 'Music Historiography and the Definition of "Renaissance"', in *Notes* 47 (1990-91), 305-30; Leofranc Holford-Strevens, 'Tinctoris on the Great Composers', in *Plainsong and Medieval Music* 5 (1996), 193-99; Christopher Page, 'Reading and Reminiscence: Tinctoris on the Beauty of Music', in *Journal of the American Musicological Society* 49 (1996), 1-31; Bonnie J. Blackburn, 'Did Ockeghem Listen to Tinctoris?', in *Johannes Ockeghem: Actes du XLe colloque international d'études humanistes. Tours, 3-8 février 1997*, ed. Philippe Vendrix (Paris, 1998), 597-640; Sean Gallagher, 'Models of *Varietas*: Studies in Style and Attribution in the Motets of Johannes Regis and his Contemporaries' (Ph.D. diss., Harvard University, 1998), ch. 2; Reinhard Strohm, 'Music, Humanism, and the Idea of a "Rebirth" of the Arts', in *Music as Concept and Practice in the Late Middle Ages*, ed. Strohm and Blackburn, 346-405; Margaret Bent, 'On False Concords in Late Fifteenth-Century Music: Yet Another Look at Tinctoris', in *Théorie et analyse musicales 1450-1650 (Music Theory and Analysis)*, ed. Anne-Emmanuelle Ceulemans and Bonnie J. Blackburn (Louvain-la-Neuve, 2001), 65-118; Sean Gallagher, 'Pater optime: Vergilian Allusion in Obrecht's *Mille quingentis*', in *The Journal of Musicology* 18 (2001), 406-57; Rob C. Wegman, '"Musical Understanding" in the 15th Century', in *Early Music* 30 (2002), 47-66; idem, 'Johannes Tinctoris and the "New Art"', in *Music & Letters* 84 (2003), 171-88; Reinhard Strohm, 'Neue Aspekte von Musik und Humanismus im 15. Jahrhundert', in *Acta Musicologica* 76 (2004), 135-57; Margaret Bent, 'The Musical Stanzas in Martin le Franc's *Le champion des dames*', in *Music and Medieval Manuscripts: Paleography and Performance*, ed. John Haines and Randall Rosenfeld (Aldershot, 2004), 91-127; Alexis Luko, 'Tinctoris on *Varietas*', in *Early Music History* 27 (2008), 99-136.

[17] Rob C. Wegman, *The Crisis of Music in Early Modern Europe, 1470-1530* (New York, 2005), 53-54, 189-91; idem, 'Tinctoris's *Magnum opus*', 771-82; Palenik, 'The Early Career of Johannes Tinctoris', ch. 3; Woodley, 'The Printing and Scope', 257: 'it is increasingly apparent that any accurate and intelligent reading of Tinctoris's life and activity must take full account of his relationship to the humanist movement, both in Italy, where he spent his most creative years, and in northern Europe, which provided the familial and educational roots on which he continued to draw throughout his career, and to which he may well have eventually returned'.

these treatises found themselves completed, circulated, and in some cases even printed.[18] Jeffrey Palenik has acknowledged that Tinctoris's strong emphasis on the classical literary tradition denotes a likelihood that 'at least part of Tinctoris's extensive and prolonged study of humanism occurred in Naples'.[19]

It is my aim to investigate what it was about Naples and those he met there that encouraged this flurry of intellectual activity, and to consider some of Tinctoris's contemporary colleagues and how their scholarly activities might have influenced him, as well as how his activities might perhaps have influenced them.[20] Drawing attention to the Neapolitan context of the completion and reception of these treatises and others by Tinctoris will allow for a comparative study of Tinctoris and some of his closest colleagues at the Aragonese court in Naples. This study will have implications for our understanding of several of his treatises, including the *De inventione et usu musice*, *Complexus effectuum musices*, and *Terminorum musicae diffinitorium*, as well as the prefaces to other treatises such as his *Proportionale musices* and *Liber de arte contrapuncti*.

'Ab eruditis existimetur'

In 1477, Tinctoris made his celebrated remark that music composed more than forty years before then had been 'deemed by the learned unworthy to be heard'.[21] 'Ab eruditis existimetur' is the phrase employed by Tinctoris. Just who were these *eruditi* discussing music and musical style? Were they musicians, scholars, courtiers, or some combination thereof? In another treatise, Tinctoris wrote that 'only musicians judge sounds correctly', supporting his claim with citations of Cicero and Aristotle.[22] We do know of such scholarly discussions of music in Naples occurring among singers and composers between late 1478 and late 1480, just around the time of Tinctoris's comment.[23] Pantaleone Melaguli's contemporary biography of Gaffurius reports that Gaffurius 'being well versed in musical studies…distinguished himself so much that he did not hesitate to discuss music very sagaciously…with Johannes Tinctoris, Guglielmus Guarnerius, Bernard Ycart, and many other distinguished musicians'.[24] To these gatherings of musicians, we

[18] Woodley, 'Renaissance Music Theory as Literature'; Tinctoris, *Proportionale musices. Liber de arte contrapuncti*, ed. D'Agostino, xlviii-l. See Palenik, 'The Early Career of Johannes Tinctoris', 136, where he claims that 'an explanation of the Neapolitan artistic and literary climate' would better contextualize Tinctoris's output.

[19] Palenik, 'The Early Career of Johannes Tinctoris', 136.

[20] The need for this type of study has been announced already by Palenik, 'The Early Career of Johannes Tinctoris', 213: 'it will be necessary to consider the theorist's relationship with Italian and specifically Neapolitan humanism as well as other contemporary intellectual movements, including Platonism and Aristotelianism. This investigation will require thorough examination of potential Neapolitan literary and artistic influences, including individuals patronized by the royal court and local intellectual institutions, such as the *Accademia Pontaniana*.'

[21] 'Neque quod satis admirari nequeo, quippiam compositum nisi citra annos quadraginta extat quod auditu dignum ab eruditis existimetur.' (Tinctoris, *Liber de arte contrapuncti*, ed. D'Agostino, 138).

[22] 'Soli igitur musici de sonis recte iudicant' (Tinctoris, *Liber de natura et proprietate tonorum*, ch. 1, in *Opera theoretica*, ed. Seay, vol. 1, 69). Nearly all fifteenth-century humanistic education treatises encouraged at least some education in music in order to fulfill Aristotle's urging in Book 8 of his *Politics* 'to practice the art of music so that, as old men, they can judge and enjoy it more correctly' (a line cited by Tinctoris himself). Boethius also includes this in his definition of a 'musicus' in *De institutione musice*, I.34. On the *eruditi* as listeners, see Wegman, 'Johannes Tinctoris and the "New Art"', 174, 180; Wegman, *The Crisis of Music*, 66-76.

[23] D'Agostino suggests a fairly limited group (almost a circle) of people with whom Tinctoris had contact (Tinctoris, *Proportionale musices. Liber de arte contrapuncti*, ed. D'Agostino, lvi-lvii).

[24] 'Ibi Philippini Bononi, regii scribae municipis et aequalis sui, hortatu, in musica meditatione exercitatus, tantum praestitit ut iam cum Ioanne Tinctoris, Gulielmo Guamerii, Bemardo Ycart et compluribus aliis clarissimis musicis

might add the abbot and music theorist Blasius Romerus de Poblet, who was in Naples at this time and whose writings on music later served as the textual source for much of Florentius de Faxolis's *Liber musices*.[25]

Tinctoris's dedications to his music treatises also make reference to conversations with fellow composers and musicians.[26] For example, the dedication of his *Liber de natura et proprietate tonorum* to Ockeghem and Busnoys requests their criticism and approval of his ideas on mode, just as he had criticized many of their works.[27] Later in the body of the same treatise, during his brief discussion of mode and polyphony, Tinctoris inserted a passage in direct speech (unique to all of his writings) that implies a certain type of conversational analysis of musical works.[28]

For a musician like Tinctoris, gaining employment at the royal court in Naples would have been a real boon. During much of his reign as king of Naples, Ferdinand I (Ferrante) sought to elevate his chapel to the highest level by recruiting and competing for northern singers.[29] Ferrante's well-known fondness for and study of music was praised by Tinctoris himself as well as by both Raffaele and Aurelio Brandolini.[30] In his

acutissime disserere non dubitaret. Theoricam tunc subtilissimum opus contexuit'. This biography is found at the end of Gaffurio's manuscript copy of his *Liber de harmonia instrumentali* of 1497 (Lodi, Biblioteca Comunale, Ms. XXVIII A 9, fols. 5-130). The text also appears, revised for the press, as *De harmonia musicorum instrumentorum opus* (Milan, 1514), and in the printed version of the treatise (Milan, 1518); translation from Atlas, *Music at the Aragonese Court*, 80. Atlas proposes the dates for these conversations according to the archival documents that note the presence in Naples of all these conversants, including Gaffurius. See also Clement A. Miller, 'Early Gaffuriana: New Answers to Old Questions', in *The Musical Quarterly* 56 (1970), 367-88 at 372 n. 33; Woodley, 'Iohannes Tinctoris: A Review', 234; Palenik, 'The Early Career of Johannes Tinctoris', 170; Gianluca D'Agostino, 'Reading Theorists for Recovering "Ghost" Repertories: Tinctoris, Gaffurio and the Neapolitan Context', in *Studi musicali* 34 (2005), 25-50 at 26 n. 2.; Carlo Galiano, 'Gaffurio, il conte di Potenza e la prima dedicatoria inedita del *Theoricum opus musice discipline* (London, British Library, Hirsch IV. 1441)', in *Medioevo Mezzogiorno Mediterraneo: Studi in onore di Mario del Treppo*, ed. Gabriella Rossetti and Giovanni Vitolo, 2 vols. (Naples, 2000), vol. 2, 271-302 at 275-76; D'Agostino, 'La musica, la cappella e il cerimoniale', in *Cappelle musicali fra corte, stato, e chiesa nell'Italia del Rinascimento: atti del convegno internazionale (Camaiore, 21-23 ottobre 2005)*, ed. Franco Piperno, Gabriella Biagi Ravenni, and Andrea Chegai (Florence, 2007), 153-80 esp. at 170. On Gaffurius, see Claude V. Palisca, *Humanism in Italian Renaissance Musical Thought* (New Haven, 1985), 166-78, 191-232, 293-98; Gaffurius, *Theorica musicae*, ed. Walter K. Kreyszig and Claude V. Palisca (New Haven, 1993); Blackburn, 'Music Theory and Musical Thinking after 1450', 333-37.

[25] For the most recent and convincing account of Blasius Romerus and his connections to music, see Leofranc Holford-Strevens, 'The Erudition of Florentius de Faxolis and Blasius Romerus', in *Uno gentile et subtile ingenio*, ed. Bloxam et al., 751-59; see also Florentius de Faxolis, *Book of Music*, ed. Bonnie J. Blackburn and Leofranc Holford-Strevens (Cambridge MA and London, 2010), xii-xvi. For another interpretation of Florentius's biography, see Francesco Rocco Rossi, 'Auctores in opusculo introducti: L'enigmatico Florentius musicus e gli sconosciuti referenti del *Liber Musices* (I-Mt 2146)', in *Acta Musicologica* 80 (2008), 165-77. We will return to the presence of Blasius in Naples again below.

[26] Tinctoris, *Proportionale musices. Liber de arte contrapuncti*, ed. D'Agostino, xlviii-l, lvii-lxi. Dedicatees include the Neapolitan singer Johannes de Lotinis, the singer Jacob Frontin, the Cambrai canon and singer in the papal and Milanese chapels Martin Hanart, and the protocapellano for the duke of Milan Guillelmo Guinandi. Otherwise, the surviving treatises are dedicated to Ferrante and Beatrice d'Aragona.

[27] 'Unde quoniam scientia et cognitio tonorum sit compositoribus utilissima, opusculum hoc de natura et proprietate eorum conscripsi. Quod quidem vobis tanquam luminibus summae claritatis inter recentiores compositores dicare in animum venit, non ut eo veram, admirabilem, rarissimamque dignitatem et auctoritatem in sublimi prudentia componendi erudire conari videar, sed ut disciplinam hanc, si vera fuerit, approbare, si falsa reprobare dignemini. Rem gratissimam mihi quidem facietis, si tales in eis operibus vos ostenderitis, qualem me ostendo in vestris.' (Tinctoris, *Liber de natura et proprietate tonorum*, prologus, *Opera theoretica*, ed. Seay, vol. 1, 66-67).

[28] 'Verbi gratia, siquis universaliter mihi diceret, "Tinctoris, peto abs te cuius toni sit carmen *Le serviteur*", responderem universaliter primi toni irregularis, quoniam Tenor pars principalis ipsius carminis sit huiusmodi toni.' (Tinctoris, *Liber de natura et proporietate tonorum*, ch. 24, in *Opera theoretica*, ed. Seay, vol. 1, 85-86).

[29] For an overview of the royal chapel at Naples, see Atlas, *Music at the Aragonese Court*, 23-57. In the prologue to his *Proportionale musices*, Tinctoris also praises Ferrante's magnificence for supporting music in Naples. On this, see D'Agostino, 'La musica, la cappella e il cerimoniale', 156-57.

[30] Raffaele Brandolini, *On Music and Poetry (De musica et poetica, 1513)*, trans. Ann E. Moyer, Medieval and Renaissance Texts and Studies 232 (Tempe, 2001), 18-21: 'Ferdinand...so zealously pursued the discipline of music both publicly and privately that not only did he often practice it himself during his leisure time, but used great rewards to call to his

De laudibus musicae et Petriboni Ferrariensis, Aurelio Lippo Brandolini applauded Ferrante for his many great qualities, one of which was his love of music: 'Huc accedebant bonarum artium studia liberalesque disciplinae, quas tu quidem quantum amaveris quantumque in illis profeceris (ut de reliquis taceamus) musica maximo documento est, quum nec veterum nec recentiorum principum quisquis eius rei fuerit studiosior' ('Here were added the study and liberal disciplines of the fine arts: music provides the highest evidence of how much you have loved these and how much you have accomplished in them (to say nothing of the rest), since not one of the ancient or more recent princes has been more studious in that matter').[31] Brandolini also highlighted the importance of the judgement of musical performance, continuing: 'Huic autem rei quae materiam abunde praeberet occurrit Petrusbonus ferrariensis, musicus quidem cum omnium tum vel maxime tui iuditio praestantissimus' ('Regarding this subject, which would offer an abundance of material, there comes to mind Pietrobono of Ferrara, a most outstanding musician in the judgement both of all and most especially of yourself').[32] This courtly support of music, its study, and accurate judgement would have been the prime seedbed for Tinctoris's writings.

Tinctoris and the Grammarians

To a motivated scholar like Tinctoris, no matter how strong his humanistic tendencies might or might not have been, the Neapolitan court must have been an exciting fount of new intellectual endeavours.[33] Francesco Filelfo had complained in 1471 that literary refinement had disappeared from Naples while hunting displaced scholarship, but Francesco Bandini wrote at the same time that if one desired an example of the liberal arts, it was in Naples in all perfection.[34] In particular, Naples was making a name for

court from all over Europe those most learned in the discipline and the most skillful makers of instruments. Indeed, he used to have (as everyone knows) a very flourishing highly selected throng of singers from France, England, Spain, and Germany, assigned solely to engage in divine services and praises.' On this, see Atlas, *Music at the Aragonese Court*, 53-54; F. Alberto Gallo, *Music in the Castle: Troubadours, Books, and Orators in Italian Courts of the Thirteenth, Fourteenth, and Fifteenth Centuries* (Chicago, 1995), 75-77, 95; D'Agostino, 'La musica, la cappella e il cerimoniale', 157-58. Raffaele also praises Neapolitans Andrea Matteo Acquaviva d'Atri and Antonello Petrucci, among others, for their support of musical performance.

[31] Aurelio Lippo Brandolini, *Prefatio in Libellum de laudibus musicae et Petriboni ferrariensis ad summum maiestatem regis Ferdinandi* (Lucca, Biblioteca Capitolare, Ms. 525, fol. 175v), ed. in Gallo, *Music in the Castle*, 114-17 (my translation).

[32] A. Brandolini, *Prefatio in Libellum de laudibus musicae et Petriboni ferrariensis*, ed. in Gallo, *Music in the Castle*, 116-17 (my translation), also cited in D'Agostino, 'La musica, la cappella e il cerimoniale', 154-55; Atlas, *Music at the Aragonese Court*, 102. In addition, a number of characters in Giovanni Pontano's dialogue *Antonius* (1487), which mostly concerns the obsessive behavior of grammarians, speak of their fondness for musical performance, calling upon a musician to sing verses to them. See Strohm, 'Music, Humanism, and the Idea of a "Rebirth" of the Arts', 355, 394. For a new edition and translation of the dialogue, see Pontano, *Dialogues* (Vol. 1), ed. Julia Haig Gaisser, The I Tatti Renaissance Library 53 (Cambridge, 2012), esp. at 260-345.

[33] On Naples, see Mario Santoro, 'La cultura umanistica', in *Storia di Napoli* (Naples, 1975-81), vol. 7, esp. 128-44; idem, 'Humanism in Naples', in *Renaissance Humanism: Foundations, Forms, Legacy*, ed. Albert Rabil, Jr., 3 vols. (Philadelphia, 1988), vol. 1, 296-331; Bentley, *Politics and Culture in Renaissance Naples*, passim, esp. 283-300; Atlas, *Music at the Aragonese Court*, 1-22.

[34] The passage by Bandini is cited in Atlas, *Music at the Aragonese Court*, xi; Gallo, *Music in the Castle*, 112. On the writing style encouraged among Neapolitan humanists, Santoro, 'Humanism in Naples', 319, observes that 'one can discern in the entire literary production of Neapolitan humanism (as indeed in all humanistic literature) the erudite use of the instruments of rhetoric borrowed from the teachings of the ancients and made the object of intensive study and theoretical reflection. Therefore, the choice of various genres was not by accident, and within each genre the choice

itself as a centre of rigorous grammatical and philological analysis.[35] While in Naples, Tinctoris must have delighted in what the humanist-jurist Alessandro d'Alessandro (1461-1523) described as the 'ludi literari' among teachers and scholars in the city, who investigated and argued over the interpretation of words and sentences.[36] Antonio Calcillo had begun teaching rhetoric at the Neapolitan university, teaching from 1466-71 until he was replaced by his student Giuniano Maio, to whom we will return at length later.[37] At Naples, the famous humanistic scholar Lorenzo Valla not only wrote much of his *Elegantiae linguae latinae* as well as his first redaction of the annotations on the New Testament, but many of his texts circulated in Naples after his departure and even after his death.[38] Valla's analytical work was continued by the next generation of Neapolitan scholars, one of whom, I will argue, would serve as a model for Tinctoris.

The tireless labours of mid-century humanists toward Latin lexicography and the clarification of Latin orthography, etymology, and pronunciation reflected a scholarly methodology (one might even say scrupulosity) that Tinctoris must have admired, given his imitation of that approach in his own writings on music, especially those concerning counterpoint, notation, and the mensural system. In the aforementioned letter to Cinico, Tinctoris paid tribute to this grammar-obsessive culture in Naples, in which Cinico played an active role. With the line, 'for every letter of yours a syllable, for every syllable a phrase, for every phrase a sentence', Tinctoris cited Priscian's first four parts of grammar that were regularly repeated in many Neapolitan grammar textbooks.[39] One such textbook was written by Giovanni Musefilo, a close friend of Cinico, some time between

of structures, divisions, stylistic levels, and even diction was carefully considered. In addition to relying on classical models for such choices, Neapolitan humanists also used important texts of fifteenth-century writers'.

[35] Bentley, *Politics and Culture in Renaissance Naples*, 294-96; Carlo de Frede, *I lettori di umanità nello studio di Napoli durante il Rinascimento*, Studi e documenti per la storia della Università degli Studi di Napoli 2 (Naples, 1960), esp. 39-80; Marco Santoro, 'Gli studi grammaticali a Napoli nel quattrocento: Approdi editoriali', in *Valla e Napoli: Il dibattito filologico in età umanistica*, ed. Marco Santoro, Istituto Nazionale di Studi sul Rinascimento Meridionale, Atti 3 (Pisa and Rome, 2007), 33-51; Giancarlo Abbamonte, 'Gli studi lessicografici a Roma e a Napoli', in *Les Académies dans l'Europe humaniste: idéaux et pratiques (Actes du colloque international de Paris (10-13 juin 2003)*, ed. Marc Deramaix (Geneva, 2008), 339-68. For a recent assessment of rhetoric in fifteenth-century Italian grammar syllabi, see Robert Black, *Humanism and Education in Medieval and Renaissance Italy: Tradition and Innovation in Latin Schools from the Twelfth to the Fifteenth Century* (Cambridge, 2001), 331-65.

[36] Alessandro d'Alessandro, *Dies geniales* (Paris, 1565), fols. 33v-34r. 'Ambulabamus in littore dum Neapoli essemus, aestivo anni tempore, cum iam advesperasset, ego et Iunius Antonius, et plerique studiosi paribus disciplinis dediti, qui illuc ociandi causa advenerant. Cumque, duos ludi literarii professores, super verbo "reperio" et "invenio", gravi contentione inter se iurgantes disceptantesque videremus, libuit eorum disceptationi interesse': see Michele Fuiano, *Insegnamento e cultura a Napoli nel Rinascimento* (Naples, 1971), 19. D'Alessandro (*Dies geniales*, fol. 16v) described one such Neapolitan teacher, Giuniano Maio, as being inclined 'in exquirendis adnotandisque verborum et sententiarum viribus'. For more on D'Alessandro, see Domenico Maffei, *Alessandro d'Alessandro: Giureconsulto Umanista* (Milan, 1956).

[37] Bentley, *Politics and Culture in Renaissance Naples*, 99; Roberto Ricciardi, 'Angelo Poliziano, Giuniano Maio, Antonio Calcillo', in *Rinascimento* (2nd ser.) 8 (1968), 277-309.

[38] Bentley, *Politics and Culture in Renaissance Naples*, 108-22; Giacomo Ferraù, 'Valla e gli Aragonesi', in *Valla e Napoli*, ed. Santoro, 3-29. On the circulation of his texts in Naples, see Ferraù, *Pontano critico* (Messina, 1983), 13-14, 98-101.

[39] 'Primus liber continet de uoce et eius speciebus; de **litera**: quid sit litera, de eius generibus et speciebus, de singularum potestate, quae in quas transeunt per declinationes uel compositiones partium orationis. secundus de syllaba: quid sit **syllaba**, quot literis constare potest et quo ordine et quo sono, de accidentibus singulis syllabis; de **dictione**: quid sit dictio, quae eius differentia ad syllabam; de **oratione**: quid sit oratio, quot eius partes, de earum proprietate; de nomine: quid sit nomen, de accidentibus ei, quot sunt species propriorum nominum, quot appellatiuorum, quot adiectiuorum, quot deriuatiuorum; de patronymicis: quot eorum formae, quomodo deriuantur, ex quibus primitiuis; de diuersis possessiuorum terminationibus et eorum regulis' (Priscianus, *Institutiones grammaticae*, prefatio, ed. Martin Hertz and Heinrich Keil, 2 vols., Grammatici Latini 2-3 [Leipzig, 1855-59], vol. 2, 3; emphasis mine). For a full list of the grammar texts written and printed in Naples in the 1470s and 1480s, see De Frede, *I lettori di umanità*, 278. Authors include Niccolò Perotti, Agostino Dati, and Aurelio Bienato, as well as Guarino of Verona's widely-circulated *Regulae grammaticae* from earlier in the fifteenth century.

1474 and 1482. Musefilo's *Institutiones Grammaticae* opens, 'Grammatica est ars recte loquendi recteque scribendi scriptorum lectionibus observata. Partes grammaticae sunt quattuor: littera, syllaba, dictio et oratio.' ('Grammar is the art of speaking and writing correctly, as observed in the readings of authors. There are four grammatical parts: letter, syllable, phrase, oration'.)[40] The first half of this passage by Musefilo also brings to mind the oft-cited quotation by Tinctoris of the *Ars Poetica* of Horace that begins his counterpoint treatise: 'Scribendi recte sapere est et principium et fons' ('Wisdom is the source and fount of writing correctly').[41]

Formed by customarily accurate grammar, Tinctoris's inclination for rhetoric and rhetorical models was first thoroughly addressed by Woodley in relation to the prologue to *Proportionale musices*, then reassessed by Page, Strohm, and Wegman.[42] More recently, Sean Gallagher and Alexis Luko have argued for understanding the body of Tinctoris's counterpoint treatise (and not simply his introductory prose), particularly his conception of musical *varietas*, as borrowing directly from Cicero, while, in a number of thoughtful studies, Margaret Bent has rightly encouraged the exploration of the grammatical and rhetorical tradition as 'a basis for the purely musical procedures of late-medieval counterpoint, both written and sung'.[43] Whether for his musical works or his writings, Tinctoris's grafting of this tradition must have been bolstered by the philological endeavours surrounding him, and grounded in his own training in legal rhetoric, an underestimated influence on his writings.[44]

Private Tutoring and the Neapolitan Studio

The centre for promoting the study of grammar and rhetoric in late fifteenth-century Naples was the *studio* (or university). Most famous for its law faculty, the university had re-opened in the 1440s under Alfonso I d'Aragona (1396-1458) but had an on-and-off existence until 1465, when it finally gained more permanence with papal backing for the conferring of degrees.[45] Until 1473, professors taught in private homes, and thereafter in

[40] Naples, Biblioteca Nazionale, Ms. V. C. 12; Fuiano, *Insegnamento e cultura*, 129. On the friendship of Musefilo and Cinico, see Fuiano, *Insegnamento e cultura*, 35-38. This citation of Priscian was repeated in Lucio Giovanni Scoppa, *Institutiones grammaticae* (Naples, 1508), fol. 1r: Fuiano, *Insegnamento e cultura*, 131. In the realm of music, one might also point out Book IV of Elias Salomo's *Scientia artis musicae* [1274]: 'Et quemadmodum se habet littera ad syllabam, syllaba ad dictionem, dictio ad orationem, ita littera sive punctus ad clavem, clavis ad tonum, tonus ad cantum.' (in Martin Gerbert [ed.], *Scriptores ecclesiastici de musica sacra potissimum*, 3 vols. [St. Blaise, 1784; reprint ed., Hildesheim, 1963], vol. 3, 20). This construction is also used throughout Aurelian's *Musica disciplina*.
[41] Horace, *Ars poetica*, 309; cited in Tinctoris, *Liber de arte contrapuncti*, ed. D'Agostino, 136.
[42] Woodley, 'Renaissance Music Theory as Literature', 215-19; Page, 'Reading and Reminiscence'; Strohm, 'Music, Humanism, and the Idea of a "Rebirth" of the Arts', 360-68; Wegman, 'Johannes Tinctoris and the "New Art"', 182-86.
[43] Gallagher, 'Models of *Varietas*', ch. 2; Luko, 'Tinctoris on *Varietas*'. On grammar and rhetoric in music works, see Bent, 'Sense and Rhetoric in Late-Medieval Polyphony', in *Music in the Mirror: Reflections on the History of Music Theory and Literature for the 21st Century*, ed. Andreas Giger and Thomas J. Mathiesen (Lincoln, 2002), 45-59 at 47. See also Bent, 'Grammar and Rhetoric in Late Medieval Polyphony: Modern Metaphor or Old Simile?', in *Rhetoric beyond Words: Delight and Persuasion in the Arts of the Middle Ages*, ed. Mary Carruthers (Cambridge, 2010), 52-71.
[44] Palenik, 'The Early Career of Johannes Tinctoris', 63-65.
[45] Romualdo Trifone, *L'università degli studi di Napoli dalla fondazione ai giorni nostri* (Naples, 1954), 29-40; Riccardo Filangieri di Candida, 'L'età aragonese', in *Storia della Università di Napoli*, ed. Francesco Torraca (Naples, 1924), 153-99 at 160-67. For a transcription of Paul II's 1465 bull, see Di Candida, 'L'età aragonese', 197-98. For a useful overview of the university in this period, see Paul F. Grendler, *The Universities of the Italian Renaissance* (Baltimore, 2002), 41-45; also Bentley, *Politics and Culture in Renaissance Naples*, 57, 77; Santoro, 'La cultura umanistica', 145-58; Santoro, 'Humanism in Naples', 300-4.

three to five rented rooms scattered across the city in different monasteries.[46] On average, the university's faculty had twenty professors (ten in law, four to five in medicine, two in natural philosophy, one in logic, and two to four in the arts).[47]

At the university, there was an appointed grand chancellor who presided over the colleges of law and medicine and, starting in 1465, a professor was appointed as rector to lead the university.[48] This lasted until 1478, when Ferrante chose to make his own confessor and chaplain responsible for the direct governance of the university.[49] This meant that, starting in 1478, Tinctoris's colleague in the royal chapel (the *archicapellanus* or *cappellano maggiore*) was the formal head (or *gubernator*) of the Neapolitan university, responsible for not only governance, but an annual review of the roster of professors and subjects offered.[50] Tinctoris would been in daily contact with the head of the university and thus able to monitor the courses being taught and those teaching them.[51]

The surviving Neapolitan archival documents for both the royal chapel and the university are spotty at best—especially, unfortunately, the records for the 1470s and much of the 1480s.[52] But I would like to draw attention to the remark in Trithemius's passage in praise of Tinctoris, in which Tinctoris is described as 'regis ferdinandi neapolitani quondam archicapellanus et cantor' ('formerly archchaplain and singer of the Neapolitan King Ferdinand').[53] Woodley and Atlas have suggested that this is an ambiguity or oversight by Trithemius concerning Tinctoris's rank, but given that Trithemius is accurate in all other respects when describing Tinctoris (his benefices, his writing of elegant letters, and so forth), we might not want to dismiss it so quickly.[54] Granting that Tinctoris never cites himself as 'archicapellanus' in his treatises from the 1470s, must we also rule out the possibility that he was in fact *archicapellanus* or *cappellano maggiore* at some point later in the 1470s or 1480s at the Aragonese court, after those treatises were completed and copied?[55] In the 1470s, Tinctoris did claim

---

[46] Ercole Cannavale, *Lo studio di Napoli nel Rinascimento* (Naples, 1895), 23-25; Grendler, *The Universities of the Italian Renaissance*, 43.

[47] Grendler, *The Universities of the Italian Renaissance*, 43. On the law faculty and legal education in Naples, see De Frede, *Studenti e uomini di leggi a Napoli nel Rinascimento* (Naples, 1957).

[48] On the leadership of the *studio*, see Filangieri di Candida, 'L'età aragonese', 168-170; Trifone, *L'università degli studi di Napoli*, 32-33; Grendler, *The Universities of the Italian Renaissance*, 43.

[49] Grendler, *The Universities of the Italian Renaissance*, 44. See Filangieri di Candida, 'L'età aragonese', 168, on Enrico da Palermo ('lettore di S. Teologia') holding this position. Filangieri also records 'magister Erricus de Panhormio hordinis predicatorum regius confexor et Studii Gubernator pro anno presenti 1479 incipendo tamen a 18 octobris 1478' [Cedole di Tesoreria, vol. 85, fol. 44ff.] ('L'età aragonese', 198-99).

[50] D'Agostino, 'La musica, la cappella e il cerimoniale', 163-64.

[51] A fragmentary list of faculty and courses offered during the 1470s is in Cannavale, *Lo studio di Napoli nel Rinascimento*, 47-51.

[52] For a list of known singers and chaplains at the court in this period, see Atlas, *Music at the Aragonese Court*, 87-97.

[53] Woodley, 'Iohannes Tinctoris: A Review', 233, 247; Blackburn, 'Music Theory and Musical Thinking after 1450', 327. Later, in the mid-sixteenth century, the Neapolitan Giovantomaso Cimello described Tinctoris as 'Cappellano e Maestro di Cappella del Re Ferrante d'Aragona Re di Napoli e di Sicilia'; this is found in Cimello's *Della perfettione delle 4 note maggiori*, cited in D'Agostino, 'Reading Theorists for Recovering "Ghost" Repertories', 27.

[54] Woodley, 'Iohannes Tinctoris: A Review', 233. See Atlas, *Music at the Aragonese Court*, 75, where Atlas gives the following reasons against Tinctoris holding this position: 'First, Tinctoris himself never claims the title. Second, he was certainly not the chapel master in 1472-1473, 1480, 1481, or, if he was still in Ferrante's service, from 1488 through June 1491, years or periods for which we know that the position was held by someone else. Third, all the chapel masters for whom there is firm documentation—Exarch, Abarells, Cortes, Pere Brusca, Epo de Tropoya [*sic*], Juliano Frangipane da Caiacza, and Jacobo da Valenza—were priests, whereas Tinctoris, it seems, was not'. See Filangieri di Candida, 'L'età aragonese', 168, for an epigraph for Giuliano Mirteo, bishop of Tropea, dated 1492, which styles him 'Ferdinando de Aragonia Siciliae Regis Maior Cappellanus et Consiliarius ac Almi Studii Neapolitani Gubernator'.

[55] D'Agostino, 'La musica, la cappella e il cerimoniale', 164-65. D'Agostino cites a hitherto unnoticed text concerning the responsibilities of the 'cappellani maggiori' as 'de omnibus nostris Capellanis cognoscere et videre, et de eis iustitiam

himself to be '[musice] artis professor minimus' and 'inter legum artiumque mathematicarum professores minimus'.[56] Unfortunately, we are missing the majority of pay records for the university from 1476 to 1487 and are not certain who held the position of *cappellano maggiore* between 1481 and the year 1488, when Juliano Frangipane da Caiacza took the position after already teaching in the university.[57] Leaving this matter of speculation aside, it cannot be denied that Tinctoris would have been well aware of the pedagogical activities at the university and perhaps been able to avail himself of the courses offered or professors teaching.

Many university professors held political and court positions while also teaching. For humanists, this usually meant tutoring royal children.[58] This double duty of courtly services also included members of the royal chapel, who were often expected to serve in other roles at court. Composer and singer Johannes Cornago (c. 1400-after 1474) was appointed chief almoner, overseeing the distribution of alms to the poor, while several singers were paid for scribal activities, both musical and non-musical.[59] Tinctoris was tapped for his translating skills and recruiting efforts for new singers from northern Europe. Such translations at the Neapolitan court were regularly commissioned, from ancient Greek to Latin, Latin to Italian, French to Italian, and even into the local Neapolitan dialect. We might compare Tinctoris's royally commissioned translation of the statutes of the Order of the Golden Fleece to Ferrante's request for a revised translation of Pliny's *Natural History* into the dialect of *napoletano misto*, completed by orator and head of the royal library Giovanni Brancati in the very same year as Tinctoris's translation.[60]

Tinctoris's talents garnered him yet another role at the Neapolitan court. Much like the more philologically grounded humanists supported by the Aragonese family, Tinctoris seems to have been enlisted for a tutoring position for Beatrice d'Aragona,

---

ministrare, sicut semper extitit consuetem'. Claiming such a leadership role required greater ecclesiastical dignity than a musician such as Tinctoris possessed, D'Agostino believes it unlikely that he ever held this title. However, we must not overlook his respected training in canon and civil law, one that most musicians did not receive. Also, the papal supplication by Tinctoris in October 1490 states that he is 'cantor capellanus' but, again, it cannot be ruled out that he held the position earlier.

[56] See n. 11 above.

[57] Records are missing for 1476-78, 1481-83, and 1485-87. For more on Frangipane da Caiacza, see Atlas, *Music at the Aragonese Court*, 48-50, 75, 94. Atlas points out that Juliano assisted in setting Cinico's salary in 1491 (50 n. 155). D'Agostino claims Frangipane da Caiacza had been *archicapellanus* for the entire decade of the 1480s in D'Agostino, 'Two Musical Letters from Aragonese Naples', in *Essays on Renaissance Music in Honour of David Fallows: Bon jour, bon mois et bonne estrenne*, ed. Fabrice Fitch and Jacobijn Kiel (Woodbridge, 2011), 66-67. However, the absence of archival documents for many of these years makes this claim difficult to believe.

[58] Elisio Calenzio (i.e., Luigi Gallucci) became tutor to Federico d'Aragona in 1465 and later his political advisor and treasurer. Panormita was appointed by Ferrante in 1463 to serve as tutor to Duke Alfonso of Calabria, earning 300 ducats per year. Pontano succeed Panormita as his tutor. Earlier on, Bartolomeo Facio had been Ferrante's tutor in 1445, producing a translation of Isocrates in 1445, while Pontano was tutor to Alfonso's nephew Juan of Navarre from 1452 to 1457. Raffaele Brandolini tutored Duke Alfonso of Bisceglie, the illegitimate son of Alfonso II, from 1493 to 1495. For a lengthy list of paid *lettori* whose specialty is uncertain, see Filangieri di Candida, 'L'età aragonese', 191-92. For discussion of professors of the *studia humanitatis* at Naples in the fifteenth century, see Trifone, *L'università degli studi di Napoli*, 36-37.

[59] On Cornago, see Atlas, *Music at the Aragonese Court*, 62-69; Bentley, *Politics and Culture in Renaissance Naples*, 72. On the activities of musicians as scribes and, more generally, of music scribes, see Atlas, *Music at the Aragonese Court*, 39, 114-25.

[60] *Napoletano misto* was a refined form of dialect in Naples, used by Diomede Carafa and other writers. On the translation by Tinctoris, see, Woodley, 'Tinctoris's Italian Translation'; D'Agostino, 'Note sulla carriere'. On the Pliny translation, see Bentley, *Politics and Culture in Renaissance Naples*, 69-71; Paolo Chechi, 'I volgarizzamenti della Biblioteca aragonese', in *Le carte aragonesi: atti del Convegno, Ravello, 3-4 ottobre 2002*, ed. Marco Santoro (Pisa, 2004), 37-52. This translation was done to replace a 1460s Italian translation by the Florentine Cristoforo Landino in the late 1460s.

although whether in music or all the arts we cannot say.[61] While the details of Beatrice's instruction are uncertain, Tinctoris's dedications of treatises and at least one composition to her give the impression of a comprehensive tutelage.[62] In his treatise on mode, dedicated to Ockeghem and Busnoys, Tinctoris spoke highly of his pupil for following Aristotle's recommendation to become learned in music:[63]

> Cuiusquidem primae auctoritatis philosophi consilio freta, diva Beatrix Aragonia, Ungarorum sacratissima regina, nec illiberale nec summa eius amplitudine indignum duxit huius scientiae studio se ferventissime dedere. Quo effectum est, ut sua paene divina maiestas forma, velut Diana nymphas, et arte, velut Calliope musas, mulieres supereminens omnes, non modo cantu et pronunciatione vehementius gaudeat. Unde tamen ex Aristotelis sententia intemperans vocari non debet, sed etiam de omni genere musicorum rectissimum proferat iudicium. Neque mirum sit velim alicui quod praetermissis reliquis nobilibus ac ignobilibus musicae scientissimis, hanc serenissimam Dominam huic opusculo meo inseruerim. Nempe quemadmodum plus aliis singulari quodam amore arti nostrae sua humanitas afficitur, ita illam singulari privilegio non solum hic, verum si possem in excelsis caelorum sedibus collocarem.[64]

> Relying upon the council of this philosopher of first authority, the heavenly Beatrice d'Aragona, the most hallowed Queen of the Hungarians, regarded it as neither ignoble nor unworthy of her highest dignity to dedicate herself most fervently to the study of this science. The result has been that her near-divine majesty, surpassing in beauty all women, as Diana the nymphs and in art Calliope the Muses, not only delights rather strongly in music and performance—whence, however, following the saying of Aristotle, she should not be called immoderate—but also proffers the most correct judgement on all types of musicians. Nor would I wish it to be a surprise to anyone that, having passed over other persons, both noble and low-born, highly learned in music, I have introduced this most serene Lady into this little work of mine. Certainly, just as her kindly feelings towards our art are touched by a particular love more than towards others, so in the same degree I would place her with particular favour not only here, but, if I were able, in the highest seats of heaven.

---

[61] Woodley, 'Iohannes Tinctoris: A Review', 233; Leeman L. Perkins and Howard Garey (eds.), *The Mellon Chansonnier*, 2 vols. (New Haven & London, 1979), vol. 1, 17-20; Palenik, 'The Early Career of Johannes Tinctoris', 142-44. Tinctoris had already gained experience teaching choirboys in Chartres; on this, see Weinmann, *Johannes Tinctoris (1445-1511) und sein unbekannter Traktat 'De inventione et usu musicae'*, 44; and Palenik, 'The Early Career of Johannes Tinctoris', 49. Although evidence is lacking, another potential pupil of Tinctoris might have been Beatrice's brother, Giovanni d'Aragona (1456-85), who despite dying at a young age served in a number of diplomatic and ecclesiastical roles, including commendatory abbot of Monte Cassino and later archbishop of Salerno and cardinal of Santa Sabina and San Lorenzo in Lucina. A serious bibliophile, Giovanni was tutored by the Dominican friar Pietro Ranzano (1426-92/3), but he is connected to Tinctoris through his ownership of one of the deluxe manuscripts of the writings of Tinctoris: University of Valencia, Biblioteca Histórica, Ms. 835. On this source and Giovanni d'Aragona, see Thomas Haffner, *Die Bibliothek des Kardinals Giovanni d'Aragona (1456-1485): illuminierte Handschriften und Inkunabeln für einen humanistischen Bibliophilen zwischen Neapel und Rom* (Wiesbaden, 1997), esp. 315-19; Tinctoris, *Proportionale musices. Liber de arte contrapuncti*, ed. D'Agostino, lv. We know that Giovanni was in Naples for much of 1480 and 1482-83, in between missions as papal legate to Hungary and elsewhere. For more on Ranzano, see Bruno Figliuolo, *La cultura a Napoli nel secondo Quattrocento: ritratti di protagonisti* (Udine, 1997), 87-200.

[62] The surviving treatises by Tinctoris dedicated to Beatrice are *Tractatus de regulari valore notarum* (before c. 1475), the stand-alone Neapolitan version of *Complexus effectuum musices* (before 1475), and the early version of *Terminorum musicae diffinitorium* (before 1475). On the composition in Beatrice's honour, *Beatissima Beatrix* (in *Liber de arte contrapuncti*, Book II, ch. 25), see Atlas, *Music in Aragonese Naples*, 161-62.

[63] On this Aristotelian citation, see n. 22 above.

[64] Tinctoris, *Liber de natura et proprietate tonorum*, ch. 1, in *Opera theoretica*, ed. Seay, vol. 1, 69; my translation. My sincere thanks to Ronald Woodley for his help with this passage.

Significance might be construed from the fact that these glowing remarks for Beatrice appear outside of the formal dedication of the treatise, but this over-the-top acclaim reads like any other royal dedication, whether to her or to her father, Ferrante. Of more importance is what Tinctoris singles out as the fruit of these tutorials in music: above and beyond her training in singing is her new ability to give 'the most correct judgement on all kinds of musicians'. The power to offer a reasoned 'iudicium' is likely to be just what Tinctoris was referring to in his statement on the music of the last forty years.[65] The tutoring offered by Tinctoris, together with Beatrice's commitment to 'dedicate herself most fervently' to her studies, should have made her one of the *eruditi* that Tinctoris mentioned. Reinhard Strohm has described the treatises of Tinctoris as forming 'a full course of instruction in the musical art, at its most critical and personal in the *Proportionale musices*, but culminating in the magisterial *Liber de arte contrapuncti*'.[66] Whether or not Beatrice was subjected to each and every volume of Tinctoris's pedagogical programme, I believe it is useful to understand each of the treatises functioning as textbooks in his 'course of instruction'.

A Model for Tinctoris: Giuniano Maio

I would now like to turn to one of the university's professors and a likely intellectual colleague of Tinctoris at the court: Giuniano Maio (c. 1435-93). Best known as a professor of 'umanità' at the Neapolitan university from 1465 until 1488, Maio was a near-contemporary of Tinctoris, born in the early to mid-1430s.[67] He is listed as teaching courses in 'rettorica', 'poesia', and 'arte oratoria', earning on average 30-40 ducats per year, far less than the top legal and medical professors in Naples.[68] After studying with Antonio Calcillo da Sessa, Maio became the master of all young Latinists in Naples and had his own grammatical textbook, a copy of which was kept in the royal library, but never published.[69] In 1490, just three years before his death, Maio was appointed tutor for Pietro d'Aragona (the second son of Alfonso, Duke of Calabria, and Ippolita Maria Sforza), but Pietro died two months later.[70]

---

[65] See n. 22 above. Bonnie Blackburn ('Compositional Process in the Fifteenth Century', in *Journal of the American Musicological Society* 40 [1987], 210-84 esp. 268-69) argues that Tinctoris in this passage is referring to hearing dissonance and judging the technique with which it is handled.

[66] Strohm, *The Rise of European Music, 1380-1500* (Cambridge and New York, 1993), 594-95.

[67] On Maio, see Erasmo Percopo, 'Nuovi documenti sugli scritti e gli artisti dei tempi aragonesi', in *Archivio storico napoletane* 19 (1884), 740ff.; Tamaro De Marinis, *Nuovi documenti per la storia del Rinascimento* (Florence, 1970); Iuniano Maio, *De maiestate*, ed. F. Gaeta (Bologna, 1956), xvii-xxx; De Frede, *I lettori di umanità*, 39-80; Filangieri di Candida, 'L'età aragonese', 186-88; Santoro, 'La cultura umanistica', 146-49; Angela Maria Caracciolo, 'Giuniano Maio', in *Dizionario biografico degli italiani* (Rome, 2007), vol. 67, 618-21.

[68] For a thorough list of the payrolls of the university, along with the listed subjects of instruction for each professor, see Cannavale, *Lo studio di Napoli nel Rinascimento*, 77-110. See also Grendler, *The Universities of the Italian Renaissance*, 43-44. The salaries of the highest paid professors ranged from 150 to 300 ducats.

[69] A 'Grammatica Iuniani Maii' is listed in the *Index regalium codicum Alfonsi regis ad Laurentium Medicem ex Neapolitana eius bibliotheca transmissus* (Biblioteca Apostolica Vaticana, Ms. Vat. Lat. 7134); cited in De Marinis, *La biblioteca napoletana*, vol. 2, 193 [Inventario B].

[70] Maio was paid 100 ducats for tutoring Pietro d'Aragona. After Pietro died, Maio took on the tutoring of Alfonso and Carlo d'Aragona (two illegitimate sons of Ferrante); in 1492, he also tutored children of a certain Joan de Cremona. See Bentley, *Politics and Culture in Renaissance Naples*, 68. For a 1486 contract with a student, see De Frede, *I lettori di umanità*, 22.

Maio was beloved by his students and colleagues, as evidenced by the verses composed in his honour by two of his more celebrated contemporaries, the humanist Giovanni Pontano (1426-1503) and the poet Jacopo Sannazaro (1458-1530). In these verses, one finds Maio praised for his shaping of many exceptionally talented spirits, his keen prophetic abilities and wise counsel, and the rejoicing song and dance offered by the Muses in his honour at his tomb.[71] Starting in 1480, Maio's rising prominence at the Neapolitan court allowed him to begin to sign his name 'eques neapolitanus' or 'cavaliero napolitano', and by 1491 Ferrante named him one of his *cortegiani*, surely a welcome status given that he turned down an offer years before to come to Provence to the court of René d'Anjou. His duties as tutor to royal children included accompanying them on long voyages, such as escorting Isabella d'Aragona, the daughter of Ferrante, to Milan to marry her cousin Duke Gian Galeazzo Sforza, to whom she was betrothed.[72]

By the time of Tinctoris's arrival in Naples in the early 1470s, Maio was already accepted as the master of Latin in Naples. Teaching at the university, and privately as well, Maio would have been just the person Tinctoris could turn to for beginning or, more likely, continuing his humanistic studies. In such a role, I would argue that Maio would have been an intellectual and courtly model for someone like Tinctoris. In the mid-1470s, while Tinctoris was writing (or certainly completing) most of his treatises on all aspects of music theory, Maio was creating his own classroom textbooks by completing his own editions of Pliny the Younger's *Epistles* and selected orations of Cicero, and then had them printed by a new local printer named Mattias Moravus de Olomouc in 1476 and 1480, just before teaching courses on rhetoric at the university.[73] If Tinctoris's exposure to Cicero had been lacking during his education at Orléans, Maio's lectures and printed course books would certainly have ameliorated any and all deficiency, elevating his acquaintance to that of his mastery of Augustine.[74] The familiarity with Cicero's *De oratore* or *Tusculan Disputations* that Tinctoris reveals in his crafted prologues to those treatises completed in Naples surely benefited from Maio's mastery

---

[71] These poems are cited in Giangiuseppe Origlia Paolino, *Istoria dello studio di Napoli* (Naples, 1753), vol. 1, 267. Pontano's Tumulus 33 from Book I of his *Tumuli* is found in Ioannis Ioviani Pontani, *Carmina*, ed. Benedetto Soldati, 2 vols., (Florence, 1902), vol. 2, 186. Pontano sent these poems to Aldus via Suardino: see Kidwell, *Pontano: Poet & Prime Minister* (London, 1991), 405 nn. 239-40. The immediately preceding *tumulus* by Pontano is in honour of 'eminent musician Perinellus' (Tumulus XXXII; vol. 2, 185-86). There is also another musician praised by Pontano: Fulco of Ferrara (Tumulus XXVII; vol. 2, 183-84). The latter is cited in D'Agostino, 'La musica, la cappella e il cerimoniale', 170. See also the 'Lyra Orphei auxilium implorat a nympha' (Tumulus LIII; vol. 1, 217-18). For the verses by Jacopo Sannazaro, see Sannazaro, *Latin poetry*, trans. Michael C. J. Putnam, The I Tatti Renaissance Library 38 (Cambridge MA. and London, 2009), 188-91, 216-21. Alessandro d'Alessandro also praised Maio for his powers of divination.

[72] On this mission, see the letter dated 25 December 1488 from Ferrante to Bartolomeo Calchi, the *Primo segretario ducale* in Milan, in *Corrispondenza di Giovanni Pontano segretario dei dinasti aragonesi di Napoli (2 novembre 1474-20 gennaio 1495)*, ed. Bruno Figliuolo (Battipaglia, 2012), 408-9. This might be compared to Tinctoris traveling to Hungary to visit Beatrice after her marriage to Matthias Corvinus.

[73] The edition of selected Ciceronian orations included *Pro lege Manilia*, *Pro Milone*, *Pro Archia*, *De lege agraria*, *Pro Marcello*, *Pro rege Deiotaro*, the four *Catiline* orations, the *Verrine* orations, and selections from the *Philippics*. For the years in which courses are listed, we know that Maio offered rhetoric courses in 1472-73, 1476-77 and 1480-81. The Milanese humanist Aurelio Bianato lectured on Quintilian's *Institutio oratoria* at the Neapolitan university from 1475-76, using Valla's commentary on the ancient text. On this, see Lucia Gualdo Rosa, 'Un seguace del Valla all'Università di Napoli nel '400: Aurelio Bienato', in *Valla e Napoli*, ed. Santoro, 171-81. Maio was also known for his Italian translation of *De arte bene moriendi*, printed in 1476 by Arnaldo de Bruxelles at Naples: see Santoro, 'La cultura umanistica', 148.

[74] Rob C. Wegman, 'Johannes Tinctoris and the Art of Listening', in *'Recevez ce mien petit labeur': Studies in Renaissance Music in Honour of Ignace Bossuyt*, ed. Mark Delaere and Pieter Bergé (Leuven, 2008), 279-96 at 286, writes: 'Tinctoris's relationship to Augustine is like that of a humanist who wants to speak like Cicero, and who knows his writings inside out, but who nevertheless wants to say his own thing. That, I think, is why Tinctoris does not bother to spell out that he is borrowing from the *Confessions*: it would not have added anything to the point he is making here'.

of Latin, not to mention Tinctoris's improved sense of eloquence since the days of the Orléans matriculation log.[75]

The new-on-the-scene Neapolitan printers made most of their income by printing textbooks for law and medical students, but Maio established an enterprise here for students in the *studia humanitatis*.[76] Maio's printer Moravus must have also recognized this financial opportunity since he was responsible for printing some of the earliest editions in Italy of Seneca, Cicero, Pliny the Younger, and others.[77] Might Tinctoris have been thinking the same with the printing of the revised extracts of his *De inventione et usu musice,* just a few years later with the very same printer, a link first identified by Woodley?[78] Perhaps so, but we do know that Tinctoris did not turn to the same printer employed by Gaffurio a year or two before, for the publication of the latter's first major treatise, the *Theoricum opus musice discipline*, printed at Naples by Francesco di Dino in 1480.[79]

Early financial backing for Moravus seems to have come from the abbot and music theorist Blasius Romerus, who offered assistance with the editions of the Bible, Seneca, and Maio.[80] As the publisher of important editions of classical texts, liturgical books, and several works by Neapolitan humanists, Moravus was understandably the clear choice by Tinctoris to print excerpts of his *De inventione et usu musice* in the early 1480s.[81] Conceivably the project was encouraged by Blasius, who was knowledgeable in music. However, it is puzzling that no evidence survives of Blasius (in the redactions of his writings by Florentius) or of Tinctoris ever citing each other. Also possible, and to me more likely, is that an introduction between Moravus and Tinctoris was made by Maio, who had been working with Moravus for at least five years.

Ever since Karl Weinmann's study of the *De inventione et usu musice* appeared, several basic questions have lingered about the Neapolitan print of the extracts by Tinctoris: why was it printed in the first place and for whom?[82] Why were these selections printed over others? Lacking the pedagogical sharpness that appears in most of Tinctoris's treatises like the *Proportionale musices* and *Liber de arte contrapuncti*, the Moravus print

[75] On Ciceronian readings of Tinctoris's writings, see Woodley, 'Renaissance Music Theory as Literature'; Wegman, 'Johannes Tinctoris and the "New Art"'; Luko, 'Tinctoris on *Varietas*'.

[76] On early Neapolitan printers, see Mariano Fava and Giovanni Bresciano, *La stampa a Napoli nel XV secolo*, 2 vols. (Leipzig, 1911-13), vol. 2, 1-127; Mario Santoro, 'I primi decenni della stampa a Napoli e la cultura napoletana', in *Primi convegno dei bibliotecari dell'Italia meridionale* (Naples, 1956), 13-28, esp. 22-25; Marco Santoro, *La stampa a Napoli nel Quattrocento* (Naples, 1984). Santoro, 'Humanism in Naples', 309, remarks that 'editions of writings by the humanists themselves…can attest the preferences and choices of university instruction, as in the intense editorial activity of Giuniano Maio with the printer Moravo;…or witness the large reading public of the works of humanists such as Pontano'. The printer Francesco del Tuppo was a student of the Neapolitan *magister puerorum* Messer Pietro Bruscia. On this, see Nino Pirrotta, 'Music and Cultural Tendencies in 15th-Century Italy', in *Journal of the American Musicological Society* 19 (1966), 127-161 at 132 n. 12.

[77] For a list of relevant Neapolitan prints by Moravus, see Fava and Bresciano, *La stampa a Napoli*, vol. 2, 92-127. Other volumes printed by Moravus include a Latin Bible (1476), a *Missale Romanum* (1477), Diomede Carafa's *Trattato dell'optimo cortigiano*, and several of Pontano's works.

[78] On Moravus and Tinctoris, see Woodley, 'The Printing and Scope', 241-45.

[79] D'Agostino, 'Reading Theorists', 26. For a facsimile edition of this work, see Franchino Gaffurio, *Theoricum opus musice discipline*, ed. Cesarino Ruini (Lucca, 1996). See also Atlas, *Music at the Aragonese Court*, 80.

[80] Blasius first appears in Neapolitan court records in 1451; on this, see Atlas, *Music at the Aragonese Court*, 32, 35-36. See also Holford-Strevens, 'The Erudition of Florentius de Faxolis and Blasius Romerus', 753, where Florentius's later indebtedness to Blasius is discussed. For further on Blasius, see n. 25 above. I expressly thank Bonnie Blackburn for sharing with me the colophon of Moravus's print of the Bible, which explicitly recognizes Blasius.

[81] On the dating of the Moravus print, see also Palenik, 'The Early Career of Johannes Tinctoris', 53-54.

[82] Woodley, 'The Printing and Scope', 239.

of *De inventione et usu musice* puzzles us as to how a collection of personal anecdotes and observations on musical instruments and musical performance would be selected for publication and, one might assume, distribution of some kind, in preference to his other completed works. This text is far from the music theory 'course of instruction' that was completed and copied for circulation in the 1470s, just years before this.

Woodley, Wegman, and Palenik have deftly painted a picture for us of a much larger encyclopedic masterpiece by Tinctoris from which these printed excerpts came, as did those that survive in a manuscript in Cambrai.[83] The genesis and state of completion of this *speculum* of music, which appears to have covered both *musica speculativa* and *musica practica*, remain to be settled. However, with so little of the text surviving, doing this will be a daunting task. What concerns us here are those passages that *were* selected for publication in Naples.

As the printed title makes relatively clear, *De inventione* concerns the history of music and the criticism of music and performance. The latter topic makes sense for a Neapolitan audience, one which sought for itself a heightened ability to judge music and musical performance. The former topic was equally fitting since it too was under debate in Naples at this time. In fact, in the fall of 1478, mere months after Tinctoris finished his *Liber de arte contrapuncti*, Aurelio Brandolini gave the inaugural oration for the academic year in which he laid out some of the uncertainties about music's origins and power:

> De musicae etiam inventione veteres dubitavere. Nam alii ab Amphione, alii Mercurio, nonnulli ab Apolline inventam existimaverunt. Proptereaquod Apollinem cum cythara veteres poetae finxerunt...Atque hinc poetae veteres cecinerunt Orpheum feras et saxa cantus dulcedine attraxisse. Hinc Amphion cythara thebanos muros aedificasse...Nam quid, obsecro, aliud est feras et saxa dulcedine carminis demulceri nisi rusticos atque agrestes homines Orphei sapientissimi viri doctrina et eloquentia informari? Quid aliud est Amphionem cithara thebanos muros aedificare nisi doctum atque eloquentem virum rusticis atque incultis hominibus sua sapentia persuadere ut in coetu ac societate vivant, moenia aedificent, civitatemque conficiant?[84]

> The ancients were also uncertain about the invention of music, since many thought it to have been discovered by Amphion. Several others made Mercury the inventor, others Apollo; therefore the ancient poets portrayed Apollo with the cithara...And so the ancient poets said that Orpheus, with the sweetness of his song, was able to move wild beasts and stones. So too they said that Amphion with the cithara built the walls of Thebes...For what else could wild beasts and stones being softened by the sweetness of song mean, if not that rustic and uncultured men are refined and trained by the teaching and eloquence of Orpheus, a most wise man? What else could Amphion building the walls of Thebes with the cithara mean, if not that a learned and eloquent man with his wisdom persuades rustic and unrefined men to live together in society, to build walls and construct a city?

---

[83] Woodley, 'The Printing and Scope'; Wegman, 'Tinctoris's *Magnum opus*'; Palenik, 'The Early Career of Johannes Tinctoris', ch. 2.

[84] Paris, Bibliothèque Nationale de France, Ms. latin 7860, fols. 19r, 23v, 57r, 62v; cited in Gallo, *Music in the Castle*, 106-107.

All of these figures, Amphion, Mercury, Apollo, and Orpheus, appear in Tinctoris's *De inventione*, all with the same oft repeated ancient tales.[85] It could be that Tinctoris, who would have known Aurelio Brandolini, was filling a void on this topic by circulating a scholarly tribute to music for Neapolitan scholars, celebrating its ancient roots, while highlighting its present-day masters. Much like with his *Liber de arte contrapuncti*, Tinctoris was surely eager to gather all of his knowledge and experience before publishing these extracts, completing *De inventione* only through 'sleepless labour'.[86] And yet the writing style in these published extracts is different from the treatises believed to come from the 1470s.

Without any doubt, Tinctoris was responding to a burgeoning practice in Naples: writing history and commentary supported by evidence of modern experience. As Strohm writes of *De inventione*, 'this work, at least, could not have been written without the experiences of Italian humanist writing about contemporary reality, pioneered by such men as Leon Battista Alberti'.[87] Closer to Naples than Alberti were humanist-minded scholars like Pontano, Maio, Cinico, Aurelio and Raffaele Brandolini, and Diomede Carafa, whose tracts are filled with references to and descriptions of recent, even present-day, battles, political intrigues, orations, festivals, and so forth. Mario Santoro remarks that in quattrocento Naples it was 'the widespread duty of the humanists to project in their writings their own understanding of reality and to express judgments, principles, and precepts that reflect specific situations and the demands of their own experience'.[88] As the first music theorist in history to regularly cite his contemporaries by name, work, and passage for fault or strength, Tinctoris imitated his kindred scholars in Naples.

The Art of Lexicography

Beyond editions of Roman authors and a connection through Moravus, Tinctoris and Maio shared common ground over particular texts. The scholarly work for which Maio gained his greatest fame was a Latin lexicon entitled *De priscorum proprietate verborum*.[89] The project for this Latin dictionary was begun by Maio's own teacher Antonio Calcillo, but revised and printed by Maio under his own name in Naples in 1475 (by the printer

---

[85] Weinmann, *Johannes Tinctoris (1445-1511) und sein unbekannter Traktat 'De inventione et usu musicae'*, 40, 43-44.

[86] 'Antequam de musica aliquid conscriberem, sapientiam rerum diversarum ad eam pertinentium audiendo, legendo cum exercitatione continua quoad potui, acquirere conatus sum.' (Tinctoris, *Liber de arte contrapuncti*, prologus, in *Opera theoretica*, ed. Seay, vol. 2, 11); Weinmann, *Johannes Tinctoris (1445-1511) und sein unbekannter Traktat 'De inventione et usu musicae'*, 28: 'pervigili labore'.

[87] Strohm, *Rise of European Music*, 594-95. Palenik, 'The Early Career of Johannes Tinctoris', 55, writes: 'In these chapters, the theorist recalled and shared his opinions of a wide range of personal experiences with some of the greatest musicians of the fifteenth century'.

[88] Santoro, 'Humanism in Naples', 320. Wegman, 'Tinctoris's *Magnum opus*', 771, describes Tinctoris as 'more relaxed, more inclined to intersperse his commentary with bits of poetry, supremely self-assured in the way he drops the names of classical authors left, right, and center, more given to telling us about his personal experiences, and more disarming in the way he reveals his private thoughts and feelings'. Also, Wegman, 'Johannes Tinctoris and the "New Art"', 187, claims that in Tinctoris's list of contemporary composers in the *Complexus*, 'there is a sense...that the achievement of the present and recent past must be held on to, preserved in recorded history'.

[89] Iunianus Maius, *De priscorum proprietate verborum* (Naples: Mattias Moravus, 1475). I consulted the copy in Harvard University, Law School Library (Historical and Special Collections: Rare unclassed).

Moravus, with the help of Blasius Romerus).[90] The dictionary saw several re-printings over the next two decades at Treviso, Brescia, Venice, and again at Naples, and was used by the famed Florentine humanist Angelo Poliziano in his lectures on Virgil's *Bucolics* and Terence's *Andria*.[91] Maio's lexicon was listed among the Neapolitan volumes sent to Lorenzo de' Medici, along with a 'Vocabularium Chalcidii' and 'Grammatica Iunianii Maii'.[92] Interestingly, an illuminated copy of Maio's printed lexicon features an image of Ferrante's musical chapel.[93] Gianluca d'Agostino has noted the striking similarity of Maio's lexicon to the title of Tinctoris's mode treatise, *Liber de natura et proprietate tonorum*, finished in Naples just one year after Moravus printed Maio's lexicon.[94]

As one of the first early modern Latin lexicons, *De priscorum proprietate verborum* offers its reader an alphabetically ordered volume of Latin terms with very brief definitions (in Latin) and occasional references to their appearance in both classical and modern Latin literature.[95] The lexicon closes with a letter to Francesco Enrico Languardo, in which Maio states his plans to supply the lexicon's terms with 'multas lucubrationes', probably in the Gellian tradition, but this project never seemed to get off the ground since the majority of terms are still lacking extensive commentary.[96]

The dedication of Maio's dictionary to Ferrante in many ways resembles the prologue to Lorenzo Valla's *Elegantiae linguae latinae*, which tells of a recent reawakening of Latin studies and philology.[97] In fact, it has been shown that Maio was closely reading and interpreting Valla's work when completing his own.[98] Maio spoke of the lengthy confusion in Latin studies at the hands of barbarians and celebrates the first flower of youth that a new age of Latin brings, resulting from the work of ingenious and learned scholars. Maio stated his purpose as finally bringing together a volume on the

---

[90] On Maio's borrowing from Calcillo's lexicon (which survives as an unicum in Oxford, Bodleian Library, Ms. Bodl. 171) and the influence of Valla's *Elegantiae*, see Gianni Antonio Palumbo, 'Valla nel *De priscorum proprietate verborum*', in *Valla e Napoli*, ed. Santoro, 223-36; Milena Montanile, *Le parole e la norma: Studi su lessico e grammatica a Napoli tra quattro e cinquecento* (Naples, 1996), 19-31; Palumbo, 'Noterelle in calce al *De priscorum proprietate verborum* di Giuniano Maio', in *Lessicografia a Napoli nel Cinquecento*, ed. Domenico Defilippis et al. (Bari, 2007), 157-76.

[91] Popularity of the lexicon is evidenced by successive printers elsewhere at Treviso (Bernardus de Colonia, 1477; Confalonerius, 1477), Brescia (Boninus de Boninis, 1480), Venice (Scotus; Peregrinus de Pasqualibus et Dionysius Bertochus; Jo. Rubeus, 1482 and 1485), and again at Naples (1490, possibly again by Moravus?): see Ricciardi, 'Angelo Poliziano, Giuniano Maio, Antonio Calcillo', 281 n. 1. On Poliziano's use of Maio's lexicon, see Anthony Grafton, 'On the Scholarship of Politian and its Context', in *Journal of the Warburg and Courtauld Institutes* 40 (1977), 150-88 at 155 n. 15.

[92] Ricciardi, 'Angelo Poliziano, Giuniano Maio, Antonio Calcillo', 291. See also De Marinis, *La biblioteca napoletana*, vol. 2, 193. Interestingly, in 1476 Lorenzo sent back to Naples a number of volumes and a letter by Poliziano to Ferrante's son, Federico d'Aragona (1452-1504), who was keen for vernacular texts, especially 'those which had been written poetically in the Tuscan language'. On this, see Santoro, 'Humanism in Naples', 310.

[93] The print is illuminated by Cola Rapicano and held in Paris, Bibliothèque nationale de France, Rés. X.132. See D'Agostino, 'La musica, la cappella e il cerimoniale', 161.

[94] Tinctoris, *Proportionale musices. Liber de arte contrapuncti*, ed. D'Agostino, xlviii-l.

[95] Ricciardi, 'Angelo Poliziano, Giuniano Maio, Antonio Calcillo', 280. Authors cited by Maio in his lexicon include Servius, Donatus, Porphyry, Ps.-Acrone, Asconio Pediano, Priscian, Macrobius, Aulus Gellius, Varro, Festus, Nonio Marcello, the Jurisconsults, and Strabo (in the Latin translation by Guarino of Verona). Fifteenth-century texts are all lexical works: Pontano's *De aspiratione*, Lorenzo Valla's *Elegantiae*, and Tortelli's *De orthographia*.

[96] Languardo was a Dominican friar who served as bishop of Policastro (1466-70), then archbishop of Acerenza and Matera until his death in 1482.

[97] *Laurentii Vallensis De linguae latinae elegantia*, ed. Santiago López Moreda, 2 vols. (Cáceres, 1999). There are prefaces to each of the six books of Valla's work. It was first printed in 1471 and reprinted nearly sixty times until 1536. Valla notes in his prologue to Book 3 that the essence of law lies in the interpretation of words; this is something Tinctoris would have certainly appreciated. On Valla's ideas of rebirth, see Strohm, 'Music, Humanism, and the Idea of a "Rebirth" of the Arts', 351, 391.

[98] Palumbo, 'Valla nel *De priscorum proprietate verborum*', 223-36.

interpretation of Latin words, building on, refining, and making more efficient the already published work of an earlier generation of philologists, Valla and Tortelli.[99]

Compare this to Tinctoris and his dedication for the *Terminorum musicae diffinitorium*, the first printed lexicon of musical terms (also, in alphabetical order), where he believes 'it very useful to define music's terms in principle and in detail so that by understanding all things concerning music, those who practice it may the more readily grasp its nature and its particulars'.[100] Ease of reference makes for efficient practice of the art.[101] Just as Tinctoris does elsewhere for music, Maio praises Ferrante for generously establishing a public readership and making it so that 'there is no discipline that is not being actively studied in the city of Naples', then also praises Mattias Moravus for bringing this new kind of printing to a supreme perfection.[102] The history of Latin, with its recent blossoming through learned hands, offered by Maio (and earlier by Valla) deserves comparison with Tinctoris's account of a new art achieved by modern-day artists like Ockeghem, Busnoys, Regis, Faugues, and Caron.[103]

While it has been established that Maio was influenced by the looming figure of Valla, I believe that Tinctoris was equally receptive to his profound scholarship and acerbic tone. Valla's infamous *De donatione Constantini* (1440), with its over-the-top temper, must have inspired Tinctoris when responding to his violent critics in the prologue to his *Liber de natura et proprietate tonorum*. Valla writes that it is his aim 'to eradicate error from people's minds, to remove persons from vices and crimes by admonition and reproof'.[104]

The earlier Neapolitan version of Tinctoris's *Diffinitorium* must have been completed very early in the 1470s, while Beatrice d'Aragona was still his student and before her betrothal in summer 1475.[105] The c. 1495 version, printed by the ex-cantor of

---

[99] The preface is edited in Ricciardi, 'Angelo Poliziano, Giuniano Maio, Antonio Calcillo', Appendix A¹, 302-3. An Italian translation is found in De Frede, *I lettori di umanità*, 49-50. Maio is referring to Valla's *Elegantiae* and Tortelli's *Commentaria grammatica de orthographia dictionum e graecis tractarum*.

[100] 'suos diffinire terminos utilissimum existimans quibus intellectis de ea acturi facilius et naturam ejus et suarum partium comprehendant' (Tinctoris, *Terminorum musicae diffinitorium*, ed. Parrish, 4).

[101] As Woodley describes it, in his review of Cecilia Panti's edition and translation of the *Diffinitorium*: 'Perhaps, in view of the sheer complexity of many of the terms elaborated in his main series of treatises since the dictionary's compilation, Tinctoris viewed the practical, instructional function of the *Diffinitorium*, with its necessarily concise but therefore potentially confusing or ambiguous definitions, as already somewhat obsolescent by the 1480s. (Tinctoris is basically operating within an ancient intellectual context in which detailed, elaborated meaning *proceeds* from definition rather than functioning to problematize definition: a somewhat more simplistic and linear epistomological construct than we might be comfortable with today.)' (Ronald Woodley, 'The First Printed Musical Dictionary', in *Early Music* 34 [2006], 479-81 at 480).

[102] 'Quippe cum ea publico stipendio, ut omnium disciplinarum usus Neapoli plurimus esset: satis ampla ex tua munificentia instituisti.' (Maio, *De priscorum proprietate verborum*, 1).

[103] Tinctoris's famous lists celebrating modern-day composers appear in the prologues to *Proportionale musices* and *Liber de arte contrapuncti*, as well as Chapter 19 of the *Complexus*. For the literature on these lists, see n. 16 above.

[104] 'ut errorem a mentibus hominum convellam, ut eos a vitiis sceleribusque vel admonendo vel increpando summoveam' (Valla, *On the Donation of Constantine*, ed. G. W. Bowersock [Cambridge, Mass., 2007], 7). Tinctoris defends the criticisms he waged against foolish composers in his *Proportionale*, claiming: 'Ac in memoriam quidquid in eo dixerim revocans, me hactenus vera praecepisse nec indigne vestros errores circa praefata proportionum signa reprehendisse constantissima mente confiteor. Ratus a viris eruditis nullum consequi vituperium, immo laudem immensam, si, ratione praevia, veritatis non vanitatis prae me ferens amorem, quod in artem nostram commissum fuerit delere pro viribus studeam. Quis enim usque adeo sensus immunem se praebet, ut in omni studiorum genere alterum alterius erronea scripta et corrigere et damnare passim ignoret?' (Tinctoris, *Liber de natura et proprietate tonorum*, prologus, in *Opera theoretica*, ed. Seay, vol. 1, 66).

[105] Woodley, 'The Printing and Scope', 239; 'Tinctoris's Italian Translation', 191-92. Blackburn, 'Music Theory after 1450', 329, believes it was written earlier, 'before Tinctoris came to Naples, perhaps for the use of his choirboys in Orléans or Chartres'. This could be, since his dedication to Beatrice only states that he is merely following the practice of

Treviso Cathedral Gherardus de Lisa included few changes or corrections from the earlier manuscript version, although, as Woodley and Cecilia Panti have noted, it remains unknown whether Tinctoris had any connection to that printing. A proposed link between Maio and Gherardus de Flandria for the printing of his lexicon in Treviso in 1477 seemed tantalizing, but has proven unfounded. Instead, Maio's lexicon, along with his edition of Seneca, were printed in Naples by Moravus, then both texts were printed in Treviso in 1478 by Bernardus de Colonia.[106]

Another Latin lexicon from late fifteenth-century Naples printed by Moravus was the text *De aspiratione* by the humanist Giovanni Giovano Pontano (1426-1503).[107] Begun in the 1450s, revised in the 1460s, and finally printed by Moravus in 1481, this compendium of Latin orthography and pronunciation is organized in roughly alphabetical order and focused on Latin words that contained aspirated consonants and their proper spelling.[108] This was a hugely important concern in the fifteenth century and saw a fierce polemic by Pontano against Leonardo Bruni for having preferred the spelling 'michi' and 'nichil' over 'mihi' and 'nihil'.[109] Pontano's treatise was intended for classroom use and would have been used by Pontano in the private school he ran in Naples from 1448 to 1457 before being appointed tutor to children at the Aragonese court.[110]

These practical manuals of instruction and reference resemble the combination of clarity, precision, and efficiency sought after by Tinctoris in many of his own treatises, which also often took to task his contemporaries for their misuse of the elements and rules of the language at hand (for Tinctoris, of music). While philological studies gripped the intellectual climate in Naples in the wake of Valla, and Maio published and circulated revisions of his teacher's masterpiece of Latin lexicography and grammar, Tinctoris was inspired to revise, copy, publish, distribute, and teach with his pedagogical writings. For music theory, this is a turning point. As Holford-Strevens and Blackburn have both shown, the methodology and writing style of the generation of Ugolino of Orvieto and his *Declaratio musicae disciplinae* in its time had passed for something new, but the broader learning of the generation of Gaffurio was yet to come.[111]

---

recording the exercise of one's talents in books: 'dum ingeniorum suorum exercitia litteris mandant' (Tinctoris, *Terminorum musicae diffinitorium*, ed. Parrish, 2; cited in Palenik, 'The Early Career of Johannes Tinctoris', 142).

[106] Any relationship has yet to be determined, but establishing any prior connection between printing houses in Naples and Treviso would be enticing.

[107] Giuseppe Germano, *Per l'edizione critica del* De aspiratione *di Giovanni Pontano* (Naples, 1985); Germano, *Il* De aspiratione *di Giovanni Pontano e la cultura del suo tempo* (Naples, 2005).

[108] Pontano's treatise was one of the few contemporary texts cited regularly by Maio in his lexicon. It is worth noting that they were printed by Moravus in possibly the same year as the Tinctoris fragments.

[109] Germano, *Il* De aspiratione *di Giovanni Pontano*, 135-51.

[110] On Pontano's early school, see Germano, *Il* De aspiratione *di Giovani Pontano*, 41-47. Notebooks from a student of Pontano include notes on Virgil, Ovid, Valerius Maximus, as well as an 'Appendix Lexicographica'. On these, see Antonietta Iacono (ed.), *Uno studente alla scuola del pontano a Napoli: Le Recollecte del Ms. 1368 (T. 5. 5) della Biblioteca Angelica di Roma* (Naples, 2005). Maio cited Pontano's lexicon regularly in his *De priscorum*. On this, see Ricciardi, 'Angelo Poliziano, Giuniano Maio, Antonio Calcillo', 280.

[111] Holford-Strevens, 'Humanism and the Language of Music Treatises', 423-28, 437-43; Blackburn, 'Music Theory after 1450', 301-3.

A Context for the Neapolitan *Complexus*?

Maio's last known work is his 1492 *speculum principis* treatise entitled *De maiestate*.[112] This treatise on majesty allowed Maio to describe the various attributes of a good prince and simultaneously praise Ferrante. Written in Italian, this treatise offers brief discussions of twenty virtues (or one might say 'effects') that are found in majesty. Some of these virtues include clemency, honesty, modesty, piety, gratitude, kindness, self-restraint, and courage. Following each description, Maio provides illuminations from classical moral thought and gives a modern example from the deeds of Ferrante or recent Neapolitan history. The classical authors and texts cited by Maio include several Ciceronian treatises, Quintilian, Ovid, Seneca, Macrobius, Livy, Virgil, Aristotle's *Ethics*, Sallust, and Pliny the Elder.[113]

At the Aragonese court, the only true monarchy on the Italian peninsula, the *speculum principis* genre was a well-traversed one, with offerings already from Pontano, Panormita, and Ferrante's political advisor Diomede Carafa.[114] Maio's listing of twenty virtues or effects and the similar model of grounding classical and medieval authorities with examples from recent memory are striking, and worthy of some comparison with Tinctoris's *Complexus effectuum musices*. While the repertory of classical authors cited by Maio and Tinctoris, although employed towards different ends, is nearly identical, establishing any direct borrowing or modeling of Maio's text with Tinctoris's already twenty- or thirty-year-old treatise (whether one is considering the Cambrai version of the list of effects from the 1460s or the later list of twenty effects from the 1470s) would be difficult to demonstrate, however intriguing. Instead, finding a common model, perhaps within the Neapolitan context, from which both Maio and Tinctoris might have drawn, would shed light on how and when the Neapolitan revision of Tinctoris's *Complexus*, which Strohm describes as his 'most classicizing work', came together.[115]

Stronger connection to music in Maio's *De maiestate* can be found when Maio writes that majesty itself comes from the 'good and sublime sciences' and is an attribute of music, eloquence, arithmetic, and others arts.[116] One also learns in Chapter 19, in the discussion of magnificence, that Maio wrote a treatise on the origins and history of

---

[112] For the only published edition, see n. 67 above. This treatise is discussed briefly by Gallo, *Music in the Castle*, 96; D'Agostino, 'La musica, la cappella e il cerimoniale', 161 n. 24, 176-77. The text survives in one illuminated manuscript, Paris, Bibliothèque nationale de France, Ms. it. 1711, for which the scribe was Giovan Matteo de Russis (dated 28 August 1492) with illuminations by Cola Rapicano (paid April 1493). On the genre of *speculum principis* in Naples, see Bentley, *Politics and Culture in Renaissance Naples*, 202-22.

[113] Other authors include Apuleius and Valerius Maximus. Modern examples are drawn from Pontano's *De bello neapolitano* and other contemporary texts on Neapolitan history.

[114] Bentley, *Politics and Culture in Renaissance Naples*, 207-8, 264. For further political analysis of Maio's *De maiestate*, see Luca Miele, 'Politica e retorica nel "De maiestate" di G. Maio', in *Quaderni* 4 (1986), 25-60. On Tinctoris's connections to the genre of the *speculum musices*, see Palenik, 'The Early Career of Johannes Tinctoris', 93-99.

[115] Strohm, *The Rise of European Music*, 594-95; Strohm, 'Neue Aspekte von Musik und Humanismus im 15. Jahrhundert', 139. See also Strohm's introduction to Cullington and Strohm (eds.), *'That Liberal and Virtuous Art'*, 14, which states that 'the literary beauty of the many quotations from great poets places the work into the receptional context of a privileged humanistic upbringing'. Strohm acknowledges Tinctoris's dependence on Carlerius's *Tractatus de duplici ritu cantus ecclesiastici in divinis officiis*, but it could well be that a Neapolitan source for Tinctoris's inclusion of classical authors in the *Complexus* came from Maio or Pontano.

[116] 'Non con manco dignitate se sole attribuine questa alma Maiestate anco a le bone e sublime scienze, a la eloquenza, a la musica, a la aristmetica et a le altre' (Maio, *De maiestate*, 16; cited in Gallo, *Music and the Castle*, 96).

hunting, *Inventione della caccia*.[117] This text is now lost, but D'Agostino has shown that such a treatise by Maio is referenced in an early sixteenth-century bequest inventory from the library of the last duke of Calabria, entitled 'A Comparison of the Practice of Hunting and of Music'.[118] This volume is found alongside a 'De musica' of Tinctoris, which is known to be the presentation manuscript of Tinctoris's writings, now housed in Valencia.[119] Other volumes concerning music housed in the royal Aragonese library included Boethius's *De institutione musica* and the musical portions of Isidore of Seville's *Etymologiae*.[120] Similar titles appear in a much earlier inventory of books at the Neapolitan court, assembled around 1480 for Lorenzo de' Medici.[121] Nevertheless, whatever observations Maio might have made about music in relation to hunting must remain in

[117] Maio, *De maiestate*, 231. On Maio's hunting treatise, see De Frede, *I lettori di umanità*, 55; Santoro, 'La cultura umanistica', 149. Elisio Calenzio stressed the importance of hunting at Ferrante's court: see Letter 98 in Lilia Monti Sabia, 'L'"humanitas" di Elisio Calenzio alla luce del suo epistolario', in *Annali della Facoltà di Lettere e Filosofia dell'Università di Napoli* 11 (1964-68), 171-251 at 239-40. See also De Frede, 'Ferrante d'Aragona e la caccia con alcune considerazione politico-sociali', in *Archivio storico per le province napoletane* 115 (1997), 1-26. Pontano also wrote about the importance of hunting for a prince, immediately following his discussion of music in *De principe*: see Pontano, *De principe*, ed. Guido M. Cappelli, Testi e documenti di letteratura e di lingua 22 (Rome, 2003), 38. Dedicated to Alfonso, Duke of Calabria, *De principe* is closely modeled on Xenophon's *Cyropedia*, a copy of which could be found in Pontano's library. In the fifteenth century, Xenephon's text was a popular text for translation from the original Greek by humanists for reading by Italian rulers.

[118] 'Uno libro de messer Iuniano Mayo cavaliero neapolitano quale fa comparacione de lo exercicio de la musica et de lo exercicio de la caza intitulato Ferdinando primo, de volume de foglio comune, scripto de littera antica in carta bergamena. Comenza la opera *Soleno li generosi et bene accostomati ingegni non nianco* [manco ?] *inclinati*, et in fine de maiuscule *finisce el libro de la musica et de caza composter* [sic] *messer Iuniano Maio cavaliero neapolitano*. Coper[t] o de coiro lionato stampato. Signato Iuniano 28; notato alo imballaturo a ff. 190, partita 2a.' Paolo Cherchi and Teresa de Robertis, 'Un inventario della biblioteca aragonese', in *Italia medioevale e umanistica* 33 (1990), 109-347 at 255; cited in D'Agostino, 'La musica, la cappella e il cerimoniale', 176-77. Cherchi and De Robertis note that this text was copied by Mariano Volpe for the Aragonese court in December 1492, just months before Maio died. See also De Marinis, *La biblioteca napoletana*, vol. 2, doc. 878. Since this text by Maio is referred to in his *De maiestate*, it must predate the latter text.

[119] University of Valencia, Biblioteca Histórica, Ms. 835; cited in Cherchi and De Robertis, 'Un inventario della biblioteca aragonese', 240-41. Three books of music, all containing *canto figurato*, are also listed in the inventory. The description of one of these polyphonic books contains details that lead us to speculate about the book's musical contents: 'Et piú un altro libro de canto figurado de volume de foglio comune, scripto et notato canzoni et muttetti alla francese in carta bergamena. Comenza *Etous biene est ma maistituisse*, et in fine *contra puis que si bien meste advenu*. Coperto de velluto negro con 12 coquiglie de rame che serveno per cantuni et per chiedende. Signato Mottetti 3; notato alo imballaturo a ff. 227, partita 2a.': cited in Cherchi and De Robertis, 'Un inventario della biblioteca aragonese', 176. The incipit work is surely *De tous biens plaine*. *Puisque si bien m'este advenu* is almost certainly a reference to the chanson attributed to Loyset Compère. The 'contra' preceding the French title is likely the voice part designation, which together with the title should be the final text on the recto side of the last page of the volume. The inventory's descriptions of the other two polyphonic sources also cite the text incipit and explicit. One, 'uno libro de canto figurato', opens with a *Salve regina* and closes with the text 'sicut erat tacet', suggesting perhaps a Magnificat (cited in Cherchi and De Robertis, 'Un inventario della biblioteca aragonese', 241; D'Agostino, 'La musica, la cappella e il cerimoniale', 176). As the description seems to indicate, it appears that the motet volume in the inventory belonged to a collection for which it was the third volume of motets. The Tinctoris volume is marked on its binding as 'Tinctoris primo' (Cherchi and De Robertis, 'Un inventario della biblioteca aragonese', 240-41).

[120] Another large portion of the royal Aragonese library was sold by Isabella del Balzo, Queen of Naples, to a book collector in Ferrara named Celio Calcagnini. On the inventory of this sale, see Santiago López-Ríos, 'A New Inventory of the Royal Aragonese Library of Naples', in *Journal of the Warburg and Courtauld Institutes* 65 (2002), 201-43 at 230 and 234. Also, an anthology of poetry, in French, was given by Queen Isabella in 1523 to a 'Joan Michael, francese, cantor del signore Duca de Ferrara' (240). On the singer, see Lewis Lockwood, 'Jean Mouton and Jean Michel: New Evidence on French Music and Musicians in Italy 1505-1520', in *Journal of the American Musicological Society* (1979), 191-246. The musical passages in Isidore's *Etymologiae* are found in Book III, 15-23.

[121] D'Agostino, 'La musica, la cappella e il cerimoniale', 176; De Marinis, *La biblioteca napoletana*, Inventario B. Other music volumes in this inventory for Lorenzo include a 'Musica Boetij', 'Musica Isidori', 'Musica Tinctoris', 'Liber diversarum cantionum', and a 'Musica Lippi'. D'Agostino proposes the 'Musica Tinctoris' is the illuminated Bologna copy of Tinctoris's writings (Biblioteca Universitaria, Ms. 2573). It could also have been a source for the copy of the *Proportionale musices* now in Florence, Biblioteca Medicea Laurenziana, Ms. Plut. XXIX. 48. For recent discussion of this source as it relates to John Hothby, see James Haar and John Nádas, 'Johannes de Anglia (John Hothby): Notes on His Career in Italy', in *Acta Musicologica* 79 (2007), 291-358 at 326. Gallo, *Music in the Castle*, 90, proposes the

the shadows, along with all of the modern exempla from musical life in Naples he might have employed. But it is compelling to imagine what Tinctoris might have been able to teach the Neapolitan master of Latin.

Tinctoris's Erudite Colleagues: The *Accademia Pontaniana*

Begun in the fifteenth century and separate from the university was another entity for scholarly collaboration and conversation in Naples: the *Accademia Pontaniana*. In many ways it was an informal alternative to the university at Naples. The surviving literary and epistolary evidence for this intellectual body shows us that discussion regularly turned to rhetoric, poetics, grammar, history, and theology.[122] Founded by Antonio Beccadelli (Il Panormita) (1394-1471) during Alfonso I's lifetime, gatherings took place in the royal library. Under Ferrante's rule, the meetings became more public, at first gathering outdoors under the arcades near Panormita's home, then often meeting at Pontano's home (a gift from Ferrante), Pontano's villa in Antignano, or his personal chapel, which housed the arm bone of Livy, given to him by Panormita.[123]

The long-time leader of the *Accademia*, Giovanni Pontano came from Umbria early in life and soon became the central figure of Neapolitan humanism during the second half of the fifteenth century.[124] His treatise *De aspiratione* has been discussed above, but overall Pontano was renowned as a Latin writer and his interests extended to astrology, astronomy, meteorology, and agriculture; his poetry often treated conjugal love and courtly life, while his prose (in the form of dialogues and treatises) concerned morals and politics, along with Neapolitan history.[125] After a long and notable career as chancellor, diplomat, and advisor to several Aragonese kings of Naples, Pontano dedicated his later life to writing treatises on social virtues, which include works on generosity, kindness, magnificence, and cooperation.[126] He also considered music to be important and says so in his *De principe*, dedicated to his pupil Alfonso duke of Calabria.[127]

Gatherings of the *Accademia* led by Pontano were informal in nature and involved readings of ancient and modern texts. It is difficult to determine membership or participation, since official membership did not seem to be required, although regular members were given or chose Latinized names for one another. We do know, however, that Giuniano Maio, Joanmarco Cinico, and Raffaele Brandolini were regular attendees, and it does seem that a majority of the participants were in the service of the Aragonese court, some as secretaries, diplomats, or other political roles, and others as tutors of

---

'Musica Lippi' to be the eulogy for Pietrobono delivered in 1473 and copied in Lucca, Biblioteca Capitolare, Ms. 525, fols. 175v-184r.

[122] On the Accademia Pontaniana, see Bentley, *Politics and Culture in Renaissance Naples*, 93-95, 133; Santoro, 'La cultura umanistica', 159-71; Shulamit Furstenberg-Levi, 'The Fifteenth Century Accademia Pontaniana - An Analysis of its Institutional Elements', in *History of Universities* 21 (2006), 33-70; Santoro, 'Humanism in Naples', 304-7.

[123] On its meeting place, see Furstenberg-Levi, 'The Fifteenth Century Accademia Pontaniana', 36-44.

[124] Carol Kidwell, *Pontano: Poet & Prime Minister*; Bentley, *Politics and Culture in Renaissance* Naples, 127-37, 176-94.

[125] Bentley, *Politics and Culture in Renaissance Naples*, 246-52; see also Pontano, *Dialogues*, vii-xxvii. On his theory of poetics, see Santoro, 'Humanism in Naples', 311-13. Many of Pontano's writings were completed following his retirement from active political life; on this period, see Kidwell, *Pontano*, 256-301.

[126] Giovanni Pontano, *I trattati delle virtù sociali. De liberalitate, De beneficentia, De magnificentia, De splendore, De conviventia*, ed. Francesco Tateo (Rome, 1965).

[127] See n. 117 above. Pontano, *De principe*, 38: 'Adhibendi sunt etiam musici qui tum cantu tum chordis oblectent animum et curas permulceant; dandum quoque aliquid istrionibus'; cited in Gallo, *Music and the Castle*, 76.

various members of the royal family.[128] Another known member was Lorenzo Bonincontri (1410-91), a political exile from Tuscany whose commentary on the astronomical text by Manilius might have been the source for Tinctoris's citation of the ancient astrologer in his *De inventione et usu musice*.[129] Formal training or higher education seems not to have been a prerequisite for membership, and friendships among members were often strong and life-long.[130]

Woodley has put forward that Tinctoris's participation in the *Accademia* seems 'intrinsically highly likely', given his certain connection to Pontano, namely the latter's 1487 instruction to Tinctoris for recruiting new singers from the north for the royal chapel in Naples.[131] Claude Palisca has also shown the likely influence of Pontano's astronomical writings on Tinctoris's views concerning the harmony of the spheres.[132] It could also be that Tinctoris's understanding of the concept of *varietas* might have come from or been influenced by Pontano's ideas on the celestial world.[133]

[128] Kidwell, *Pontano*, 57-59; Camillo Minieri Riccio, *Biografie degli accademici alfonsini detti poi pontaniani dal 1442 al 1543* (Naples, 1881); Furstenberg-Levi, 'The Fifteenth Century Accademia Pontaniana', 50-58 esp. at 53. The 'core members' listed by Furstenberg-Levi include Pontano, Compatre, Poderico, Altilius, Sannazaro, Giovanni Pardo, Chariteo, Girolamo Carbone, Marino Tomacelli, Marullus, Andrea Matteo and Belisario Acquaviva, Tristano Caracciolo, Crisostomo Colonna, Galateo (Antonio de Ferraris), Franceschello Marchese, Elisio Calenzio, and Summonte. Kidwell adds Theodore Gaza and Lorenzo Bonincontri.

[129] For more on Bonincontri, see Kidwell, *Pontano*, 58. On Manilius, see Santoro, 'Humanism in Naples', 309. On Tinctoris and Manilius, see Leofranc Holford-Strevens, 'Tinctoris on the Great Composers', in *Plainsong and Medieval Music* 5 (1996), 193-99 at 195 n. 13.

[130] Furstenberg-Levi, 'The Fifteenth Century Accademia Pontaniana', 54 observes that 'many other academy members had no formal higher education, but obtained a humanistic education from private lessons, either from Pontano himself or from other teachers. The following academy members were in that category: the Acquaviva brothers, Caracciolo, Federico Poderico, and Compatre. Thus, as Gothein affirmed, "Per appartenere a questo circolo era quasi più necessario essere un uomo addestrato alla pratica della vita che un dotto"' (Everardo Gothein, *Il Rinascimento nell'Italia meridionale*, trans. T. Persico [Florence, 1915], 256). On friendships of members, see Furstenberg-Levi, 'The Fifteenth Century Accademia Pontaniana', 55-58.

[131] Transcribed and discussed in Woodley, 'Iohannes Tinctoris: A Review', 235, 245; Atlas, *Music at the Aragonese Court*, 73; D'Agostino, 'La musica, la cappella e il cerimoniale', 172. Palenik, 'The Early Career of Johannes Tinctoris', 167: 'Assuming that the theorist made the trip—there is no reason to believe that he did not—such a journey would have taken well over a year, and probably closer to two. Evidence of Tinctoris's return to Naples first reappears in a document of February 1491 concerning one of his canonries'. See also Woodley, 'Tinctoris and Nivelles', 112-13. This letter might be compared with the instructions and letters of introductions borne northward by Gaspar van Weerbeke from the Sforza court in Milan; these are edited, translated, and discussed in Paul A. Merkley and Lora L. M. Merkley, *Music and Patronage in the Sforza Court* (Turnhout, 1999), esp. 77-79. Woodley, 'Renaissance Music Theory as Literature', 218 n. 34: 'No specific evidence has yet to emerge linking Tinctoris with Pontano's renowned Academy, though some participation on Tinctoris's part seems intrinsically highly likely'.

[132] Palisca, *Humanism in Italian Renaissance Musical Thought*, 181-85; Strohm, 'Neue Aspekte von Musik und Humanismus im 15. Jahrhundert', 138-39. For a corrective on Palisca's interpretation of Tinctoris's views on the harmony of the spheres, see Palenik, 'The Early Career of Johannes Tinctoris', 72, 82-83. Cinico would have become familiar with medieval texts on astronomy when copying an anthology of astronomical writings for Ferrante in 1469; this manuscript is New York, Morgan Library, Ms. M. 389.

[133] See also Charles Trinkaus, 'The Astrological Cosmos and Rhetorical Culture of Giovanni Gioviano Pontano', in *Renaissance Quarterly* 38 (1985), 446-72 at 456-57: 'For Pontano, the celestial world was, as it were, a great society of intersecting voices, agreeing and disagreeing with each other and arriving at some momentary equilibrium only to pass rapidly into a continuing dance of debate and reconciliation. He compared it to the world of human culture, which also varied according to talents, peoples, geographic regions, and history. He draws a marvellous metaphor, comparing heavenly things to the variety produced by the arts and trades, especially those of painting and dyeing, in which such richly varied effects can be gained from different mixtures of the few primary colors: "Such diligence can be seen in every art." He especially sees this to be the case in his own art of poetry'. Pontano, *De rebus coelestibus*, Lib. VI, sig. M5: 'Haec autem ipsa varietas tam diversa morum ingeniorumque...maxime apparet in pictura...Itaque ab ipsa commistione, proque commistionis temperatura cuncta haec profiscuntur, quod mathematici est non secus ac medici, omni arte diligentiaque perspicere'. Pontano first drafted this work in 1475-76, then revised it completely after 1495, with an edition published at Naples posthumously in 1512 by Sigismund Mayr. Cited in Wegman, 'Johannes Tinctoris and the "New Art"', 176-77. For the current account of Tinctoris's understanding of *varietas*, see Gallagher, 'Models of *Varietas*', ch. 2; Luko, 'Tinctoris on *Varietas*'.

The Tinctoris-Cinico Letter

The strongest evidence for Tinctoris interacting with this circle of Neapolitan scholars comes in his aforementioned letter to Joanmarco Cinico. It offers us the most extensive surviving example of Tinctoris's life outside of music. The body of his letter to Cinico raises moral and social issues, which Woodley and Wegman have both observed reveal a certain dismay or frustration by Tinctoris with courtly life. Given Tinctoris's apparent unemployment or retirement from the royal chapel by the mid-1490s, this could be the case. However, it should also be noted that each of these moral and social issues raised by Tinctoris is the subject of much discussion by Pontano in his writings and correspondence. In fact, many of them are the topics of entire treatises or dialogues by him, composed in and around the time of this letter.[134] Moreover, the rejection of each of the conventional desires in favour of a virtuous life was central to leading a life according to the Cynics. Given that his addressee took the name 'il Cinico', or was given it (perhaps by the *Accademia*), Tinctoris praised him for his spurning of these desires and for 'encouraging and stimulating others to act likewise'.[135] With this letter, Tinctoris sought not only to show him that he understood true Cynicism, but to offer an epistolary contribution on the topic.

Referencing Cicero, Augustine, and Varro, Tinctoris opened his letter with two proverbs: 'nothing should be sought from him who is unable to give it' and foolish is he who places 'happiness as the highest fulfilment of all'.[136] This served as an introduction into his railing against wealth, renown, honours, power, and pleasures in order to achieve a virtuous life. Providing examples from classical literature and modern-day history (as recent as the imprisonment of the French cardinal Jean la Balue [1469] or the Turkish siege of Belgrade [1456]), Tinctoris turned to the Neapolitan model of fortifying an account or argument with recent and personal experiences.[137] Whether or not Tinctoris was griping about his state in life or work, these concepts were hotly debated by Tinctoris's colleagues at the Neapolitan court: the diplomats, the administrators, the counsellors, and so forth. And, as Tinctoris noted in the letter, he was writing in response to Cinico's own 'ornate and fitting' letter on these matters.

Proposing a stronger connection between Tinctoris and the *Accademia Pontaniana* can be strengthened by the very end of the letter between Tinctoris and Cinico. As seen in the passage here, Tinctoris wrote to Cinico from the town of Pozzuoli, a town on the Bay of Naples:

> Quibus me (inspectis templo Sybille, colosso Bayano, ponte Gallicule, operibus mirificis penitus dirutis) monitum vis considerare nihil (preter officium virtutis) duraturum, in quo mihi tecum convenit, eo quod ipsa virtus qua recte vivitur sit gradus unicus quo ad felicitatem finis insciam animi mortalium diis effecti similes conscendunt.[138]

---

[134] The descent of Charles VIII into Italy has been considered a turning-point for Italian intellectuals and the consciousness of Neapolitan humanists. Santoro, 'La cultura umanistica', 323, writes: 'This event marked a transformation in Pontano's intellectual and moral itinerary, as reflected in his late writings, *De fortuna*, *De prudentia*, the dialogue *Aegidius*, and *De immanitate*'. Other moral treatises by Pontano from this period are *De liberalitate* (1493) and *De beneficentia* (1493).

[135] Tinctoris addresses Cinico as 'cynicorum perfectissimo' and 'tu rarissime virtutis Cynice', then later closes his letter, 'For in this way, as befits your Cynic discretion and propriety, you will of your abundant good nature pardon me… Farewell, then, most singular example of the Cynics' (Woodley, 'Tinctoris's Italian Translation', 236, 243-44).

[136] Woodley, 'Tinctoris's Italian Translation', 236-37.

[137] Woodley, 'Tinctoris's Italian Translation', 200-202, argues that Tinctoris is modeling his letter on the genre made famous by Seneca.

[138] Woodley, 'Tinctoris's Italian Translation', 243-44.

In this you advise me, having visited the Temple of the Sibyl, the Colossus at Baiae and the Bridge of Caligula—all astounding constructions now completely in ruins—and express the wish that I consider nothing capable of enduring, save the duty of virtue; in this regard I am quite in agreement with you, on the grounds that virtue, through which an upright life is led, is the one and only ladder by means of which the spirit of mortal man can approach godhead and ascend to happiness knowing no end.

Tinctoris notes that he has gone there on Cinico's advice and visited three ancient sites: (1) the Temple of the Sibyl; (2) the Bridge of Caligula; and (3) the Colossus at Baiae. Together with Cinico's recommendations, Tinctoris might have used a guidebook for his travels in Pozzuoli: a text printed by Arnaldo da Bruxelles in December of 1475, *Libellus de mirabilibus Puteolorum*, generally attributed to Giovanni Elisio, a text that Woodley points out is bound with the sole surviving copy of Tinctoris's letter.[139] The Temple of the Sibyl is likely to be Avernus, a site of frequent pilgrimage by humanists, and cited as an entrance to the Underworld in Book VI of Virgil's *Aeneid*, a text and author frequently referenced by Tinctoris.[140] As Woodley clarifies, what Tinctoris calls the bridge of Caligula was not actually the ancient Roman pontoon bridge built in A.D. 39, as Suetonius, Dio, and others say, to cross several miles of a portion of the Bay of Naples from present-day Pozzuoli over to the Baiae as an elaborate and expensive part of his becoming emperor of Rome.[141] Instead, Woodley rightly suggests that the 'bridge' was made of 'the remnants of the stone piles which supported the great ancient mole or pier of Puteoli'.[142] Finally, the Colossus at Baiae seems to refer to a statue or sculpture at Baiae, the ancient beach resort on the Bay of Naples frequented by wealthy ancient Romans and the site of legendary debauchery. The Romans (including Cicero) covered the coastline and surrounding hills with luxurious villas, one of which was occupied centuries later by none other than Pontano, to be used regularly for meetings of the *Accademia* as well as long periods of isolated study.[143] Horace wrote that nothing in the world compared to splendid Baiae.[144] Pontano himself loved the Baia and even composed two books of hendecasyllabic poetry to his friends, family, and lovers with the title of *Baiae*.[145]

[139] Fava and Bresciano, *La stampa*, vol. 2, 67-87. Woodley, 'Tinctoris's Italian Translations', 194-95, discusses this text; the Arnaldo printing date, however, should read 1475, not 1485.

[140] The illuminator Cola da Rapicano, who regularly collaborated with Cinico in preparing manuscripts, illuminated at least one manuscript of another famous guidebook to the baths of Pozzuoli, Petrus de Ebulo's *De balneis Puteolanis*, currently Milan, Biblioteca Ambrosiana, Ms. I. 6. inf.

[141] Suetonius, Cal. 19.1-2, records that the bridge was constructed 'by bringing together merchant ships from all sides and anchoring them in a double line, after which a mound of earth was heaped upon them and fashioned in the manner of the Appian Way'. On this, see also Marc Kleijwegt, 'Caligula's "Triumph" at Baiae', in *Mnemosyne* (4th ser.) 47 (1994), 652-71.

[142] Woodley, 'Tinctoris's Italian Translation', 243 note to lines 201-2.

[143] For a useful modern-day guide to the ancient sites, see Paola Miniero, *Baia: il castello, il museo, l'area archeologica* (Naples, 2000).

[144] Cited in Pontano, *Baiae*, ed. Rodney G. Dennis, The I Tatti Renaissance Library 22 (Cambridge MA, 2006), introduction.

[145] Pontano, *Baiae*, ed. Dennis. On the Baia and Pontano's fondness for the area, see Kidwell, *Pontano*, 118-25. Pontano's *Hendecasyllaborum libri seu Baiae* were published in Venice by Aldus and in Naples by Pietro Summonte in 1505, two years after Pontano's death.

Conclusion

This letter by Tinctoris not only proves Trithemius accurate in praising Tinctoris as a writer of elegant letters, but also further exemplifies Tinctoris's fascination with the ancient world. Perhaps more importantly, this letter shows a connection between Tinctoris and the scholarly activities of his Neapolitan colleagues, such as Cinico, Pontano, and several of the tutors of Aragonese children like Elisio Calenzio, Raffaele Brandolini, and others. If one is disinclined to believe any direct connection with them or with the activities of the *Accademia* beyond his friend Cinico, his treatment of themes common to their intellectual circle and his visiting of sites they frequented (almost as a tourist) shows a Tinctoris who wanted to imitate his Neapolitan colleagues, even if he had already left the service of the Aragonese court.

We know from Tinctoris's dedication of his musical dictionary to Beatrice in the early 1470s that he took pleasure in 'achieving knowledge in various subjects, not being satisfied with a single art' and that he knew he probably could not excel those who put their energies and devotion toward one particular art.[146] Tinctoris, the unabashed polymath, would have shared a great deal with the scholars he encountered during his two decades in Naples, from the professors at the university like Giuniano Maio, to Giovanni Pontano and his think-tank of friends and colleagues, along with Joanmarco Cinico the scribe, collaborator, and friend. While we can see the impact of Tinctoris's years of singing, teaching, and a rather scholastic legal education on his theoretical writings, it becomes evident that the intellectual and courtly life of late quattrocento Naples would have pushed Tinctoris to share that learning with his new students, readers, and erudite colleagues in Naples.

Abstract

The explosion of Johannes Tinctoris's treatises over the course of about five years in the mid-1470s has been shown to be not necessarily the inspired fruit of his employment at the royal court of Naples, beginning in or around 1472-73, but rather the result of several years of singing, instructing, reading, and even drafting treatises before his arrival there. However much his years of training and experience in musical practice and theory before Naples might have shaped Tinctoris, it is nevertheless only at Naples that these treatises found themselves completed, circulated, and in some cases even printed. Drawing attention to the Neapolitan context of the completion and reception of several of Tinctoris's treatises allows for a comparative examination of Tinctoris and some of his closest colleagues at the Aragonese court in Naples, namely Giuniano Maio, Giovanni Pontano, and Joanmarco Cinico. This study has implications for our understanding of several of his treatises, including *De inventione et usu musice*, *Complexus effectuum musices*, and *Terminorum musicae diffinitorium*, as well as the prefaces to his *Proportionale musices*, *Liber de natura et proprietate tonorum*, and *Liber de arte contrapuncti*.

---

[146] Tinctoris, *Diffinitorium musice*, ed. Cecilia Panti (Florence, 2004), 4, prologus: 'Unde quom, diversis naturaliter gaudens non unica arte contentus, plurium cognitionem attingere, sicut tua iam discretio novit, in dies animo ferventi pretendam, non mirum si in qualibet adeo perfectus non evadam, ut illos, qui singulariter in singulis artibus operam et curam efficacissime ponunt, vincere possim.' (my translation).

Tinctoris's Family Origins:
Some New Clues

■

RONALD WOODLEY

The joint preoccupations of music and law were fundamental to the trajectory of Tinctoris's career. In a rare glimpse into the theorist's long-standing emotional, as well as intellectual, attachment to music, he tells us in the Prologue of his *Complexus effectuum musices*, addressed to another keen young student of music, Princess Beatrice of Aragon, that he had dedicated himself to music from his earliest years ('musicen cui me ab ineunte aetate dedidi').[1] Frustratingly, though, it has proved impossible so far to identify where, and by whom, this youthful commitment to music was nurtured, other than by surmising that his early training probably took place at one of the *maîtrises* within a plausible radius of his home village in French-speaking Brabant, Braine-l'Alleud. Although I made a similar point elsewhere many years ago,[2] it is perhaps worth repeating that future research here may usefully focus further on Saint-Vincent, Soignies, or Sainte-Waudru, Mons, or even his more local collegiate church of Sainte-Gertrude, Nivelles—though early exposure to high-quality polyphonic repertories and influential senior musicians, such as seems implicitly to underlie Tinctoris's reflection, may diminish somewhat the likelihood of this last-named, at least as a primary source of his experiences. In view of Tinctoris's later, though ambiguous, association with Cambrai cathedral in 1460,[3] alongside eminent and clearly admired figures there such as Du Fay, Regis, and

---

[1] *Egidius Carlerius [and] Johannes Tinctoris: On the Dignity & the Effects of Music*, ed. Reinhard Strohm and J. Donald Cullington, Institute of Advanced Musical Studies Study Texts 2 (London, 1996), 51 and 67; *Johannis Tinctoris opera theoretica*, ed. Albert Seay, 2 vols. plus vol. 2a, Corpus scriptorum de musica 22 (s.l. & Neuhausen-Stuttgart, 1975-78), vol. 2, 165. The classical phrase 'ab ineunte aetate' used by Tinctoris can sometimes mean 'from an early age' and sometimes the more precise 'from the coming of age' (i.e., upon reaching adulthood). In the context of Tinctoris's address to the young Beatrice, who was in her mid-to-late teens at the time and on the verge of betrothal to Matthias Corvinus of Hungary, it is a moot question which particular emphasis Tinctoris had in mind, since he is partly seeking to draw a parallel between his own youthful experience, looking back in the 1470s as an established figure in his early middle age, and his obsequious appreciation for the young princess's own talents. I am grateful to Jeffrey Dean for pointing out that Tinctoris may here be recasting a passage from Cicero, *De oratore* 1.96-7, which would tend to reinforce the interpretation as 'from an early age'.

[2] Ronald Woodley, 'Iohannes Tinctoris: A Review of the Biographical Evidence', in *Journal of the American Musicological Society* 34 (1981), 217-48 at 225.

[3] The payment from the account of the *petits vicaires* at Cambrai to Tinctoris for four months' service to the cathedral was first reported in Craig Wright, 'Dufay at Cambrai: Discoveries and Revisions', in *Journal of the American Musicological Society* 28 (1975), 221. The misinterpretation (including by the present writer) that this necessarily indicated that Tinctoris was actually functioning as *petit vicaire* for this period was corrected in Alejandro E. Planchart, 'The Early Career of Guillaume Du Fay', in *Journal of the American Musicological Society* 46 (1993), 367-68; Planchart informs us that the 'need for capitular approval indicates that the payment is, in effect, a gift to Tinctoris' (ibid., 368). The terminology employed, according to which Tinctoris 'servivit in habitu ecclesie' for these four months, clearly implies some kind of genuine, attendant service to the cathedral, which, since the account that year was controlled by Du Fay, Planchart suggests may have been a period of working or studying with the composer (ibid.). Joshua Rifkin, on the other hand, considers that 'the document [Planchart] cites does not indicate that Tinctoris "had been a beneficiary of [Du Fay's] tutelage," except perhaps in the most general sense.' ('Compere, "Des Pres," and the Choirmasters of Cambrai: *Omnium bonorum plena* Reconsidered', in *Acta Musicologica* 81 [2009], 55-73 at 60-61). I am grateful to Jeffrey Dean for alerting me to Rifkin's comment, and for the suggestion, particularly in view of n. 4 below, that Tinctoris had perhaps been connected more with Gilles Carlier than Du Fay during his months at Cambrai.

Gilles Carlier (Egidius Carlerius),[4] we cannot rule out the possibility that at least part of his boyhood training had also already taken place there, or at the collegiate church of Saint-Géry in the same town.[5]

An analogous situation is observable when it comes to Tinctoris's parallel attachment to the law. We have a reasonably clear basic outline of his university career at Orléans, though this is not without its anomalies and still unanswered questions.[6] There can be no doubting, too, that his experience and qualifications to licentiate (later doctoral) level in canon and civil law would have contributed materially to his ability to progress socially and economically through his career as working musician, teacher, chaplain, and legal adviser at Orléans, Chartres, and Naples, as well as inflecting the language and structuring of his theoretical writings. But just as we are still very much in the dark as to the institutional circumstances in which Tinctoris first became exposed to the music that took hold of him from such an early age, before his appointment in the late 1450s to the cathedral of Sainte-Croix at Orléans,[7] so it has been equally difficult to build any kind of real context or motivation for his legal studies before his recorded matriculation as member (albeit not fully paid-up) of the German nation at the University of Orléans at some point between July and September 1462.[8]

Part of the reason, therefore, that I have chosen, as a contribution to this quincentenary celebration issue, to try and sweep out such an apparently small corner of Tinctoris's long and illustrious life is that, as our new digital edition of his writings gets properly under way,[9] there seems a certain appropriateness in revisiting the very beginnings of the project's subject from this little-explored angle. But a more immediate and substantive motivation is that there has recently come to light a repository of fifteenth-century documents that I have been attempting to locate for over thirty years, which at least begin to shed some light on Tinctoris's family context in these still very elusive early years. The new information, first signalled in an earlier article on Tinctoris's

[4]   For this last-named, and in particular the relationships between Tinctoris's *Complexus* and Carlerius's *Tractatus de duplici ritu cantus ecclesiastici in divinis officiis*, see especially *On the Dignity & the Effects of Music*, ed Strohm and Cullington. All three of these figures, further triangulated with the *L'homme armé* tradition and Tinctoris's writings, are discussed in Sean Gallagher, *Johannes Regis*, Collection 'Épitome musical' (Turnhout, 2010), esp. 59-85.

[5]   I am extremely grateful to Alejandro Planchart for sharing with me his listings, accrued over many years of archival research, of the choirboys cited sporadically in the fifteenth-century Cambrai cathedral records (personal communication of 23 June 2012). It is worth noting that a number of other appointments relating to Braine-l'Alleud are recorded in the Cambrai archives: for instance, Jehan Daussy (Jehan de Douai), who is recorded as chorister between 1477 and 1479, was collated to a chaplaincy at Braine-l'Alleud by 1493; Jehan de la Porte (Johannes de Porta), *petit vicaire* from 1462 to 1474, was collated to a chaplaincy at the hospital in Braine-l'Alleud in August 1480 (see also Figure 1 and nn. 32, 40, and 49 below); and Nicole de Berquier, documented as former chorister in 1456, resigned a chaplaincy at the hospital of Saint-Philippe in Braine-l'Alleud on 17 September 1493. (I am again very grateful to Alejandro Planchart for these details.) On the significance of Saint-Géry, with respect to the early musical experience of Josquin in the 1460s, see David Fallows, *Josquin*, Collection 'Épitome musical' (Turnhout, 2009), 23-24 and 35.

[6]   See, for instance, Woodley, 'Iohannes Tinctoris: A Review', 225-29; also the important recent contribution of Jeffrey S. Palenik, 'The Early Career of Johannes Tinctoris: An Examination of the Music Theorist's Northern Education and Development' (Ph.D. diss., Duke University, 2008), which enlarges and corrects some of the present writer's earlier work.

[7]   As discussed by Marlène Britta, 'Contribution à l'étude des années passées par Johannes Tinctoris à Orléans : 1458-65', forthcoming in the following issue of this Journal.

[8]   It is likely that Tinctoris had already commenced his law studies a little in advance of this formal matriculation, by May 1462: see Palenik, 'The Early Career', 17, and n. 13 below. We also need to bring back into any discussion of Tinctoris's education the probability that before moving to Orléans he had already pursued an arts degree, perhaps even to masters level (ibid., 16); in this case we should seriously reconsider, with Palenik, the two individuals of the correct name and diocesan origin whose matriculations are recorded at the University of Leuven in c. 1446 and c. 1448 (ibid., 36-40; Woodley, 'Iohannes Tinctoris: A Review', 219).

[9]   See Introduction above.

obit at Sainte-Gertrude, Nivelles,[10] is principally of an historical rather than strictly musical nature. One of the documents to emerge, however, suggests something, albeit very indirectly, about Tinctoris's treatise *De inventione et usu musice*, which by a nice coincidence meshes with recent investigations of this work that other Tinctoris scholars, notably Rob Wegman and Jeffrey Palenik, have carried out. I shall return to these implications for *De inventione* towards the end of this article.

We have known for a long time that Tinctoris's father was called Martin. In the unique surviving copy of the printed extracts from *De inventione* printed in Naples around 1481-83, the heading placed after the initial letter of salutation from Tinctoris to Johannes Stokem, immediately before the first extract from Book 2 of the treatise, states that the author dedicated the work 'to the most blessed soul of Martin Tinctoris, his most highly honourable father'.[11] A number of specific issues need to be teased from this apparently innocuous inscription. First and foremost, who wrote it, and on what basis? It is clearly not of Tinctoris's own authorship, at least not in its entirety: his own conventional literary habit of self-abasement in his treatise prologues as, for instance, 'inter musice professores minimus' or close equivalent, would scarcely allow of a self-styling as brazen as 'musicus prestantissimus'. Yet the wording of the actual dedication to his father shows all the signs of having been lifted—perhaps by the printer Matthias Moravus himself, acting here, as was not uncommon at the time, in a quasi-editorial capacity—more or less directly from some authorial exemplar. Secondly, the 'quos' clearly refers back to 'librorum', which is to say, implicitly the complete set of books constituting the treatise (or at least the printer/editor's perception thereof), from which the subsequent extracts from Books 2, 3, and 4 (out of five in total) are taken. This being the case, the dedication by the author to his late father seems itself to refer to this whole work, and not just to the printed extracts. What cannot be inferred from this wording with any degree of certainty is whether or not the dedication implies that his father was only relatively *recently* deceased. In principle this would be just about plausible in the early 1480s, if Tinctoris himself were born in the early to mid-1430s, as has been generally supposed; but such a level of detail has frankly never seemed to matter all that much, as far as musicological discussion of the treatise's actual content and gestation are concerned. We shall see later, however, that the relationship between the evolution of *De inventione* and its author's father may be less tangential than suspected.

Tinctoris's geographical origins are known, fortunately, from the author's own hand. Despite the years of claims and counter-claims in more modern times, especially

---

[10] Ronald Woodley, 'Tinctoris and Nivelles: The Obit Evidence', in this Journal 1 (2009), 110-21 at 117 n. 29.

[11] With the original punctuation: 'Ex secundo librorum de inventione et usu musice: quos Johannes Tinctoris brabantinus: iurisperitus: poeta: musicusque prestantissimus: anime beatissime Martini Tinctoris: patris eius quamplurimum honorandi: conscribendo dicavit.' Regensburg, Bischöfliche Zentralbibliothek, Die Proskesche Musikabteilung [D-Rp], Th 33 (*olim* H 15), fol. 2; Karl Weinmann (ed.), *Johannes Tinctoris (1445-1511) und sein unbekannter Traktat 'De inventione et usu musicae': Historisch-kritische Untersuchung*, 2nd edn. with foreword by Wilhelm Fischer (Tutzing, 1961; original edition Regensburg and Rome, 1917), with facsimile of this folio as frontispiece. A new edition and English translation of the surviving text of this treatise will appear later in 2013 as part of the new digital edition cited above. For a study of the typography and dating of the print, see Ronald Woodley, 'The Printing and Scope of Tinctoris's Fragmentary Treatise *De inventione et usu musice*', in *Early Music History* 5 (1985), 239-68; for a more recent investigation of the contents and textual history of the treatise, see Rob C. Wegman, 'Tinctoris's *Magnum opus*', in *Uno gentile et subtile ingenio: Studies in Renaissance Music in Honour of Bonnie J. Blackburn*, ed. M. Jennifer Bloxam, Gioia Filocamo, and Leofranc Holford-Strevens, Collection 'Épitome musical' (Turnhout, 2009), 771-82; also the extended treatment, building on Wegman's work, in Palenik, 'The Early Career', 51-128.

in the nineteenth century, which I have written about elsewhere[12]—first between France and Belgium, and then within Belgium between Nivelles and other regions—we can be sure that Tinctoris thought of himself as coming from the village (now *commune*) of Braine-l'Alleud, lying around twenty kilometres south of Brussels, and, unlike Nivelles itself, only a few kilometres down the road, just within the bounds of the diocese of Cambrai. He is quite explicit about his place of origin in his own (once again artificially self-abasing, though linguistically extravagant) entry in the matriculation register of the German nation at the University of Orléans on 1 April 1463 (new style), marking his period of office as procurator: 'me Johannem tinctoris, pangeristarum ymum ast ecclesie sancte crucis Aurelian[ensis] choralium pedagogum, quem terra branie alodii cameracensis dyocesis ecastor genuit'.[13]

In the late 1970s, when the Orléans matriculation books began to be published, one of the editors, Hilde de Ridder-Symoens, inserted an intriguing aside into her commentary, suggesting that Tinctoris was probably the son of one Martin le Taintenier, who was recorded as *échevin* of Braine-l'Alleud. No date was given, but the source of her information, transmitted to her via a third party, was given as the parish archives of Braine-l'Alleud ('A.P. Braine-l'Alleud, n° 60; voir aussi n° 76').[14] At this point, however, the trail for other researchers wishing to follow up the lead went quite cold, and remained so for an unfortunate number of years. De Ridder-Symoens' informant, named as 'L[éon?] van Dormael', proved impossible to contact; the Archives générales du Royaume in Brussels, and their main regional repository for French-speaking Brabant in Louvain-la-Neuve, were for a long time unable to suggest where such a *fonds* of documents might be held; and as recently as 2009, while I was carrying out the research on Tinctoris's obit at Sainte-Gertrude in Nivelles, cited above, I was informed that all the relevant archives for Braine-l'Alleud were destroyed in the town fire of 1661, and that the parish registers commenced only in 1809.

With the invaluable help, however, of several colleagues with a particular interest in the local history and genealogy of the area,[15] I have finally managed to track down this collection of documents to a strong-box in the archives of the *Cure* of Braine-l'Alleud (effectively, the town's rectory), a fine house next to the church of Saint-Étienne, which would certainly have been Tinctoris's own baptismal parish church, though it was

---

[12] Ronald Woodley, 'Brussels, Bibliothèque Royale, MS II 4147: The Cultivation of Johannes Tinctoris as Music Theorist in the Nineteenth Century', in *Ars musica septentrionalis: De l'interprétation du patrimoine musical à l'historiographie*, ed. Barbara Haggh and Frédéric Billiet, with Claire Chamiyé and Sandrine Dumont (Paris, 2011), 121-58 (based on a paper delivered at the international conference of the same name, Association Ad Fugam with University of Paris IV-Sorbonne, Douai, and Cambrai, November 2005).

[13] 'me, Johannes Tinctoris, lowliest of panegyrists [*or* musicians], yet choirmaster at the church of the Holy Cross in Orléans, whom by heaven the soil of Braine-l'Alleud, in the diocese of Cambrai, begat': full text and initial discussion in Woodley, 'Iohannes Tinctoris: A Review', 225-27 and 243; further elaborated in Leofranc Holford-Strevens, 'Humanism and the Language of Music Treatises', in *Renaissance Studies* 15 (2001), 415-49 at 424-28, and Palenik, 'The Early Career', esp. 20-29. A reproduction of Tinctoris's procuratorial entry is given in Woodley, 'Brussels, Bibliothèque Royale, MS II 4147', 126.

[14] Hilde de Ridder-Symoens, Detlef Illmer, and Cornelia M. Ridderikhoff, *Premier livre des procurateurs de la nation germanique de l'ancienne université d'Orléans (1444-1546)*, Tome 1, Pt. II: Biographie des étudiants, vol. 1 (1444-1515) (Leiden, 1978), 69.

[15] I record here my enormous gratitude to, first, Claudine Lemaire for initially alerting me to the likely existence of the documents discussed below, and for providing a preliminary handlist from Jean Bosse of potentially relevant items; subsequently to Jean-Marie Laus, President of the Cercle d'histoire et de généalogie de Braine-l'Alleud (Brania), for tracing the documents' actual whereabouts; and to André Crickx, for kindly arranging permission from the Dean, Alain de Maere d'Aertrycke, for me to photograph the documents *in situ* in June 2011.

substantially rebuilt in the sixteenth and following centuries.[16] As a result, we now have access to a run of nearly two hundred documents from the fifteenth century relating to various acts of the *échevinage* of the town, that is, the body functioning as the principal agents of local administration and the judiciary; these do, indeed, confirm the activities not only of Martin le Taintenier, but also numerous other members of the same family. (As an aside at this point, it should be noted that the documents concerning Tinctoris's time at Orléans cathedral, discussed in the following issue of this Journal by Marlène Britta, consistently give his vernacular name as Le Teinturier. But it is clear enough from genealogical and glossary sources consulted that the two names, and indeed trades, in this period were essentially the same, *taintenier* being a local Brabantine and north-eastern French variant of what in most of central France was called *teinturier*.[17] The name Teinturier, originally associated of course with the trade of cloth-dyeing, seems simply not to have been used in French-speaking Brabant at this time; so the apparent disparity of spelling should not cause us any particular anxiety.) The purpose of this article, however, is not merely to attempt a lesson in Belgian parochial history. Rather, if we look more closely at the function, structure, and evolution of the *échevinage* at Braine-l'Alleud in the fifteenth century, we can, I think, glimpse something of the circumstances that may have induced the musician Tinctoris to pursue legal studies so assiduously, in parallel to his dedication to the world of music.

The *seigneurie* of Braine-l'Alleud in the fifteenth century should be considered, so far as its governmental and juridical structures are concerned, as divided into two domains. The central part, the more built-up village or *bourg* itself (Figure 1) was a clearly delineated, and legally distinct, *franchise*, or *franche ville*, scarcely 400 metres by 200 metres in extent, and circumscribed by a combination of natural and man-made boundaries, including ditches and the river now called the Hain (previously the Braine), after which the village and other Braines in the region are named.[18] This central *bourg* or *franchise* was administered by a group of seven *échevins*, appointed for a year at a time on the feast of St. John the Baptist by the principal *seigneur* of Braine-l'Alleud, himself directly answerable to the duke of Brabant, who at this point in history was one and the same person as the duke of Burgundy. The larger, more sprawling rural area of the *seigneurie* of Braine-l'Alleud, beyond the physical and judicial limits of the *franchise*, was known as the *foraineté* or the *afforaineté*, that is, the collection of hamlets constituting the 'outside' part, which extended for some fifteen kilometres from Tourneppe, Rhode-Saint-Genèse, and Halle in the north-west to Lillois-Witterzée and Plancenoit to the

---

[16] See in particular Jean Bosse and Ernest Pays, *L'Église Saint-Étienne à Braine-l'Alleud* (Braine-l'Alleud, 1992).

[17] For example, Jean-Baptiste-Bonaventure de Roquefort, *Supplément au Glossaire de la langue romaine* (Paris, 1820), 288: '*Taintenier* s'est dit pour teinturier; *tinctor*'; Gabriel Antoine Joseph Hécart, *Dictionnaire rouchi-français* (Valenciennes, 1834), 443: 'Taintenier, [=] teinturier. Hors d'usage' ('rouchi' being the dialect of the Valenciennes region, related to Picard and the 'ch'ti' of the Lille area); [Pierre] Feuchère, 'La bourgeoisie lilloise au moyen âge', in *Annales. Économies, sociétés, civilisations* 4/4 (1949), 421-30 at 424, citing the 1301-2 account of Baude le Borgne listing professions at Lille: 'un teinturier, bien appelé Philippe le Taintenier'; for an early Ypres ordinance (1292-1309) prescribing a recipe for the trade of hot cauldron dyers ('ch'est des tainteniers à la caudière'), see J.-B. Weckerlin, *Le drap 'escarlate' au moyen âge* (Lyons, 1905), 57; also online genealogical resources such as GeneaNet: 'Taintenier…Porté dans le nord de la France et en Belgique, le nom désigne un teinturier (ancien français "teintenier"). Avec le même sens: Teintenier, Tintenier, Tintigner', (<http://www.geneanet.org> accessed 11 July 2012).

[18] See Bosse and Pays, *L'Église Saint-Étienne à Braine-l'Alleud*, 13. Although this overlaid reconstruction by Pays, reproduced here as Figure 1, is not provided with a scale indication, some idea of the relatively compact area of the village can be gained from a comparison with the size of the church itself.

south and east.[19] This area was separately administered by a second group of seven *échevins*, again appointed by the local lord, not annually but (at least in principle) for life, or in case of misdemeanour at the pleasure of the *seigneur*; these *échevins forains* were headed by a *maire* or *mayeur/maieur*, though there is no sign of the *échevins de la franchise* having a similar senior position until a much later period.[20] For most of the fifteenth century the *seigneur*, and therefore the *échevinage* itself, exercised the rule of *la justice basse* and *la justice moyenne*, until 1489 when the right to administer *la haute justice* (that is, including capital punishment) was also devolved from the duke to the local lord.

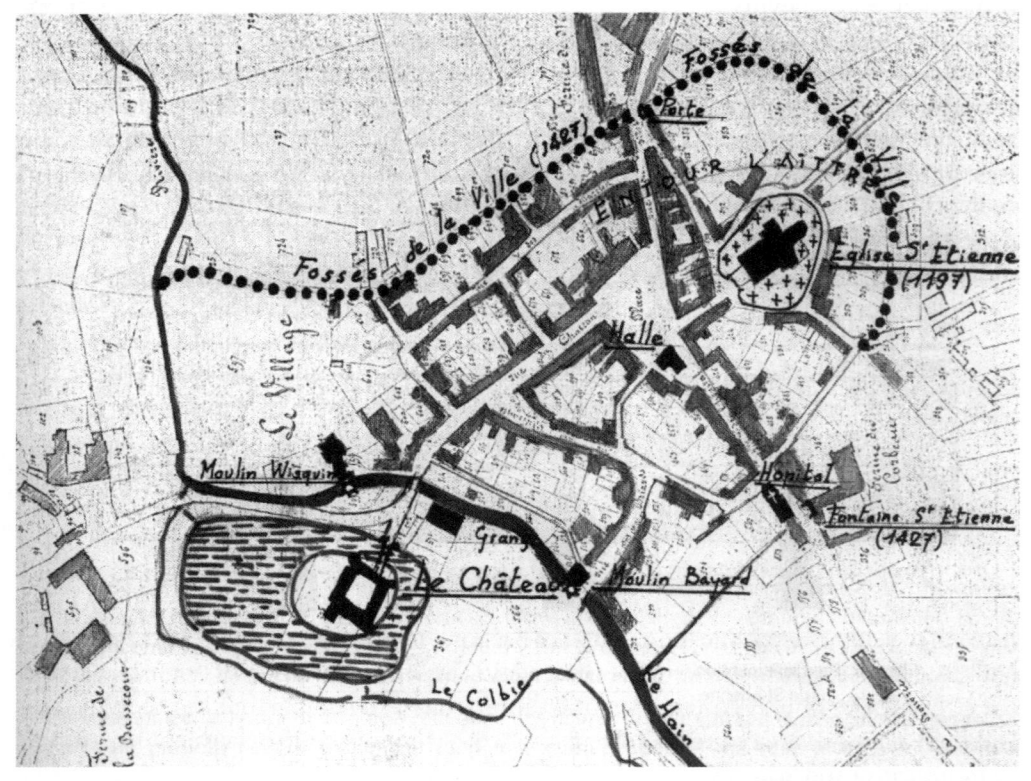

Figure 1. The *bourg* of Braine-l'Alleud, showing natural and man-made boundaries and principal sites, c. 1450: reconstruction by Ernest Pays. From Jean Bosse and Ernest Pays, *L'Église Saint-Étienne à Braine-l'Alleud: Histoire de l'église. Des origines à nos jours* (Braine-l'Alleud, 1992), 13. Reproduced by permission of the Cercle d'histoire et de généalogie de Braine-l'Alleud (Brania)

[19] See, for instance, the map of the *commune* in Fabienne Mariën et al. (eds.), *Braine l'Alleud: son histoire d'hier et d'aujourd'hui. Milieu et vie* (Brussels, 1982), 55.
[20] Much of the contextual information here is indebted to Fabienne Mariën, *La franchise de Braine-l'Alleud au moyen âge* (Braine-l'Alleud, 1975). See also Mariën et al. (eds.), *Braine l'Alleud*, esp. Pt. II, Ch. 2: Fabienne Mariën, 'Les principales institutions d'origine médiévale', 123-82. According to the declaration of Henri de Witthem, dated 10 September 1440 (Archives de la cure de Braine-l'Alleud, No. 50), formally stating the structure of the two bodies of *échevins* at that time, 'sont les eschevins de la franchise mis de loffice de lesquevinage la nuict Saint Jehan et apres ce le Seigneur y peult mettre des aultres si se luy plaist comme ont faict ses devantrains…et tant que des eschevins afforains chyaulx sont eschevins tout leur vie sil ne le fourfont ou il passent de vie a trespassement et adont y peult le Seigneur mettre des aultres come ont faict ses devantrains'. Quoted from [Jean Bosse,] 'Les échevins et conseillers de Braine-l'Alleud (I)', in *Braine-l'Alleud et son histoire*, fasc. 9 (1982), 25-43 at 26.

Martin le Taintenier appears named in the new documents, mainly overseeing land and property transactions, for the first time as one of the *échevins de la franchise*, in an act dated 18 April 1456, relating to the sharing out of houses, lands, and other heritable property to Stienne (Étienne), Ostart, and Colle (Nicole) Stassart,[21] following the death of their brother Hanon Stevenart (Archives de la cure de Braine-l'Alleud [henceforth ACBA], No. 61).[22] Martin le Taintenier is recorded again in an act of 23 May 1460 (ACBA, No. 64), detailing the sale of land to the priory of Sept-Fontaines, in which he is cited as among the *échevins*, along with the *maire*, of the court and lordship of Le Ménil, one of the local courts within a separate *seigneurie* in the parish: 'pardevant nous le maire et les eschevins del court et signourie dou maynilh en le paroche de braine laleut' ('before us, the mayor and *échevins* of the court and seigniory of Le Ménil in the parish of Braine-l'Alleud').[23] A few months later, on 10 August 1460 (ACBA, No. 65; a particularly clear document to read: see Figure 2),[24] Martin heads the list of the *échevins de la franchise* who oversee the sale of a *courtil* (curtilage) of land and tenement by Adam le Feure and his wife Liize (Élise), tenants acting for the *seigneur* of Braine-l'Alleud, Henri de Witthem, to Hene Ber and Jehan le Molnier:

> A Tous ceulx qui ces presentes lettres veiront et oront Nous martin le taintenier, ostart stassart, Henry del halle, Ernault touzin, Willaume bacheler, Jehan coulon, et pierart Julianne, Eschevins de le franquise de braine laleut, salut, et cognoissance de verite, savoir faisons, que pardevant nous, Sont venus en leur personnes, Adam le feure, et liize se femme, dune part, hene ber, et Jehan le molnier, dautre part[.][25]

> To all those who will see and hear these present letters, we, Martin le Taintenier, Ostart Stassart, Henry del Halle, Ernault Touzin, Willaume Bacheler, Jehan Coulon, and Pierart Julianne, *échevins* of the *franchise* of Braine-l'Alleud, [send] greeting and cognizance of truth. We make it known that before us came in their own persons Adam le Feure and Liize his wife on the one part, [and] Hene Ber and Jehan le Molnier on the other part[.]

A further reference to Martin can be found in a rental agreement of 18 March 1461 (ACBA, No. 66), in which he is once more acting as one of the *échevins* of the local court of Le Ménil. The impression is given, therefore, from these documents of the mid-1450s and early 1460s, that, despite the formal division of responsibilities between the *échevins de la franchise* and *échevins de la foraineté*, in practice there was some cross-territorial flexibility of personnel—dependent, one may presume, on practical exigences of

---

[21] Various members of the Stassart family (e.g., Étienne, Ostart, Philippe, Jean) were central to the *échevinage* of Braine-l'Alleud throughout the fifteenth century, and were clearly a powerful force in the *commune* (Mariën, *La franchise*, 31-36).

[22] Document also outlined in Mariën, *La franchise*, 59.

[23] On the structures of the primary and various secondary *seigneuries* within Braine-l'Alleud at this time, see Mariën, 'Les principales institutions', 137-55.

[24] A number of these acts from the *fonds* of ACBA, including this one, still retain the attached wax seal of the *échevinage*; some earlier and later seals are reproduced in Mariën, 'Les principales institutions', 169-72. Some other acts were drawn up in *chirographe* format, in which duplicate texts have been separated by a unique pattern of decoration and cut, as a guarantee of authenticity when the two parts are reunited. It seems to have been a general policy for the *échevins de la franchise* to seal their acts (see, for instance, Figure 2), and for the *échevins de la foraineté* to use *chirographe* format (Mariën, *La franchise*, 37).

[25] Also outlined in Mariën, *La franchise*, 59-60. Punctuation by oblique stroke in the original is reproduced here as commas.

availability and/or expertise.[26] Whether or not the gradual move from *franchise* to *foraineté* represented in any sense a career progression or promotion, it is apparent from another new document, found in a different repository of medieval Braine records, relating to rental incomes inherited by one Katerine Jonet on the death of her brother Jaquemart, registered in Brussels, that by 3 October 1466 Martin le Taintenier had attained the position of *maire* of the *foraineté*: '[*top:*] Sachent tout presenttes et advenier que pardevant le maieur et les eschevins forains de braine laluet' ('May all present and future know that before the mayor and the *échevins forains* of Braine-l'Alleud'); '[*bottom:*] comme maire martin le taintenier' ('as mayor Martin le Taintenier') (Louvain-la-Neuve, Archives générales du royaume, Greffes scabineaux de l'arrondissement de Nivelles [henceforth GSAN], No. 5153, Act 10: see Figures 3a and 3b).[27] Finally, he is named again as holder of this office in similar terms the following year, on 10 March 1467 (new style), in a rental transfer agreement surviving as part of the rediscovered collection at Braine-l'Alleud: '[*top:*] pardevant le maire et les eschevins forains de braine laluet' ('before the mayor and the *échevins forains* of Braine-l'Alleud'; '[*bottom:*] comme maire martin taintenir' ('as mayor Martin Taintenir') (ACBA, No. 70).[28] (This last spelling, which, together with '-iir', shows up as a frequent alternative in the documents, suggests that the name Le Taintenier may have been commonly pronounced this way, rather than as something closer to the modern French *-ier* termination. Note also that the 'le' has been dropped from the name on this occasion.)

Was this Martin le Taintenier the musician's father? We still lack the clinching evidence, but the chances are extremely high that he was. Of all the individuals named in this run of new ACBA documents, of which there is a complete inventory,[29] covering all the most prominent transactions and geographical locations of property in this small town, there is only one Martin le Taintenier. The given name Martin, too, is curiously extremely rare in the Braine records: I have so far found only two other individuals with the name from the whole collection of fifteenth-century acts, one from 1429 (Martin le Hoir: ACBA, No. 40), the other from 1445 (Martin de Pospol or Pospot: ACBA, No. 53),[30] and neither relating in any way to the Taintenier family. In another piece of the jigsaw, the association of this vernacular name (Le) Taintenier with the Latin Tinctoris has been up to now presumed but not proven. But we can, in fact, now be all but certain about this: another member of the family, indeed another Jehan le Taintenier, this one a priest—possibly an uncle or great-uncle of the musician—is cited in the ACBA acts in the vernacular, as owner or tenant of a curtilage in the town in 1451: 'ung petit courtilh qui est a sire Jehan le tainteniir prestre' ('a small curtilage belonging to Mr. Jehan le

[26] A similar observation is made by Jean Bosse, 'Les échevins et conseillers de Braine-l'Alleud', in *Braine-l'Alleud et son histoire* (Association du musée de Braine-l'Alleud), fasc. 9 (1982), 25-43 at 26; kindly communicated by Jean-Marie Laus. Fabienne Mariën has noted that the distinctions gradually broke down further over succeeding centuries, so that by 1559 the full complement included three *échevins* each for the *franchise* and the *foraineté*, with a further four straddling the two jurisdictions; and by the eighteenth century the eight *échevins* were employed with no distinction at all (Mariën, 'Les principales institutions', 169).

[27] Document outlined without reference to Martin le Taintenier in Mariën, *La franchise*, 60.

[28] Document outlined, again without reference to Martin le Taintenier, in Mariën, *La franchise*, 60.

[29] The typescript inventory, *Inventaire des archives de la cure de Braine-l'Alleud. Première partie: Archives qui se trouvent dans le coffre-fort* (152 pp.; no date), is held in the *Cure* at Braine-l'Alleud. I am again very grateful to Jean-Marie Laus and André Crickx for making available a copy of this typescript, drawn up probably by Lieut.-Col. BEM Jean Bosse, founding president of the Association du Musée Brainois, perhaps some time in the 1970s or 1980s.

[30] Outlined in Mariën, *La franchise*, 58; in this case I have not seen the original document, and so am unable to clarify the full name in question.

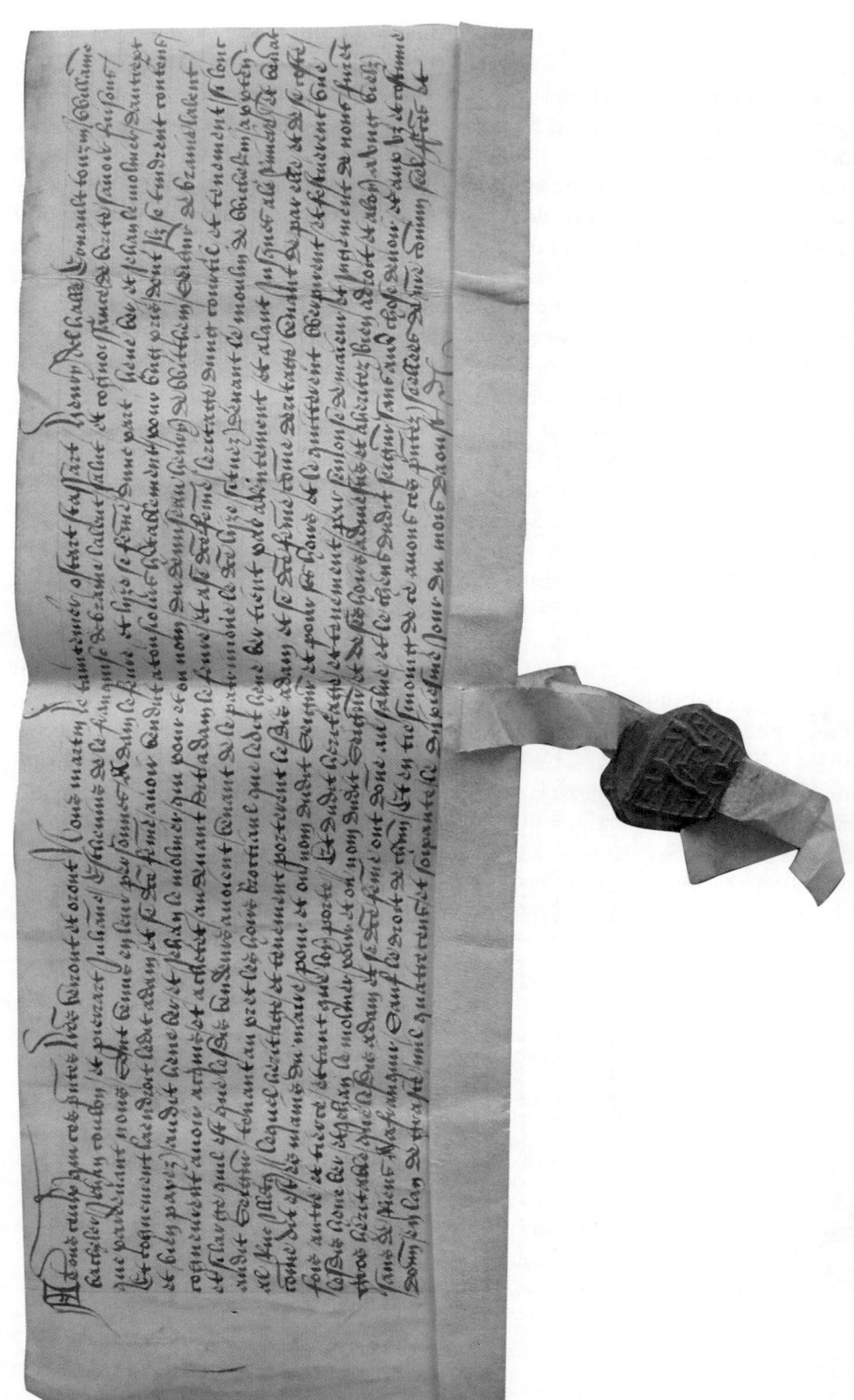

Figure 2. Braine-l'Alleud, Archives de la cure, No. 65 (10 August 1460). Reproduced by permission of the Dean of Braine-l'Alleud/Braine-le-Château

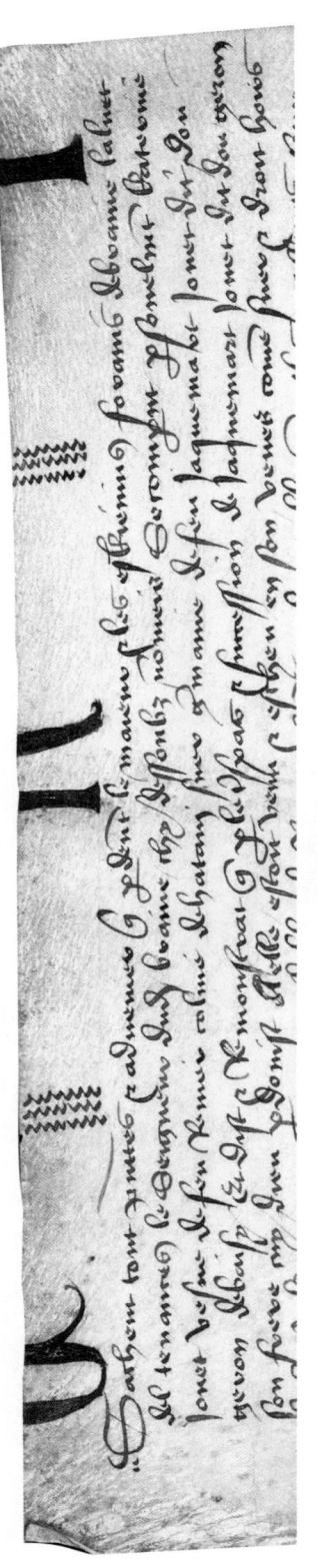

a. Detail identifying signatories of *chirographe* as *maieur* and *échevins forains* of Braine l'Alleud (top)

b. Detail identifying *maieur* as Martin le Taintenier (bottom)

Figure 3. Louvain-la-Neuve, Archives générales du royaume, Greffes scabineaux de l'arrondissement de Nivelles, No. 5153, Act 10 (3 October 1466).
Reproduced by permission

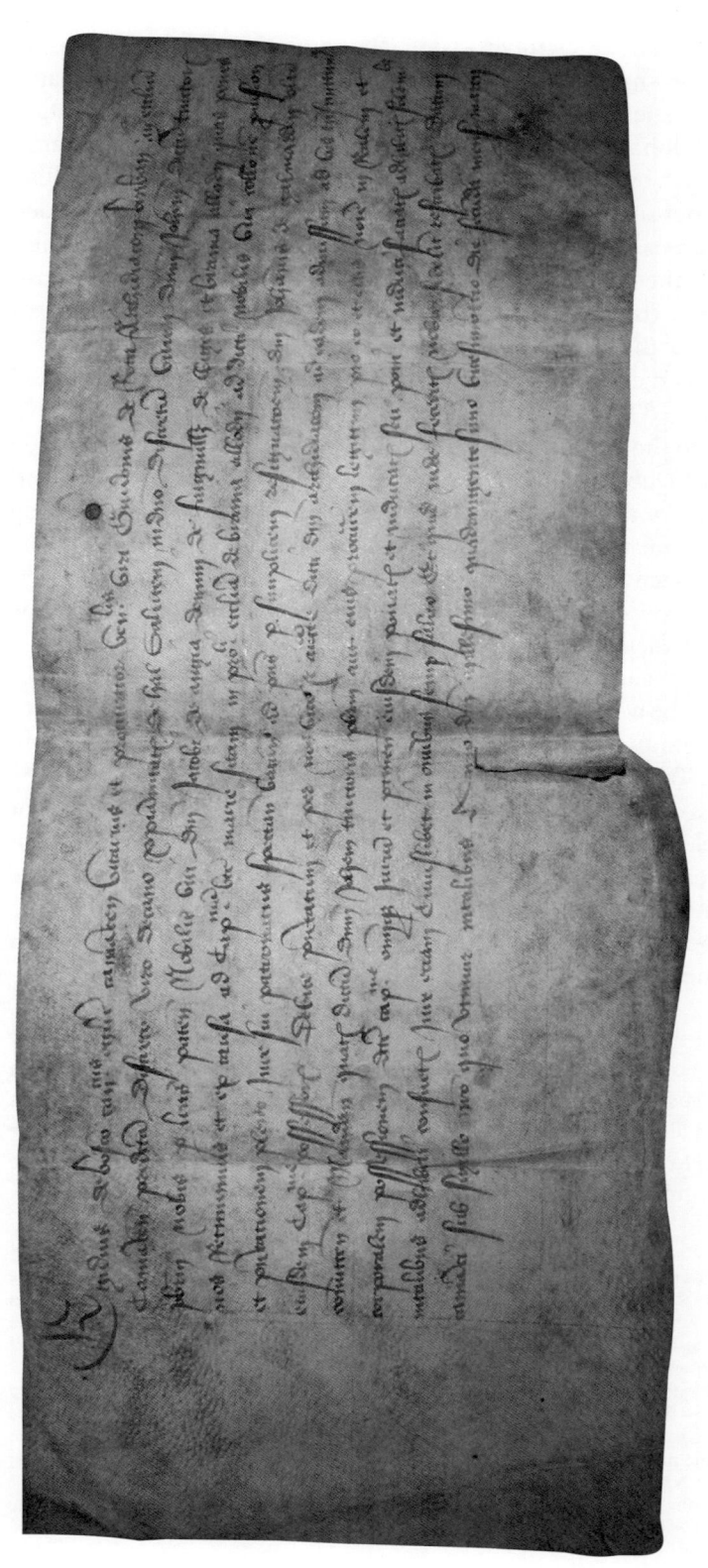

Figure 4. Braine-l'Alleud/Braine-le-Château, Archives de la cure, No. 36 (2 March 1424 new style). Reproduced by permission of the Dean of Braine-l'Alleud/Braine-le-Château

Tainteniir, priest') (ACBA, No. 60: 6 October 1451).[31] The same man—at least, we have no reason to think otherwise—had earlier been granted the chaplaincy of Notre Dame in the parish church of Saint-Étienne at Braine-l'Alleud, vacant following the resignation of the previous chaplain, Johannes of Galmaarden: 'discretum virum dominum Johannem dictum tinctoris presbyterum…ad capellaniam beate marie sitam in parochiali ecclesia de brania allodii…per simplicem resignationem domini Johannis de galmarden ultimi eiusdem Capellanie possessoris' ('the distinguished gentleman Mr. Johannes, called Tinctoris, priest…to the chaplaincy of the Blessed Mary situated in the parish church of Braine-l'Alleud…through the simple resignation of Mr. Johannes of Galmaarden, last possessor of the same chaplaincy') (ACBA, No. 36: 2 March 1424 new style; see Figure 4). Le Taintenier's candidature for the chaplaincy had been presented by letters patent from Jacques d'Enghien, *seigneur* of Braine-l'Alleud and patron of this benefice, and the mandate to the dean of Halle to collate the chaplaincy had been made by Egidius de Bosco (Gilles Dubois), canon of Cambrai cathedral, acting as vicar and procurator for Guido de Rota, archdeacon of Brabant. Interestingly, the 'dictum' tag attached to Le Tainteniir's name in this latter document suggests that, even though the family name Tinctoris had been generally current in northern Europe for many years, at least in written Latin contexts, such a Latinization of this particular vernacular in this region at this time was nevertheless not yet fully embedded in normal usage.

What is of even greater value, though, to our overall survey of the Tinctoris family, is that the primary force of the act of 6 October 1451 cited here (ACBA, No. 60) was to record the rental to Jehan Symon of a house and land belonging to a Zegre le Taintenier, son of the late Ernault le Taintenier, the former having appeared personally at the proceedings of the *échevins de la franchise* for the purpose: 'Sachent tout que pardevant nous se comparut personelement Zegre qui fut fils de feu Ernault le tainteniir' ('May all know that before us appeared in person Zegre who was son of the late Ernault le Tainteniir').[32] This house and land, further identified by its location—which incorporates the reference to the property of Jehan le Taintenier, priest, cited above—had been previously in the possession of Reniir le Taintenier:

> par aRentissement heritable a Jehan Symon…une maison…et tenure sy longhe et sy large quil se contient et estent qui fut Reniir le taintenier Jadis Joindant ale Riviere du moulin de baiart dun costeit et dautre aux maisons du signeur et Joindant aux tenements de le maison de baiart Et arrencquez ce le moitiet de le grainge acosteit par derriers le moullin Et le courtilh tout seloncq le grainge jusquez a ung petit courtilh qui est a sire Jehan le tainteniir prestre et joindant a gromt fosseit qui vat a pont de mariry [etc.]

[31] In recent musicological discussions it has been presumed that, for want of any concrete evidence to the contrary, the musician Tinctoris was not a priest; but the wording of some of the documentation from Orléans cathedral, discussed in the forthcoming issue of this Journal by Marlène Britta ('Contribution à l'étude des années passées par Johannes Tinctoris à Orléans'), once more raises the possibility that he may have been an ordained priest after all. (I am grateful to Bonnie J. Blackburn for this observation during discussion at the 2011 Barcelona conference at which the present paper was first given.) There can be no question, of course, of the priest cited in these two documents of 1424 and 1451 being identified with the musician—the date of the former is far too early—even though, as I have suggested here, the likelihood is very high that the two were closely related members of the same family. It is not impossible, though, that this Jehan le Tainteniir is the same man as that appearing in Nivelles on 4 February 1454 as procurator for Piérart Remi: see Woodley, 'Tinctoris and Nivelles', 117 n. 29.

[32] The *échevins* are named as: Mychaut le Cambreloim, Ernault dele Porte, Jehan Jermal, Nychaize dele Porte, Stiene Stassart, Hostart *fils [de]* Jehan Stassart, and Gilliart dele Tour. On the De la Porte family (spelt in various ways), cf. n. 5 above and nn. 40 and 49 below.

through heritable rental to Jehan Symon…a house…and tenure as long and as wide as it comprises and exists, which belonged formerly to Reniir le Taintenier, adjoining the stream of the Bayard mill from one side, and from another side the houses of the lord, and adjoining the tenements of Bayard House, and this set out across half of the grange alongside behind the mill and the curtilage all the way along the grange, as far as a small curtilage which belongs to Mr. Jehan le Tainteniir, priest, and adjoining the great ditch which goes to the Mariry bridge [etc.]

(ACBA, No. 60: 6 October 1451)

So here we have four members of the Le Taintenier family named together in the same document: Zegre (or Siger) is the son of the late Ernault; Reniir is another family member of unknown relationship but possibly of an older generation; and the priest Jehan, whose own name and property is mentioned in passing here simply as an aid to identifying the main property's location, is clearly of a generation born around the turn of the century. The approximate site of the various lands and houses owned by the Le Taintenier family can be estimated by mapping the detail of the above description on to Ernest Pays's reconstruction of the bounds of the *franchise* in Figure 1, that is, on the south-west fringe of the village, adjoining the River Hain on one side and some unspecified houses belonging to the local lord, Henri I de Witthem, whose castle lay just beyond the river boundary, on another side.[33] The orientation of the lands further involves the Bayard mill and house, the grange, and the 'Pont de Mariry', which is probably the bridge taking the road from the seigneurial castle across the river.[34] It is difficult to be sure from the description on which side of the river the Le Taintenier properties were situated: one might have thought it likely that the river marked a natural and absolute boundary of the jurisdiction of the *échevins de la franchise*, before whom the rental agreement had been brought; but there is some evidence that their remit extended to some of the land on the other side of the river,[35] and in view of the significance of the grange in the location details of the properties of both Zegre and Jehan le Taintenier, we should not rule out the possibility that these encompassed land on the southern or south-western bank. On the other hand, even as late as the middle of the nineteenth century the parcelling of land in this area of Braine-l'Alleud had not changed significantly (see Figure 5),[36] which would seem to indicate the greater likelihood of the Le Taintenier lands stretching along the riverbank on the *bourg* side, bounded by the Hain itself and the path running parallel to the river, between the Bayard mill and the road leading to the main town square (Figure 1 again). In today's town, the same area is taken up by the small collection of houses running along the narrow Rue de la Trairée (the equivalent of the old pathway), bounded to the north-west by the Rue de la Chiennerie, and to the south-east by the Rue Bayard, with a works car-park occupying the site of the old grange along the south-western bank of the River Hain (map reference: 50° 40' 54" N, 4° 22' 03" E).

---

[33] For an outline of the holders of the *seigneurie* of Braine-l'Alleud, including the long De Witthem dynasty of which this Henri was the first, see Mariën, 'Les principales institutions', 137-47.

[34] Cf. Mariën, *La franchise*, 25, citing this same document.

[35] Mariën, *La franchise*, 27.

[36] Mariën et al. (eds.), *Braine-l'Alleud*, 156, reproducing part of Philippe Christian Popp, *Atlas cadastral de Belgique* (Bruges, c. 1842-79).

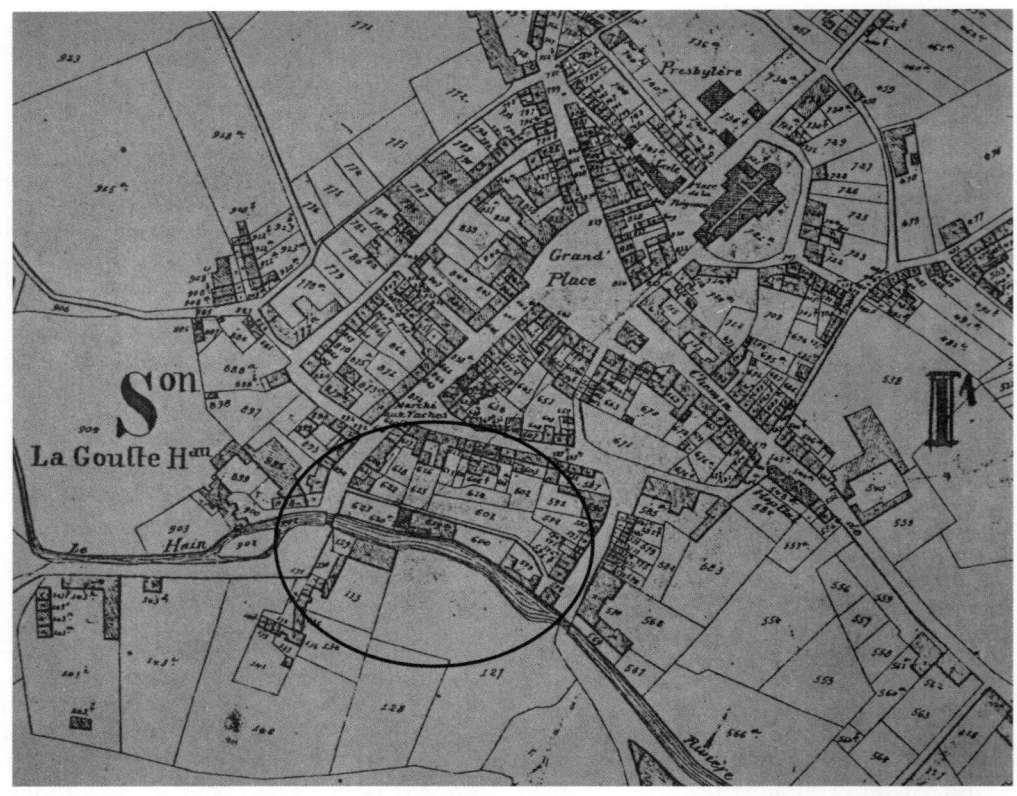

Figure 5. Braine-l'Alleud in the mid-nineteenth century: indications of land division in the area of fifteenth-century Le Taintenier property (circled). From *Braine l'Alleud: son histoire d'hier et d'aujourd'hui. Milieu et vie*, ed. Fabienne Mariën, Jean-Marc Doyen, Georges-Henri Everaerts, A.-Henry Smets, and Jean-Louis Van Belle (Brussels, 1982), 156

A little more detail of these and other members of the family can be sketched in. Reniir le Taintenier (variously spelt Renier, Reynier, Regnier, etc.) was himself a long-standing *échevin* at Braine-l'Alleud: his first appearance in the records seems to be in an act of 14 February 1421 (1422 new style: GSAN, No. 5153, duplicated in ACBA, No. 35); here, named as 'reniirs li teinteniirs', he is counted among the *échevins* of the court of Evrard T'Serclaes, lord of Le Ménil: 'nous les esqueveins del court messire everart serclaies'.[37] Over the following twenty-five years, he remains active as *échevin* at the court of Le Ménil, where, as we have seen, Martin le Taintenier himself acted at a slightly later period. He is also cited as the owner of further property near the poor lands in the Le Ménil *seigneurie*, in a document of 12 October 1437 from the *échevinage* of Leuven outlining debts owed by Jacques d'Ardenne of the parish of Hennuères, and his wife Jeanne, to Jean Block of Turnhout: 'Item ad dimidium bonnarium terre situm supra campum de manyl Inter terras Reneri le tentenier et terras pauperum de braine' ('Item, with respect to a half-*bonnier* of land situated above the plain of Le Ménil, between the

---

[37] A slightly earlier reference to 'Renier le taintenier' as *échevin* at the court of Le Ménil on 14 February 1420 (old style?) in the repository of Archives ecclésiastiques du Brabant (henceforth AEB) at Anderlecht (No. 15603) has not been verified at the time of writing.

lands of Renier le Tentenier and the poor lands of Braine') (ACBA, No. 44; also in French as AEB, No. 12564, fol. 32v).[38] The latest act found so far which carries the name of Reniir as *échevin* at the court of Le Ménil dates from around 1446 (AEB, No. 12564, fol. 21v); it seems likely that he died at some point between this date and the rental agreement of 6 October 1451, discussed above, by which time the property by the river in Braine-l'Alleud which had formerly ('jadis') belonged to him was now owned and rented out by Zegre le Taintenier.

Zegre or Siger later appears several times more in the Braine archives. For instance, on 17 February 1480, in the presence of the *échevins* of Brussels, an act in Flemish records the sale by Ostart Stassart, son of the late Jean Stassart and husband of Jeanne del Porte, to the *seigneur* of Braine, Henri de Witthem, of a *bonnier* of land[39] in the parish of Braine-l'Alleud, in a place called 'Flohay' between the property of 'nycasiis vander poerten' (Nicaise del Porte)[40] and 'Zegers teyntenier', as well as two other parcels (ACBA, No. 124). On 13 June 1496, before the 'eschevins de la ville et francquhyze de Braine laliux' Joseph du Fief, his wife Anne de Horembecq, and her brother Jehan rent out to Heyne le Tailleur and his wife Jehanne Meyselet a house and land called 'les teynneries' (Les Tanneries) situated near the Bayard mill, adjoining the property of the *seigneur* of Braine, the river, and a field remaining to Zegre: 'seant enpres le moulin de Bayart Joindant dung costet au Signeur de braine et Daultre alle Riviere et Du tr[oisiem]e au pre le Remanant Zegre le taintenier' ('sited next to the Bayard mill, adjoining from one side [property belonging to] the lord of Braine, and from another side the river, and from the third side the field [that is] the remnant possession of Zegre le Taintenier' (ACBA, No. 191). This last-named field, from the location given, is clearly part of the same property cited earlier as inherited from Reniir, the house on the land having perhaps been sold in the interim period; it is cited again twice across the subsequent eighteen years in the context of sales transactions of adjoining property, first on 17 September 1499 (ACBA, No. 196), and then again on 28 February 1514 (new style; ACBA, sixteenth-century series, No. 13).

Two further members of the Le Taintenier family appear more fleetingly in these records. In a Flemish act of 22 May 1445 a 'Heinric teyntenier' (presumably Henri as part of the same French-speaking family) is cited as 'scepenen van Aleide' (AEB, No. 12564, fols. 20v-21r),[41] indicating that he, too, functioned as *échevin*, probably in another local seigneurial court in the area of the chapel of L'Ermite (Ter Cluysen) in the Forêt de

---

[38] Documents citing Renier le Taintenier during this period, and in this capacity, include: AEB, No. 15496 (1425); ACBA, No. 40 (18 May 1429); AEB, No. 15603 (7 May 1430); AEB, No. 12564, fol. 21v (2 December 1432); AEB, No. 15496 (1435); AEB, No. 12564 (20 October 1443 and 22 May 1445). Some of these references have not yet been finally verified.

[39] Grace Lucile Wakelin, 'Standards of Living in the Commune of Namur, 1263-1429' (Ph.D. diss., University of Toronto, 1998), vi: 'It is convenient to think of a bonnier as between one and one-half and three acres.'

[40] Present-day Flohaye is an area on the south-western edge of Braine-l'Alleud, beyond the Le Taintenier lands, by the river mentioned previously. Del Porte is himself cited as *échevin* of both the *foraineté* and the *franchise* on several occasions between around 1445 and 1475 (cf. n. 32 above and n. 49 below), as were other members of the same family both earlier and later in the century, such as Jean del Porte li Jovenes (between 1408 and 1418), Arnould (between 1437 and 1456), Sébastien (*maire de la foraineté* 1485-86, *échevin* 1484, 1496): see Mariën, *La franchise*, 31-36. These are in addition to the Jeanne married to Ostart Stassart mentioned here; Nicaise del Porte must therefore have been well acquainted with the Le Taintenier family. Moreover, it seems very likely that the Jean de la Porte, *petit vicaire* at Cambrai cathedral from 1462 to 1474 and appointed chaplain at the hospital of Braine-l'Alleud in 1480 (see n. 5 above), was part of the same family; this valuably confirms another direct route linking the family networks at Braine, including the Le Tainteniers, and musical personnel at Cambrai.

[41] Information from hand-written notes by Jean Bosse kindly provided by Claudine Lemaire: original document unverified.

Soignes to the north-west of the region.[42] Finally, a Cathérine le Teintenier is cited as married to Gérard le Bourgoys in an act of 20 February 1483 (ACBA, No. 136) detailing the sale to Jean Baceler of a field held in fief from the *seigneur* of Braine, sited in the *foraineté* beyond the Neuf Moulin, between the properties of the *seigneur*, those of Jean Giriniau, and the river. As guarantee they cede the rental, worth one *couronne* of seventy-two *plaques*, of a pasturage located in a place called 'Toure de Vaux' (Tour-des-Veaux: a little to the west of the *bourg*).[43] No other information on Cathérine is known.[44]

Although it is still impossible to be sure of the precise family relationships to which these various documents bear witness, a few more or less informed hypotheses can be ventured. The likelihood that in Martin le Taintenier we have the musician Tinctoris's father must, I think, be regarded as, if not conclusive, at least very high. Reniir is clearly of the previous generation, and the continuity of service to the *échevinage* at Braine-l'Alleud from him to Martin, which parallels other dynastic continuities such as we can see, for instance, in the Stassart, Bacheler, Blokerie, and De la Halle families,[45] suggests that Reniir may well have been Martin's father, hence Tinctoris's grandfather. It seems that the priest Jehan le Taintenier was probably of the same generation as Reniir, perhaps therefore his brother, hence great-uncle to the theorist; he may, however, have been Martin's brother, hence Tinctoris's uncle. It might be thought at first that Ernault le Taintenier, since he had died by October 1451, was of this same older generation as Reniir; but since his son Zegre, perhaps only just of an age to inherit Reniir's property in that year, survived until at least 1514, we might also consider that Zegre was of the same generation as the musician (who died in 1511); and so Ernault could in that case have been a brother or close cousin of Martin who had died relatively young, hence uncle or more remote cousin of Tinctoris. Henri, as *échevin* in 1445, could have been a brother or cousin of either Reniir or Martin: without further information it is impossible to divine. Again, Cathérine, involved in land transactions with her husband Gérard in 1483, may have been of the same generation as Tinctoris, perhaps a cousin to him, as daughter of Ernault and sister to Zegre, though this again is pure speculation, and she may equally have been of the next-younger generation of the family.

One further document, too, is highly suggestive in a different way, and brings us back much closer to the musician Tinctoris, who is ultimately the focus of our interest. On 9 March 1472 (new style) letters were drawn up by Frankart Stassart, *rentier* of Braine-l'Alleud,[46] with Henri de la Halle, Bernart Baceller, and Pierre Giriniaux, *allowiers*, according to the terms of which an area of six *bonniers* of heathland just outside the north-east bounds of the *franchise*, in a place called Le Roussart, was sold to the *seigneur*

---

[42] See Fabienne Mariën, 'Les sites et monuments archéologiques et touristiques', in Mariën et al. (eds.), *Braine-l'Alleud*, 205-42 at 205-13. This geographical region brings to mind another area of land once owned by a Jehan le Taintenier in 'Audegier' (perhaps present-day Auderghem on the edge of the Forêt de Soignes) and described as 'jadis hiretaige de lostellerie': see Woodley, 'Iohannes Tinctoris: A Review', 225 n. 13, where Soignies is given erroneously for Soignes. It has not so far been possible to identify which member of the Le Taintenier family this refers to, and in any case the lands of this Jehan and the other Henri would have been separated by a considerable distance, as the Forêt de Soignes was much more extensive in the fifteenth century than it is today.

[43] Outlined in Mariën, *La franchise*, 69: document unverified.

[44] She is probably of too young a generation within the fifteenth century to be identified with the Catheline 'le Tintenneresse', daughter of Jehan Trikart/Tickart, *dit* le Tintenier, who seems to belong to a quite different branch of the wider family complex in the Nivelles region: see Woodley, 'Tinctoris and Nivelles', 117 n. 29.

[45] See especially Mariën, *La franchise*, 31-36, with annexed documents at 46-78.

[46] The personal seal of Frankart Stassart, in his capacity as *rentier*, survives in Brussels, Archives générales du royaume, Cabinet de Sigillographie, Moulages, No. 34107; reproduced in Mariën, 'Les principales institutions', 172.

of Braine, Henri de Witthem.[47] The sale was brought about by the death of Martin Taintenier—as in the 1467 rental transfer agreement cited above, the 'le' has here been dropped—and was registered by the personal attendance of two named children of his, a son Evrart and a daughter Jehanne:

> A Tous ceux quy ces presenttes lettres veront ou Oront, Jou frankart stassart Renthier de braine laluet et des appertenances, Et nous messires henry dele halle presbyter prieur delle halle bernart baceller et pierre giriniaux allowiers a treshault tresnoble trespuissant Seigneur et prince monsigneur le ducq de bourgogne et de brabant Salut et congnissance de verite. Sachent tout que pardevant nous Se comparurent personelement Evrart tainteniers et Jehanne se suer germaine enfant de feu martin tainteniers Et la endroit de leure bonne, pure et francq volente Sans forche, et sans nulle constrainte disent que il avoient vendu, bien et loyaulment et Werpit[48] a touiours perpetuelement…Siix bonnier de terres lors gisant en bruyers ou Roussart quy leur estoit parvenu et escheux de martin taintenirs leur peres Joindant ces dite terre et bruyers dun costet a nicaise dele portte[49] par desseur dun costet et daultre au courtil con dist le beghyne et a Jehan serclaies daultre a pierre ale plices dit poindeur…[*ends:*] Che fu fait en le ville de braine laluet lan mil quattre cent Soisante onze le neufysme Jour de marche.

> To all those who will see or hear these present letters, I, Frankart Stassart, *rentier* of Braine-l'Alleud and its appurtenances, and we, Messrs. Henry dele Halle, priest, prior of Halle, Bernart Baceller and Pierre Giriniaux, *allowiers* to His Most High, Most Noble, Most Powerful Lord and Prince, My Lord the Duke of Burgundy and of Brabant, [send] greeting and cognizance of truth. May all know that before us appeared in person Evrart Tainteniers and Jehanne his natural sister, children of the late Martin Tainteniers; and of their good, pure and free volition, without force or any constraint, they state that they have sold properly and faithfully, and given over for ever in perpetuity…six *bonniers* of land at the time lying as heathland in Le Roussart, which had passed down to them and come into their possession from Martin Taintenirs their father; these said lands and heath adjoining from one side [the property of] Nicaise dele Portte from above one side, and from another side the curtilage called 'Le Beghyne' and [the property of] Jehan Serclaies, and from another side [the property of] Pierre ale Plices, called Poindeur… [*ends:*] This was done in the town of Braine-l'Alleud in the year one thousand, four hundred and seventy-one, the ninth day of March.

(ACBA, No. 76: 9 March 1472 new style; underlining as in Ms.)

This whole document is reproduced as Figure 6; see also details in Figure 7.

---

[47] For an estimate of the extent of this land, cf. n. 39 above.

[48] A regional legal term with the sense of 'giving over possession to' or 'vesting'; related antonymically to the modern French 'déguerpir': see, for instance, Philippe Antoine Merlin, *Répertoire universel et raisonné de jurisprudence*, 36 vols. (Brussels, [5]1825-28), vol. 36, 490.

[49] Note that this is presumably the same Nicaise dele Porte whose land was cited earlier as close to that of Zegre le Taintenier, and so the heathland in question here may have related to the latter. There is a Chemin du Roussart still extant on the north-eastern outskirts of Braine-l'Alleud.

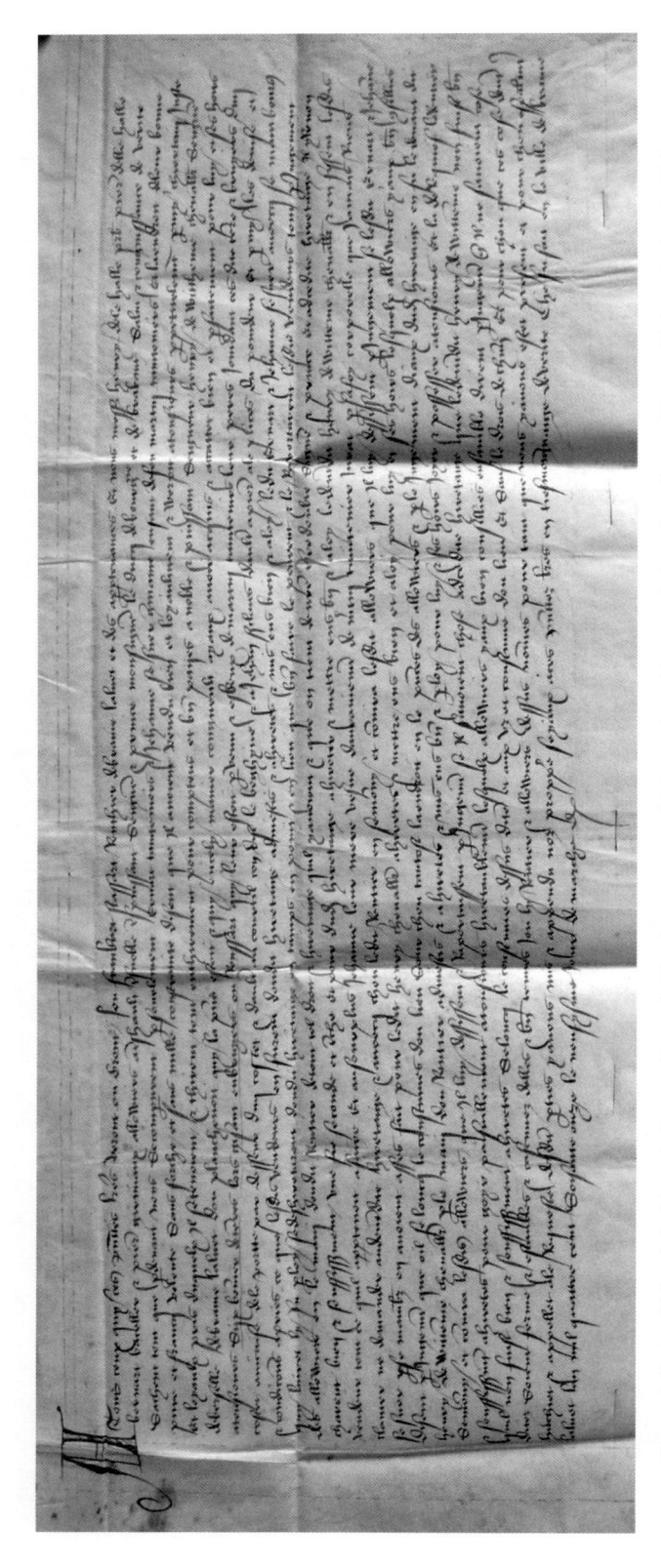

Figure 6. Braine-l'Alleud, Archives de la cure, No. 76 (9 March 1472 new style). Reproduced by permission of the Dean of Braine-l'Alleud/Braine-le-Château

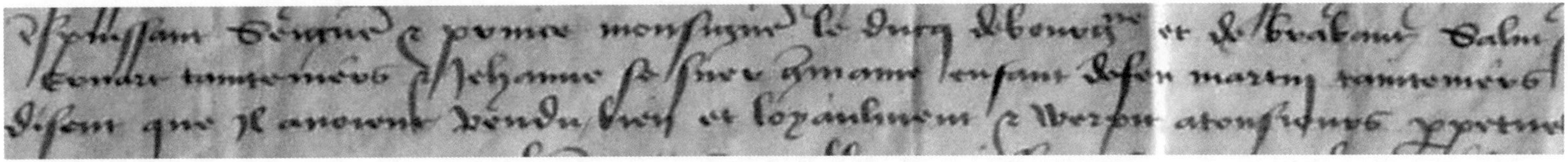

a. Detail citing Evrart and Jehanne (*fille*) as children of the late Martin Taintenier

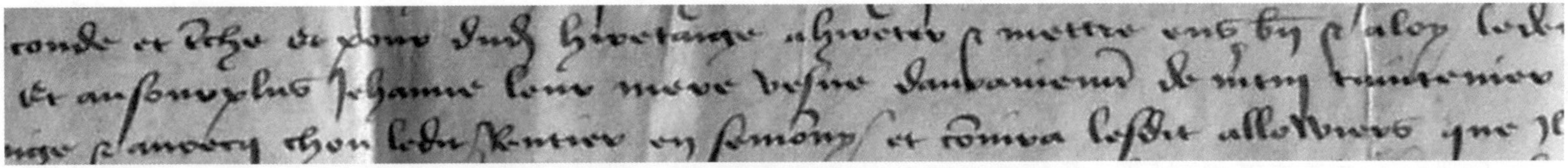

b. Detail citing Jehanne (*mère*) as widow of Martin le Taintenier

Figure 7. Braine-l'Alleud, Archives de la cure, No. 76 (9 March 1472 new style). Reproduced by permission of the Dean of Braine-l'Alleud/Braine-le-Château

Furthermore, Martin's surviving widow (hence probably Tinctoris's mother), also called Jehanne, is cited in this act as swearing an oath that she has no personal claim on the property herself: 'Et ausourplus Jehanne leur mere vesve dauranievant de martin taintenier Jurat par sa foy corporelle que Jamais Riens clamer ne demander audevant dite hiretaige' ('And furthermore, Jehanne their mother, henceforth widow of Martin Taintenier, swears by her bodily faith never to have any claim or demand in respect of the said inheritance') (partial detail in Figure 7b). It would be most convenient for us, of course, if another son, Jehan, had been included in the transaction: this would have been the clinching evidence. His absence, though, by no means vitiates the notion that the three of them were all children of Martin and Jeanne: after all, by March 1472 the musician Tinctoris was certainly far distant, perhaps already in Naples, perhaps on the way there from central France after his time as *magister puerorum* at Chartres,[50] but in any case doubtless beyond the reach of the legal requirements involved in the sale of his late father's local assets.[51]

Fortunately, the document also survives in which Martin's original acquisition of this property is registered, again by Frankart Stassart as *rentier* of the duke of Burgundy at Braine-l'Alleud and the other *allowiers*, on 2 March 1467 (new style: ACBA, No. 69 *ter*; see Figure 8). Here he is recorded as paying the *relief*, a kind of inheritance or acquisition tax, on the land, which had previously belonged to the duke of Burgundy himself (Philip the Good, until his death three months later in June 1467). Although Martin's own position is not stated explicitly here, he was presumably *maire de la foraineté* at the time, as we have already seen him as such only a week later in ACBA, No. 70, dated 10 March 1467 (new style). The location of the land acquired by Martin is described in slightly different (and more obscure) terms than in the later sale by Martin's children, but there can be little doubt that this refers to the same parcel of heathland in the Le Roussart area:

> Jou frankart stassart Rentiir de mon tres Redoubte Signeur le duc de bourgogne et de branbant a braine laleux et de appendance dicelle offiss fai savoir a tout qui ces veront et oront que en le pressence de moy et de plussieurs alowiers a tres Redoubte Singneur et prince monssigneur le ducq de bourgogne et de brabant cest assavoir sont Willaume baceller, Ernalt ly bacre Sire henry delle halle Willaume massariet [?] Se comparut en personne martin ly taintenir ly quelx Releva amoy soufiissament et par le gugement desdits alowiirs Siix bonniers de terre gisont en bruwirz au lieu condist le Roussart tenus en aleux de mon tres Redoubtez singneur qui a luy appartenoient de lonctampz comme il dist se Joindent lesdite terre a bois madame dun leis[52] et al terre Ernalt le bacre dautre

[50] See, for example, Woodley, 'Iohannes Tinctoris: A Review', 231-32; also idem, 'Renaissance Music Theory as Literature', in *Renaissance Studies* 1 (1987), 209-20 at 211; and Palenik's extended exploration of various interrelated lines of enquiry in 'The Early Career', 129-207.

[51] It may well be that some of the Le Taintenier properties in Braine-l'Alleud, particularly in view of their location close to the river and castle, were damaged or destroyed in 1488, when rebels from Brussels invaded the village in protest against the *seigneur* Henri de Witthem's espousal of the cause of Maximilian of Austria: 'les rebelles bruxellois envahirent ses terres et détruisirent de nombreux bâtiments. En ce qui concerne la seigneurie de Braine-l'Alleud, y furent détruits "*et mesmement ses chasteau court et molins audit lieu de brayne laleu / avecques aussi grant partie de son villaige audit lieu*"' (Bosse and Pays, *L'Église Saint-Étienne*, 15, citing ACBA, No. 175, dated 10 June 1489). This incursion and destruction of his home village would coincidentally have taken place at much the same time that Tinctoris obtained his canonry at Sainte-Gertrude, Nivelles: see Woodley, 'Tinctoris and Nivelles', 112.

[52] From Latin *latus* = side, normally expressed in these documents as 'coste(it)'.

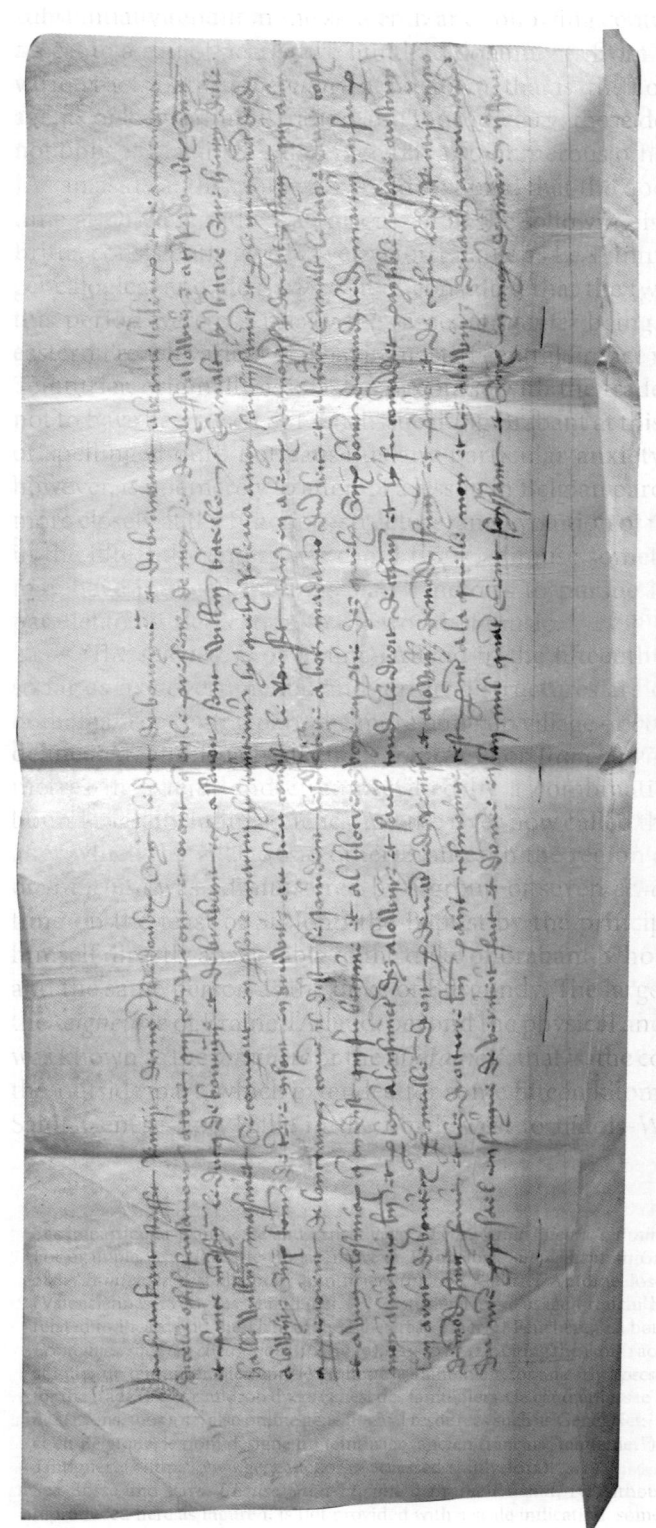

Figure 8. Braine-l'Alleud, Archives de la cure, No. 69 ter (2 March 1467 new style).
Reproduced by permission of the Dean of Braine-l'Alleud/Braine-le-Château

coste et a ung elosinia[re][53] que on dist qui fu beguine et al blocrenzvoye...[*ends:*] fait et donnee en lan mil quatre Cent soyssant et Siix en moys de mars ii[e] Jour.

I, Frankart Stassart, *rentier* of My Most Redoubtable Lord the Duke of Burgundy and of Brabant at Braine l'Alleud, by appendance to this office, make it known to all who will see and hear these same, that in the presence of myself and of several *allowiers* to the Most Redoubtable Lord and Prince, My Lord the Duke of Burgundy and of Brabant, that is to say Willaume Baceller, Ernalt ly Bacre, Mr. Henry delle Halle, William Massariet [?], there appeared in person Martin ly Taintenir, who paid to me the *relief*, sufficiently and by the judgement of the said *allowiers*, on six *bonniers* of land, lying as heathland in the place called Le Roussart, held in allod from my Most Redoubtable Lord, which for a long time belonged to him, as he states; the said lands adjoining the woods of My Lady from one side, and the land of Ernalt le Bacre from another side, and an [almshouse?], as it is called, which was the Béguine, and the [return block?]...[*ends:*] done and given in the year one thousand, four hundred and sixty-six, on the 2nd day of the month of March.

It is time to return to a more explicitly musicological perspective, and recall the context outlined at the opening of this article. For if Tinctoris's father Martin had died by early 1472, as now seems almost incontrovertible, the dedication of *De inventione et usu musice* is thrown into a different light. The view has been accruing for some time now—most recently voiced in print by Rob Wegman in his important article on Tinctoris's '*magnum opus*' published in 2009, but also in the 2008 dissertation on Tinctoris's early career by Jeffrey Palenik[54]—that a significant proportion of the content of this originally very large compilation, probably including versions of, or draft material for, at least some of his surviving treatises, may in fact date back to Tinctoris's time studying and teaching in the north of Europe in the 1450s and '60s, before his moving to Italy and eventually taking up his post at the Neapolitan court around the early 1470s. The evidence adduced by Wegman strongly indicates that the material of the treatise transmitted separately from the Moravus print of 1481-83, in Cambrai, Médiathèque municipale, Ms. 416,[55] represents portions of early versions of the text, whose intellectual focus, *auctoritates*, and writerly style belong to Tinctoris's northern education and reading.[56] It was only later that his concentrated exposure to other classical Latin and Italian vernacular literatures had a significant effect—though whether profound or superficial is still a matter of debate—on some of the peritextual elements, such as the

[53] Difficult to interpret: possibly 'clos-'; or perhaps a contracted variant of 'elemosina' = almshouse, or reference to a tenure held 'in elemosina' (cf. Audrey W. Douglas, 'Tenure *in elemosina*: Origins and Establishment in Twelfth-Century England', in *The American Journal of Legal History* 24 [1980], 95-132). The property referred to here is presumably the 'courtil con dist le beghyne' cited above in ACBA, No. 76 five years later. If the 'elosinia[re]' was an actual (old?) building in 1467—perhaps a small ex-Beguine community vacated and turned temporarily into an almshouse?—it may have gone by 1472 with the original name persisting for the land.

[54] Rob C. Wegman, 'Tinctoris's *Magnum opus*', 771-82; Palenik, 'The Early Career'.

[55] See, as precursor to Wegman, 'Tinctoris's *Magnum opus*', Woodley, 'The Printing and Scope'; also Latin text, English translation, and commentary in Palenik, 'The Early Career', 215-35.

[56] Wegman's arguments are further reinforced, extended, and debated in the extensive treatment of Palenik, 'The Early Career', esp. 51-128. (Although Palenik's dissertation bibliographically predates Wegman's article, it was informed by a pre-publication draft of the latter.) Palenik explores not only the implications of Tinctoris's intellectual and educational history for the evolution of the text(s) of *De inventione* itself, but also patterns suggesting the repurposing of material from the early version of this work for use in some of the other individual treatises. In addition, he suggests, drawing again on Wegman's perceptive work on Tinctoris's sources, that the lack of reference to the *Decretals* at certain points in the *Complexus* indicates that the Cambrai or 'northern' version of this treatise may even predate Tinctoris's law studies at Orléans (Palenik, 'The Early Career', 64-65).

dedications, prologues, and conclusions, of his own writings, and on the revisions to *De inventione* and the *Complexus* carried out in his Neapolitan period. It is, nevertheless, still more than a little mysterious what happened to the remainder of the revised version of *De inventione*, other than that it may have occupied a lost first volume of Tinctoris's complete works from the early-to-mid 1480s, of which the present Valencia codex is the surviving sibling.[57] We have no real reason to doubt the *prima facie* import of Tinctoris's own words, in which he describes to the recipient of the letter prefacing the surviving printed *unicum*, Johannes Stokem, how the treatise had only recently been completed after 'sleepless labour', and following Tinctoris's return to Naples after the meeting of the two musicians in Liège:

> [A]d me nuper ex Pannonia scribens: musarum suavissime cultor: rogasti obsecrastique: ut si quicpiam ad ingenuam artem sonoram pertinens recentius condissem: illud tibi mittere curarem...te scire velim: quod ab eo tempore quo abs te ex Leodio digressus: divino munere feliciter Neapolim regressus sum: tractatum quendam: cui de inventione et usu musice: nomini ac titulo est: pervigili labore confeci. Cuius quidem tractatus quinque libros continentis: in quibus nimirum (quoad mei fieri potuit) dulci utile miscui: licet editionem haud precipitare: sapientum consilio statuerim: de tuo tamen insigni studio: ac erga me parta virtutibus amicitia: que sola immortalis est: certissimus securissimusque: menti mee cupiditas incessit: quadamtenus parte: tue morem gerere voluntati.[58]

> Writing to me lately from Hungary, sweetest devotee of the Muses, you implored and beseeched me that if I had recently put into words anything relating to the noble art of sound, I should take care to send it to you...I should like you to know that from the time that I left you in Liège and returned by divine gift to Naples, I have completed with sleepless labour a treatise, whose name and title is 'On the invention and practice of music'. Although I determined, on wise advice, not to rush the publication of this treatise, comprising five books, in which (so far as it could be achieved on my part) I have undoubtedly mingled the useful with the pleasant, the desire nevertheless entered my mind, quite sure and certain as I was of your outstanding zeal and of a friendship born of virtues which alone is immortal, at least to some extent to gratify your wish.[59]

[57] As suggested in Woodley, 'The Printing and Scope', 254-55, and taken up as at least plausible in Palenik, 'The Early Career', 103.

[58] D-Rp Th 33, fol. 1v; Weinmann, *De inventione et usu musicae*, 27.

[59] The reference in the early 1480s to Tinctoris and Stokem having met in Liège, after which Tinctoris had 'returned' ('regressus') to Naples, is still a little mystifying. (The word 'munere' in this passage also carries the sense of 'duty', 'post', or 'employment', reinforcing the notion that Tinctoris had already been working at court before undertaking this journey north.) As discussed in Woodley, 'Iohannes Tinctoris: A Review', 234-35, it remains unlikely that the Johannes Tectoris recorded by José Quitin at St. Lambert, Liège, in September 1474 and between May 1481 and January 1483—during part of which time Stokem was a singer there—is to be identified with the theorist, since the dates, as well as the formation of the name (and signatures reproduced by Quitin) are difficult to reconcile with our other knowledge of Tinctoris's movements and various comments in his writings (José Quitin, 'Les maîtres de chant de la cathédrale St. Lambert à Liège aux XVe et XVIe siècles', in *Revue belge de musicologie* 1 [1954], 14-18). Palenik has postulated that an otherwise undocumented visit to northern Europe may well have taken place around 1478-79, encompassing work related to the 'reorganization of the Burgundian court following Charles's death and Mary of Burgundy's marriage', the meeting with Stokem in Liège, hearing the *viola cum arculo* duo Carolus (Charles) and Johannes (Hennequin) Fernandes in Bruges, as recorded in *De inventione*, and his documented stay in Ferrara—in Palenik's scenario on the way back to Naples—in May 1479 (Palenik, 'The Early Career', 168-71; cf. Woodley, 'Iohannes Tinctoris: A Review', 234).

But the coincidence of date between Tinctoris's likely arrival in Naples, and his father Martin's death by March 1472, taken together with the wording of the *De inventione* dedication cited earlier, is certainly intriguing. Perhaps an original compilation, painstakingly put together during his period jointly of legal studies and cathedral-based music teaching at Orléans and Chartres from the late 1450s through at least part, if not all, of the 1460s, did have a material existence by around 1472—possibly to be identified with the enigmatic *Speculum musices* cited by the theorist himself in his *Expositio manus*[60]—at which point Tinctoris could have added a relatively eleventh-hour dedication to his father shortly after learning of his death. Whether this process would have taken place while Tinctoris was still working in France (perhaps inflected by closer contacts with the Burgundian court), or whether he was already somewhere in Italy, and shortly to revise and redistribute the treatise's contents in a radical way, to form the bulk of his output as recognized today, it is not yet possible to say. But none of the surviving versions of his other treatises bears a personal, family dedication: by this point he is very much assuming a new kind of role and persona as writer at the Neapolitan court, building his reputation with his new employers and with a conscious regard to his increasingly internationalized nexus of contemporary musicians. If this scenario is remotely correct, he clearly looked on the original, paternal dedication as of sufficient personal importance to have it reaffirmed, both upon completion of the full treatise, and again when the extracts from this finished *De inventione* were printed by Mathias Moravus ten years after his father's death in the early 1480s. Alternatively, though—especially since Tinctoris clearly regarded the arduously completed and very substantial five-book version of this treatise, whatever its contents, as the definitive, final recension—we cannot entirely rule out the possibility that the posthumous dedication to his father had been reserved (a tenth anniversary in late 1481 or early 1482?) and accorded only to this largely lost *summa* of the author's (post-pedagogical?) musical writings.

One final thought arises regarding the relationship between what I have surmised of Tinctoris's early family origins and his later career. I have tried to make it clear that the structure of the *échevinage* at Braine-l'Alleud was really quite complex in its administrative distinctions between the *franchise* and the *foraineté*. In fact, it was even more complex than I have so far outlined, for each of these two domains operated according to quite different legal frameworks. The nature of the 'freedom' implied in the title *franchise* relates to the fact that it had long been granted exemption from the normal local judicial system, and was bound instead by the urban law of Brussels. The *foraineté*, by contrast, was governed by the rural law and customs of the nearby town of Uccle.[61] Although we are not well informed about the level of legal knowledge and general education or qualifications that the two bodies of *échevins* would have been required to possess, it is not hard to imagine that the nuances and distinctions of judgement, and the practical application of the two systems of governance, would have been often quite

---

[60] *Opera theoretica*, ed. Seay, vol. 1, 56. Palenik discusses at length the possible relationships between this *Speculum* (whether or not a treatise of this actual title) and the evolution of the contents of *De inventione* ('The Early Career', 95-100); it remains the case, though, that, from Tinctoris's cross-reference in his *Expositio manus*, this *Speculum* must have contained specific technical material discussing in detail the various genera and species of *coniunctio*, and therefore could hardly equate entirely to a 'speculative', non-pedagogical treatise.

[61] See especially Mariën, 'Les principales institutions', 159, and Mariën, *La franchise*, 28.

complicated, especially for those *échevins*, like Martin le Taintenier and several others whom we have encountered here, who crossed between the two bodies at different points of their careers. Furthermore, if we look at the evolution of the *échevinage* across the wider region during the course of the fifteenth, sixteenth, and seventeenth centuries, we can see an explicit, increasing awareness of the need to appoint at least a proportion of the *échevins* from those with university qualifications or other formal legal expertise.[62] In this context, it is not difficult to see the young Jehan le Taintenier at home in Braine-l'Alleud, surrounded by family members and other local worthies distinguished in local government and already of modest land-owning status, perceiving the importance and value of a full, university legal education, in addition to his more subjective (if no less professional, and for the family doubtless unanticipated), attraction to music. The move to Orléans University—perhaps after a first degree in arts at Leuven—to study canon and civil law properly, and to take his family's long-standing expertise in local governance to a higher level, would surely have seemed an entirely natural, aspirational path to follow, in terms of its professional continuity and the obvious personal and financial career advantages that it promised.[63] As suggested, though, at the opening of this article, in musicological research terms an important quest now will be to try to put in place some evidential base for his parallel, early musical education, which would see him sufficiently experienced and knowledgeable in music by the later 1450s to take up his new teaching responsibilities, still in his twenties, at the cathedral of the same city, and pave the way for the successful, multifaceted career that lay ahead.

Abstract

Although a reasonable amount of information has been accruing over the past thirty years or so concerning Tinctoris's life, especially in France and Italy, it has been difficult to root his musical and legal careers in terms of family background in fifteenth-century Brabant. A newly recovered repository of documents in Tinctoris's home town of Braine-

---

[62] It is worth citing, by way of analogy, the situation of the *échevinage* of Liège over this same period, as described by Le Chevalier Camille de Borman in 1892: 'Quant à la capacité requise, il est difficile, sinon impossible, de la préciser. Le bon sens pratique de nos aïeux et l'intérêt que tous avaient à pourvoir la justice de magistrats de valeur, résolvaient cette question, il faut le croire, à la satisfaction générale. Du moins, n'avons-nous trouvé nulle trace de plaintes qui se seraient élevées dans le cours des ages sur l'incapacité de ces juges. Toujours, au contraire, nous les voyons entourés d'un grand prestige, d'une haute autorité. Il faut arriver au XVIe siècle pour rencontrer, parmi les échevins, l'un ou l'autre *maistre ès arts*, *licencié* ou *docteur ès droits*. Mais bientôt, ce qui n'était qu'exception, devient règle générale et, à partir du XVIIe siècle, tous les échevins de Liège sont *licenciés* ou *docteurs en droit*.' (Camille de Borman, *Les échevins de la souveraine justice de Liége*, 2 vols. [Liège, 1892], vol. 1, 4-5).

[63] An early instance of this joint need for career advancement and financial security was the inclusion of Tinctoris's name in a list of Orléans University hopefuls who were put forward to Pope Pius II in May 1462 for various expectative benefices (Woodley, 'Iohannes Tinctoris: A Review', 227). Palenik reasonably suggests that in Tinctoris's case this may have been driven primarily by financial need, arising from the very high costs of his legal studies, combined with his relatively modest background (as we have seen here) and income from Sainte-Croix ('The Early Career', 9), though career ambition and furtherance of status would doubtless have played their part. It has not been noted before that the expectative(s) earmarked for Tinctoris in this document refer(s) to unspecified collations in the archdiocese of Reims and diocese of Cambrai ('et pro Johanne Tintoris [*sic*] ad Remensis et Cameracensis [diocesis <collationem>]': Vatican City, Archivio Segreto Vaticano, Reg. Vat. 523, fol. 200). We have no evidence that any such benefices materialised, or indeed why Reims should have been singled out in addition to Tinctoris's home diocese of Cambrai, other than for reasons of geographical proximity and jurisdictional hierarchy.

l'Alleud, along with some others from the Belgian state archives, now enables some early context to be sketched for at least some aspects of his later, multi-faceted working life, in particular as local background to his later law studies at the University of Orléans. These documents, mainly relating to the échevinage of Braine-l'Alleud, show clearly that various members of the Tinctoris (Le Taintenier) family, including his father, had an established involvement with the local governance of both the *franchise*, or village itself, and its surrounding *foraineté*. As an indirect consequence of some of the detail suggested by this new archival material, we can also fill in a little more of the context to the process and timeline underlying the compilation of Tinctoris's treatise *De inventione et usu musice*.

Free papers

„Omnia denuò multò quàm antehac correctius edita."
Zu Leonhard Lechners Redaktion der *Selectissimae cantiones* am Beispiel seiner Lesart der Vertonung des Wortes „patibulo" in Lassos Motette *Vexilla regis* LV 225

■

BERNHOLD SCHMID

Für Peter Bergquist

Bekanntlich hat Leonhard Lechner die zweite Auflage der *Selectissimae cantiones, qvas vvlgo motetas vocant* redaktionell betreut. Die erstmals 1568 erschienene zweibändige Sammlung mit Motetten Lassos[1] wollte Katharina Gerlach wieder auf den Markt bringen, was dann im Jahr 1579 in erweiterter, vor allem aber in korrigierter Form auch geschehen ist.[2] Lechner sagt dies im Titel des Drucks, wo es heißt: „Omnia denuò multò quàm antehac correctius edita"; alles sei also bei weitem korrekter als in der ersten Auflage herausgegeben worden. Deutlicher freilich äußert er sich in seiner an den Leser gerichteten Vorrede, die im folgenden vollständig abgedruckt sei:[3]

> LEONHARDVS LECHNERVS ATHESINVS ARTIS MVSICÆ STVDIOSIS S.
> In prima, omnium præstantissimi Musici, Orlandi di Lassus, Motetarum harum collectione & editione, sæpè (vt fieri solet) accidit, vt propter varietatem exemplorum & incuriam describentium plurimæ irrepserint mendæ, nonnulla etiam, vel in textus applicatione, vel in notularum aut etiam integrarum vocvm permutatione & transpositione, errata. Cum autem honesta Gerlachij nostri, Iohannis Montani, de arte Musica optimè meriti, successoris, vidua, has cantiones typis suis recudere vellet, concedere nolui, vt hoc verè diuinum opus denuò deprauatum & incorrectum in lucem prodiret, sed priorem

---

[1] Horst Leuchtmann und Bernhold Schmid, *Orlando di Lasso: Seine Werke in zeitgenössischen Drucken 1555-1687*, 3 Bde. (Kassel etc., 2001), Bd. 1, 207-14: 1568-3 und 1568-4. RISM 1568 a [L 815 und 1568 b [L 816. Wolfgang Boetticher, *Orlando di Lasso und seine Zeit 1532-1594. Repertoire-Untersuchungen zur Musik der Spätrenaissance. Band I: Monographie. Neuausgabe mit einem Fortsetzenden Literaturbericht 1958-1998, Verzeichnis der Kontrafakturen, Addenda und Emendata* (Wilhelmshaven, 1999), 759-60: 1568 γ und 1568 δ.

[2] Leuchtmann und Schmid, *Lasso: Seine Werke*, Bd. 2, 21-29: 1579-2 und 1579-3. RISM 1579 a [L 915 und 1579 b [L 916. Boetticher, *Lasso und seine Zeit*, 781: 1579 β und 1579 γ. Drucke mit Musik Lassos werden im folgenden nur mit den bei Leuchtmann und Schmid, *Lasso: Seine Werke* verwendeten Siglen zitiert.

[3] Vgl. die Faksimiles in Orlando di Lasso, *Sämtliche Werke. Zweite, nach den Quellen revidierte Auflage der Ausgabe von F.X. Haberl und A. Sandberger*, Band 5: *Motetten III (Magnum opus musicum, Teil III)*, neu hrsg. von Bernhold Schmid (Wiesbaden etc., 2006), LXXXIX (im folgenden zitiert als GA² V), und in Orlando di Lasso, *The Complete Motets 6: Motets for Four to Eight Voices from* Selectissimae cantiones *(Nuremberg, 1568)*, hrsg. von Peter Bergquist, Recent Researches in the Music of the Renaissance 110 (Madison, 1997), [xxxvi] (im folgenden zitiert als CM 6); hier auch eine Übersetzung ins Englische. Beide Faksimiles aus dem Tenor-Stimmbuch des Exemplars der Bayerischen Staatsbibliothek München, Musikabteilung, 4 Mus.pr. 458.

editionem ex iustis & emendatis exemplis recognoui, vitia etiam obiter inserta & aspersa, qua potui diligentia, vt opus hoc musicum pristino nitori restituerem, semoui, atq[ue] vt prælis Gerlachianis subijceretur permisi. Quod tibi, Musices Orlandicæ amator, paucis significandum duxi, teq[ue] officiosè, vt hunc qualemcunq[ue] laborem candido & grato animo accipias, oro.

Leonhard Lechner aus dem Etschtal den die Musik Studierenden mit Gruß.
In der ersten Sammlung und Auflage dieser Motetten des bedeutendsten von allen Musikern Orlando di Lasso geschieht es oft (wie es vorzukommen pflegt), dass aufgrund der unterschiedlichen herangezogenen Vorlagen und der Schlamperei der Kopisten sich eine große Anzahl von Fehlern eingeschlichen hat. Nicht wenige Fehler finden sich entweder in der Textunterlegung, oder als Verwechslung oder Verschiebung von Noten oder ganzen Stimmen. Da aber nun die ehrenhafte Witwe unseres Gerlach, des Nachfolgers von Johannes Montanus, der sich um die Musik höchst verdient gemacht hat, diese Gesänge in ihrem Verlag neu herausgeben wollte, konnte ich nicht zulassen, dass dieses wirklich göttliche Opus noch einmal in verderbter und nicht korrigierter Form erscheinen sollte. Ich habe stattdessen die erste Auflage durchgesehen und mit richtigen und korrigierten Quellen verglichen, dabei die offenkundigen eingestreuten Fehler mit größter Sorgfalt entfernt, um diesem musikalischen Werk seinen früheren Glanz zurückzugeben, und gestattet, dass es der Gerlachischen Druckerpresse übergeben würde. Ich habe gedacht, dass ich Dir, der Du die Musik Orlandos liebst, dies mit wenigen Worten anzeigen mußte; und ich bitte Dich nachdrücklich, dass Du diese Arbeit – wie auch immer sie beschaffen sein möge – mit Freude und Gefallen annehmen mögest.[4]

Lechner stellt also fest, dass die erste Auflage aufgrund unterschiedlicher Quellen als Vorlagen und auch aufgrund der Schlamperei von Kopisten fehlerhaft gewesen sei. Eine unkorrigierte Neuauflage habe er deshalb nicht zulassen wollen; er habe die erste Auflage stattdessen mit besseren Quellen verglichen („priorem editionem ex iustis & emendatis exemplis recognoui") und dabei Fehler mit größter Sorgfalt entfernt („vitia etiam obiter inserta & aspersa, qua potui diligentia…semoui". Dies ist für die Überlieferung von Lassos Motetten von großer Bedeutung: Die *Selectissimae cantiones* in Lechners Redaktion sind eine außerordentlich wichtige und einflußreiche Quelle, und zwar schon deshalb, weil die gegenüber Lechners Version von 1579 unveränderte Auflage aus dem Jahr 1587[5] als eine der Vorlagen für das *Magnum opus musicum* auszumachen ist, also für die „Gesamtausgabe" der Motetten Lasso, die seine Söhne Ferdinand und Rudolph im Jahr 1604 bei Heinrich in München[6] herausgegeben haben.[7] Vom *Magnum opus* führt ein direkter Weg zur Gesamtausgabe, wie schon der Titel der Motettenbände verrät: *Magnum opus musicum von Orlando di Lasso. […] In Partitur gebracht von Carl Proske,*

---

4 Eine Durchsicht der Übersetzung hat dankenswerter Weise Michael Bernhard vorgenommen.
5 Leuchtmann und Schmid, *Lasso: Seine Werke*, 1587-2 und 1587-3.
6 Leuchtmann und Schmid, *Lasso: Seine Werke*, 1604-1. 1587-2 und 1587-3 wurden als Quellen für 1604-1 herangezogen, da einerseits Lechners Lesarten übernommen wurden und andererseits einige wenige in 1587-2 und 1587-3 neu dazugekommene Fehler auch in 1604-1 zu finden sind. Vgl. dazu Orlando di Lasso, *Sämtliche Werke. Zweite, nach den Quellen revidierte Auflage … Band 3: Motetten II …* (Wiesbaden etc., 2004), LXX (im folgenden zitiert als GA² III); GA² V, XX-XXI und LXI im kritischen Bericht zu Nr. 172; Orlando di Lasso, *Sämtliche Werke. Zweite, nach den Quellen revidierte Auflage … Band 7: Motetten IV …* (Wiesbaden etc., 2007), LI (im folgenden zitiert als GA² VII).
7 Zur Bedeutung der *Selectissimae cantiones* vgl. auch Orlando di Lasso, *Sämtliche Werke. Zweite, nach den Quellen revidierte Auflage … Band 11: Motetten VI …* (Wiesbaden etc., 2012), (im folgenden zitiert als GA² XI), LXII-LXVIII: Die im ersten Teil der *Selectissimae cantiones* 1568-3 erstgedruckten Motetten und ihre Überlieferung.

kritisch durchgesehen und redigirt von Franz Xaver Haberl. Proske hat bekanntlich die Motetten Lassos nach der Ausgabe von 1604 spartiert, Haberl ließ Proskes Partitur kopieren, unterlegte den Text bei nicht aufgelösten Idemzeichen und setzte Herausgeberakzidentien.[8]

Peter Bergquist hat in einem Aufsatz über die Ausgaben der *Selectissimae cantiones* von 1568 und 1579 Lechners Tätigkeit untersucht und dargestellt, was er korrigiert hat.[9] Einige wenige Korrekturen beziehen sich auf Fragen des Rhythmus: So hat er zwei kleinere Notenwerte auf einer Tonhöhe zu einem größeren Wert zusammengezogen, wenn die Textunterlegung nur eine Silbe vorsieht; korrigiert sind außerdem einige falsche Notenwerte.[10] Häufiger finden sich Korrekturen bei der Tonhöhe, wobei entweder die Noten überhaupt auf der oder zwischen den falschen Linie/n sitzen,[11] oder Vorzeichen fehlerhaft gesetzt sind bzw. ganz fehlen.[12] Schließlich hat Lechner in großer Anzahl Textunterlegungsfehler beseitigt, etwa Unklarheiten bei der Zuordnung, die sich aufgrund des dichten Notensatzes zwangsläufig ergeben.[13]

Bergquist stellt zudem die Frage, ob bzw. auf welche älteren Quellen Lechner zurückgegriffen haben kann, oder ob er auch selbst korrigiert hat. Dass Lechner Emendationen vorgenommen haben muß, wenn ihm keine ältere, bessere Quelle zur Verfügung stand, ist offenkundig; ein vom Verfasser der vorliegenden Zeilen schon früher diskutiertes Beispiel sei als Beleg angeführt: In der ersten Auflage der *Selectissimae cantiones* ist erstmals das *Nunc gaudere licet* (1568-3,36, LV 339)[14] überliefert, wo Lechner die unsinnige Formulierung „ut lex post ut lex post iubet magister laetitiae" zum sprachlich korrekten „ut lex postulat et iubet magister laetitiae" geändert hat. Dass es sich bei der Korrektur um eine Eigenleistung Lechners handeln muß, wird klar, wenn man aus anderen Quellen den Originaltext kennt: „Ut lex Pothumiae iubet magistrae laetitiae" heißt es dort; und dass dies der Originaltext ist, erhellt sich aus der Tatsache, dass wir es dabei mit einem Zitat aus einem Gedicht Catulls zu tun haben.[15] Bergquist versteht gar die Formulierung der Vorrede, er (Lechner) habe „priorem editionem ex iustis & emendatis exemplis recognoui, vitia etiam obiter inserta & aspersa, qua potui diligentia ... semoui", in dem Sinn, dass Lechner damit andeuten wollte, er habe auch emendiert.[16]

---

[8] Vgl. auch Haberls Vorwort zu Band I der Lasso-Gesamtausgabe, wieder abgedruckt in Orlando di Lasso, *Sämtliche Werke. Zweite, nach den Quellen revidierte Auflage ... Band 1: Motetten I ...* (Wiesbaden etc., 2003), XXVII (im folgenden zitiert als GA² I).

[9] Peter Bergquist, „The Two Editions of Lasso's *Selectissimae Cantiones*, 1568 and 1579", in *Yearbook of the Alamire Foundation* 6 (2008), 147-57.

[10] Bergquist, „The Two Editions", 153.

[11] Bergquist, „The Two Editions", 153.

[12] Bergquist, „The Two Editions", 153-54.

[13] Bergquist, „The Two Editions", 154-56. Er berücksichtigt dabei auch die aus dem *Thesaurus musicus* (Nürnberg, 1564; Leuchtmann und Schmid, *Lasso: Seine Werke*, 1564-5 bis 1564-9) in die zweite Auflage der *Selectissimae cantiones* aufgenommenen Motetten. Der *Thesaurus* war unter der Leitung von Johannes Montanus und Ulrich Neuber, den Vorgängern von Gerlach in der traditionsreichen Nürnberger Offizin, entstanden.

[14] In Orlando di Lasso, *Sämtliche Werke*, Band XIX: *Magnum opus musicum, Lateinische Gesänge für 2, 3, 4, 5, 6, 7, 8, 9, 10 u. 12 Stimmen. In Partitur gebracht von Carl Proske, kritisch durchgesehen und redigirt von Franz Xaver Haberl.* Teil X (Leipzig, [1908]), Nr. 472, 66-68.

[15] Catull, Gedicht Nr. 27: *Minister vetuli puer Falerni.* Vgl. Bernhold Schmid, „Lassos ,Nunc gaudere licet': Zur Geschichte einer Kontrafaktur", in *Compositionswissenschaft. Festschrift Reinhold und Roswitha Schlötterer zum 70. Geburtstag,* hrsg. von Bernd Edelmann und Sabine Kurth (Augsburg, 1999), 47-56, hier 50.

[16] Bergquist, „The Two Editions", 152: „His preface states that he 'revised the previous edition from accurate and corrected exemplars and ... removed in the process obvious mistakes'. This suggests that he received better texts from an outside source as well as exercising independent judgment on his own."

Auf welche Quellen Lechner zurückgegriffen haben könnte, wissen wir nicht, da er ja nicht angibt, was er benutzt hat.[17] Andererseits aber lassen sich, wie Bergquist betont, ab etwa 1579 engere Beziehungen zwischen Lasso und der Gerlachschen Offizin feststellen; Lechners „richtige und korrigierte Quellen" könnten also direkt von Lasso gekommen sein. Dafür spricht auch, dass die *Selectissimae cantiones* von 1579 in ihrem zweiten Band fünf erstbelegte, vielleicht gar erstgedruckte Sätze enthalten, die von Lasso an Katharina Gerlach oder Leonhard Lechner gegeben worden sein könnten.[18] Auch zwei gegenüber der ersten Auflage weggelassene Stücke, *Zachaee festinans descende* und *Gloria patri*[19] sind evtl. geeignet, Lassos direkte Einflußnahme auf die Auflage von 1579 zu erhärten: Bergquist hält beide Sätze sowohl aus stilistischen Gründen als auch aufgrund ihres Fehlens in der Auflage von 1579 für Falschzuschreibungen. Sollte dies tatsächlich zutreffen, dann könnte Lasso selbst veranlasst haben, die beiden Stücke nicht mehr abzudrucken.[20]

Im folgenden soll die soeben angeschnittene Problematik, ob Lechner Vorlagen hatte oder selbst korrigierend tätig war, anhand eines im Detail zu untersuchenden, aussagekräftigen Beispiels diskutiert werden. Eine zumindest hypothetische Lösung lässt sich dabei vorstellen, die freilich keine letztgültige Sicherheit bietet. Klar wird allerdings ein weiteres Mal, wie schwierig eine einigermaßen eindeutige Entscheidung ist, wenn man nicht entweder eine Vorlage für Lechner nachweisen kann, oder – wie im Fall des oben kurz angerissenen Catull-Zitats in *Nunc gaudere licet* – aufgrund des Textes und seiner Herkunft offenkundig sein dürfte, dass die von Lechner gegebene Lesart auch von ihm selbst erstellt worden ist.

Besprochen sei die Vertonung des Wortes „patibulo", mit dem die erste Strophe des Hymnus *Vexilla regis prodeunt* endet. Lasso hat diesen Venantius Fortunatus zugeschriebenen Text als großangelegte Motette komponiert:[21]

> I. *Vexilla regis prodeunt* à 6
> II. *Impleta sunt quae concinit* à 6
> III. *Beata cuius brachiis* à 2
> IV. *O crux, ave, spes unica* à 6

In folgenden Quellen ist das Stück überliefert (Tafel 1).[22] Nach der ältesten Quelle, dem *Liber secundus* bei Scotto in Venedig, erscheint das Stück also viermal bei Gardano (Venedig) in dessen *Liber secundus*, geht in die drei Auflagen der *Selectissimæ cantiones* bei Gerlach ein und wird davon abhängig schließlich in die „Gesamtausgabe" von Lassos Motetten, das *Magnum opus musicum* bei Heinrich in München, übernommen.

---

[17] Diese und die folgenden Überlegungen nach Bergquist, „The Two Editions", 152-53.

[18] Leuchtmann und Schmid, *Lasso: Seine Werke*, 1579-3 enthält erstmals als Nr. 47 *Si bene perpendi* (LV 642), als Nr. 48: *Agimus tibi gratias* (LV 643), als Nr. 54 das vorher bisher nicht mit originalem Text nachweise Kontrafakt *Ave Iesu Christe alta stirps* = nach Ausweis der Überschrift im Druck *Ave Maria alta stirps* (LV 644), als Nr. 61 *Proba me Deus* (LV 645) und schließlich als Nr. 71 *Anna, mihi dilecta, veni* (LV 646), ein Satz, der mutmaßlich schon früher entstanden sein dürfte; vgl. GA² III, XCI und Peter Bergquist in Orlando di Lasso, *The Complete Motets 18: Motets from Printed Anthologies and Manuscripts, 1570-1579*, hrsg. von Peter Bergquist, Recent Researches in the Music of the Renaissance 124 (Middleton, 2001), xxi.

[19] Leuchtmann und Schmid , *Lasso: Seine Werke*, 1568-4,10 (LV 252) und 1568-3,32 (LV 193, III. pars).

[20] Bergquist, „The Two Editions", 153; dort Verweis auf Peter Bergquist in Orlando di Lasso, *The Complete Motets 5: Motets from* Quinque et sex perornatae sacrae cantiones *(Venice, 1565)*. *Motets for Five to Eight Voices from* Sacrae cantiones, liber secundus, tertius, quartus *(Venice, 1566)*, hrsg. von Peter Bergquist, Recent Researches in the Music of the Renaissance 109 (Madison, 1997), xvi-xix (im folgenden zitiert als CM 5).

[21] LV 225, GA² XI 333, 172-79. Peter Bergquist hat in CM 5, 56-71 ebenfalls eine Edition dieser Motette vorgelegt.

[22] Nicht berücksichtigt sind dabei die zwei Biciniendrucke Leuchtmann und Schmid, *Lasso: Seine Werke*, 1591-5 und 1612-2/II, die jeweils nur den zweistimmigen dritten Teil der Motette *Beata cuius brachiis* überliefern.

Quelle nach Leuchtmann/Schmid	Kurztitel	Verlag und Ort
1565-4,10	*Orlandi Lassi [...] Sacræ cantiones nunc primum omni diligentia in lucem editæ, à Iulio Bonagiunta Musico Ecclesiæ diui Marci Venetiarum. liber secundus*	Girolamo Scotto, Venedig
1566-7,15	*Orlandi Lassi Sacræ cantiones [...]. Liber Secvndvs*	Antonio Gardano, Venedig
1568-3,10	*Selectissimæ cantiones [...] per excellentissimum Musicum, Orlandum di Lassus*	Theodor Gerlach, Nürnberg
1569-21,15	*Orlandi Lassi Sacræ cantiones [...]. Liber Secvndvs*	Antonio Gardano, Venedig
1572-1,15	*Orlandi Lassi Sacræ cantiones [...]. Liber Secvndvs*	Söhne Antonio Gardanos, Venedig
1579-2,13	*Selectissimæ cantiones [...] per excellentissimum Musicum Orlandum di Lassus*	Katharina Gerlach und Erben Johannes Montanus', Nürnberg
1584-1,15	*Orlandi Lassi Sacræ cantiones [...]. Liber Secvndvs*	Angelo Gardano, Venedig
1587-2,13	*Selectissimæ cantiones [...] per excellentissimum Musicum Orlandum di Lassus*	Katharina Gerlach, Nürnberg
1604-1,333	*Magnum Opvs Mvsicvm Orlandi de Lasso [...] Complectens omnes cantiones qvas Motetas vulgo vocant*	Nikolaus Heinrich, München

Notenbeispiel 1a zeigt die Fassung des ältesten Drucks 1565-4, Beispiel 1b stellt synoptisch die Version Leonhard Lechners aus 1579-2 gegenüber. Zunächst ist festzustellen, dass in Lechners Ausgabe, außerdem in 1587-2 und davon abhängig in 1604-1, aber schon in der ersten Auflage der *Selectissimae cantiones* der Bassus in der Sexta vox steht und umgekehrt die Sexta vox im Bassus-Stimmbuch. Sodann nimmt Lechner in den T. 30-32 des Cantus eine Änderung der Notenwerte vor, indem er die Semibrevis und die Minima *h'* zur punktierten Semibrevis verbindet und im Gegenzug die punktierte Semibrevis *a'* (T. 32) zu zwei Noten aufteilt, woraus sich eine Verschiebung der Textunterlegung ergibt: Er passt den Cantus ganz einfach an den Altus und die Quinta vox an (ebenso in 1587-2 und 1604-1). Doch dies tut nichts zur Sache, da sich an den Tonhöhen bzw. den Zusammenklängen ja nichts ändert. Hier geht es um krasse klangliche Unterschiede bei „patibulo" in beiden Fassungen.

Beispiel 1. Orlando di Lasso, *Vexilla regis prodeunt*

a. T. 27-34 aus 1565-4,10

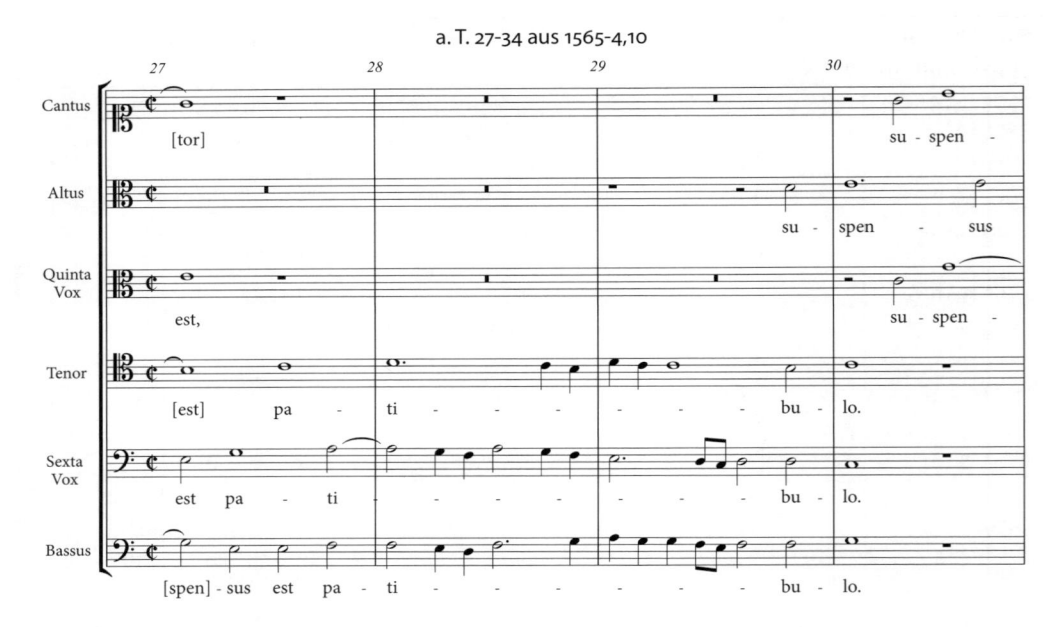

Die Stelle ist jeweils zweimal vertont; sie wird zuerst vom Tiefchor, dann vom Hochchor vorgetragen. Nicht eingegangen wird auf die Takte bis 28 Mitte (Tiefchor) und 32 Mitte (Hochchor), darzustellen ist jedoch, was ab T. 28 Mitte bzw. ab T. 32 Mitte geschieht. Die Außenstimmen, also Tenor und Sextus/Bassus (ab T. 28 Mitte) sind in beiden Fassungen identisch mit Cantus und Quintus/Quinta vox (ab T. 32 Mitte). Die Passage wird lediglich um eine Quinte nach oben verlagert. Unterschiede sind hingegen bei den Mittelstimmen festzustellen: In 1565-4 ergibt sich eine Verschiebung (Beispiel 2a und 2b).

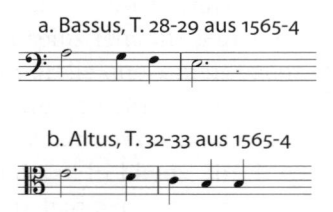

Beispiel 2 Lasso, *Vexilla regis prodeunt*

a. Bassus, T. 28-29 aus 1565-4

b. Altus, T. 32-33 aus 1565-4

Die Minima *a* wird an der Analogstelle zur punktierten Minima *e'*, die punktierte Minima *e* zu zwei Semiminimen *h*, innerhalb der Passage ergibt sich also rhythmisch eine Verschiebung um eine Semiminima nach rechts. Dies hat massive Auswirkungen auf die Klanglichkeit: Die scharfen Dissonanzen im Tiefchor (*f* gegen *g* etc., vgl. Beispiel 3a) lösen sich im Hochchor in Wohlgefallen auf (Beispiel 3b).

Beispiel 3. Lasso, *Vexilla regis prodeunt*

a. Tenor, Bassus, Sextus, T. 28-29 aus 1565-4

b. Cantus, Altus, Quintus, T. 32-33 aus 1565-4

Beispiel 4. Lasso, *Vexilla regis prodeunt*

a. Sexta vox, T. 28-29 aus 1579-2   b. Altus, T. 32-33 aus 1579-2

Lechner wollte die Dissonanzen im Tiefchor offenbar nicht hinnehmen: er passte deshalb den Tiefchor an den Hochchor an und lieferte eine Version, die vor ihm quellenmäßig nicht greifbar ist (Beispiel 4a und 4b). Es stellt sich die Frage, ob die Fassung in 1565-4 fehlerhaft ist, außerdem, ob Lechner nach besseren Quellen (woher auch immer er sie haben hätte können) korrigiert hat oder ob er selbst emendiert hat. Zu bedenken ist dabei vor allem, dass die scharfen Dissonanzen evtl. auf die Absicht des

Komponisten schließen lassen, das Wort „patibulo", also Kreuzesbalken, im Tiefchor musikalisch besonders drastisch auszudeuten – was Lasso durchaus zuzutrauen ist – um dann im Hochchor zu zeigen, wie die Stelle satztechnisch regulär zu gestalten wäre. Wenn dem so ist, dann hätte Lechner entweder Lassos Absicht nicht erkannt und deshalb auf einen Fehler geschlossen, oder es wäre ihm die Dissonanz zur Textausdeutung dann doch zu krass gewesen. Bei der Diskussion der Frage, ob wir es mit Textausdeutung oder mit einem Fehler zu tun haben, ist die Überlieferungslage mit einzubeziehen: Zunächst ist kurz auf den ältesten Druck (1565-4, Scotto) für unser Stück und die Widmungsvorrede einzugehen, die der Herausgeber Giulio Bonagiunta, Musiker an S. Marco in Venedig, unterzeichnet hat. Er schreibt, dass er von Lasso Motetten zur freien Verfügung erhalten und diese mit Widmung an Dominicus Paruta drucken lassen habe („itaque cum ab Orlando Lasso […] cantiones aliquę, vulgo Mottetta nuncupata, mihi donata fuissent, quibus authoris liberalitate mihi pro meis vti licet, typis mandare, ac tui pręclarißimi nominis inscriptione illustrata emittere, publicareque volui.").[23] Tatsächlich sind fast alle im Druck enthaltenen Motetten hier auch erstbelegt (zehn von insgesamt zwölf), wodurch seine Behauptung, er habe die Stücke von Lasso erhalten, gestützt wird. So gesehen kommt dem Druck natürlich ein vergleichsweise hoher Quellenwert zu. Andererseits kann die Publikation nicht als gänzlich unproblematisch bezeichnet werden: Bergquist stellt fest: „The text of RISM 1565c is good on the whole; its biggest problems are in text underlay, which is sometimes imprecise, as noted in the 'Critical Report'".[24] Für *Vexilla regis prodeunt* sind zudem geringe Fehler im Notentext festzustellen.[25] Die Art der Fehler deutet auf eine gewisse Flüchtigkeit bei der Redaktion; insbesondere die kleinen Probleme bei der Textunterlegung sind meist leicht zu durchschauen und zu korrigieren.[26] Mit der zweitältesten Quelle für Lassos Motette, Gardanos *Secundus liber* 1566-7, liegt ein um vier Motetten erweiterter Nachdruck von 1565-4 vor, zu dem Bergquist feststellt: „Gardano […] often improved Scotto's text by correcting wrong words and incorrect or unclear underlay."[27] Allerdings ist auch dessen Ausgabe der Motette nicht durchgängig fehlerfrei; hingewiesen sei auf einen Textfehler in allen Stimmen der IV. pars (T. 30-39), wo das korrekte „salvas rege" durch „salva reges" ersetzt wird. Für unseren Zusammenhang ist wichtig, dass Gardano trotz

---

[23] Vgl. Bergquist in CM 5, xi. Im selben Band [xxxi] ein Faksimile der Widmungsvorrede (Plate 2) und eine Übersetzung ins Englische. Vgl. auch Horst Leuchtmann, *Orlando di Lasso: Sein Leben. Versuch einer Bestandsaufnahme der biographischen Einzelheiten* (Wiesbaden, 1976), 128. Leuchtmann bezeichnet Bonagiunta als Organisten an S. Marco in Venedig, Bergquist hält ihn für einen Sänger und beruft sich dabei auf Denis Arnold, „Bonagiunta [Bonagionta], Giulio", in *The New Grove Dictionary of Music and Musicians*, hrsg. von Stanley Sadie (London, 1980), Bd. 3, 14. Vgl. auch den Artikel von Andrea Marcialis, „Bonagiunta [Bonagionta], Giulio", in *The New Grove Dictionary of Music and Musicians*, hrsg. von Stanley Sadie und John Tyrell (London, ²2001), Bd. 3, 847. Horst Leuchtmann bezeichnet Bonagiunta in seinem Artikel „Bonagionta, Bonagiunta, Giulio", in *Die Musik in Geschichte und Gegenwart*, hrsg. von Ludwig Finscher (Kassel etc., ²2000), Personenteil 3, Sp. 314 ebenfalls als Sänger. Bonagiunta selbst nennt sich im Titel des Drucks „Musico Ecclesiæ diui Marci Venetiarum."

[24] CM 5, xi-xii; vgl. dort auch den Critical Report auf 304. Vgl. auch die Anmerkungen zum Notentext zu *Vexilla regis prodeunt* in GA² XI, CIX-CXI.

[25] Vgl. die vorausgehende Fußnote. Ein klarer Fehler z.B. in der I. pars im Sextus, wo in T. 36 als dritte Note ein G in 1565-4 statt ein F steht. Gardano übernimmt in 1566-7 diesen Fehler.

[26] Vgl. Anmerkungen zum Notentext GA² XI, CIX-CXI.

[27] CM 5, xii. Bergquist, xix Anmerkung 5, zitiert zudem einschlägige Arbeiten von Mary S. Lewis, die sich zwar auf Publikationen Scottos und Gardanos vor 1550 beziehen, „but their comments can be considered valid for these later editions also." Vgl. Mary S. Lewis, *Antonio Gardano, Venetian Music Printer, 1538-1569: A Descriptive Bibliography and Historical Study* (New York, 1988-), Bd. 1, besonders 30-33. Mary S. Lewis, „Twins, Cousins, and Heirs: Relationships among Editions of Music Printed in Sixteenth-Century Venice", in *Critica Musica: Essays in Honor of Paul Brainard*, hrsg. von John Knowles (Amsterdam, 1996), 193-224.

offenkundiger Redaktion und Korrekturen gegenüber seiner Vorlage 1565-4 die beschriebenen Dissonanzen bei „patibulo" unverändert übernimmt; mutmaßlich wurde die Stelle also nicht als fehlerhaft angesehen.

Die erste Auflage der *Selectissimae cantiones* aus dem Jahr 1568 ist für *Vexilla regis prodeunt* mit größter Sicherheit von Gardanos *Secundus liber* abhängig.[28] Ein starkes Indiz dafür ist, dass Gardanos Textfehler „salva reges" übernommen wird; ferner findet sich im Tenor der IV. pars in den T. 14-16 erstmals bei Gardano 1566-7 die Unterlegung „reisque dona ueniam", die 1568-3 übernimmt. 1565-4 (und auch die von Lechner redigierte zweite Auflage der *Selectissimae cantiones* 1579-2) drucken stattdessen „auge piis iustitiam".

Zusammenfassend sei wiederholt:

- Dem Scotto-Druck mit den Dissonanzen beim ersten „patibulo" kommt einige Autorität zu, da der Herausgeber Bonagiunta nach eigener Aussage die Motetten von Lasso erhalten hat, was durchaus wahrscheinlich ist.
- Der redaktionell gegenüber Scotto eingreifende Gardano übernahm die „patibulo"-Stelle unverändert, dürfte sie also wohl für korrekt gehalten haben; aus der Version im Hochchor (T. 32-33) wären die Mißtöne in T. 28-29 ja problemlos zu korrigieren gewesen. (Zu ergänzen ist, dass die späteren Auflagen von Gardanos *Liber secundus* 1569-21, 1572-1 und 1584-1 das erste „patibulo" ebenfalls so abdrucken, wie es 1565-4 erstmals überliefert ist.)
- Gardanos Druck ist mit einiger Sicherheit die Vorlage für die *Selectissimae cantiones* von 1568.
- Dass mit Lechners 1579-2 eine Redaktion von 1568-3 vorliegt, in der er die Dissonanzen beim ersten „patibulo" beseitigt, wurde oben ausführlich dargelegt. Die bei ihm überlieferte Fassung ist vorher nicht nachweisbar. (Sekundär ist in unserem Zusammenhang, dass das *Magnum opus* 1604-1 über 1587-2 auf 1579-2 zurückgeht).

Wiederum sei die Frage gestellt, ob die Fassung in 1565-4 fehlerhaft ist, außerdem, ob Lechner emendiert hat oder ob ihm tatsächlich eine ältere Vorlage zur Verfügung stand, um die Stelle zu „korrigieren". Es müßte sich dann um einen heute verlorenen Druck handeln, oder aber er hätte tatsächlich Material von Lasso erhalten.

Nimmt man alle oben angestellten Überlegungen zusammen, so ist mit einer gewissen Wahrscheinlichkeit anzunehmen, dass die dissonante „patibulo"-Stelle tatsächlich so von Lasso stammt und nicht als Fehler in 1565-4 anzusehen ist:

- Für die Richtigkeit von Bonagiuntas dissonanter Version aus dem Jahr 1565 spricht seine Aussage, er habe die Motetten von Lasso erhalten; 1565-4 dürfte wohl tatsächlich ein Erstdruck sein.
- Der redigierende Gardano griff bei der fraglichen Stelle nicht ein; wenn seiner Meinung nach ein „Fehler" vorgelegen hätte, wäre er aus der Paralellstelle im Hochchor problemlos zu korrigieren gewesen.
- Vor allem aber macht die Dissonanz als Textausdeutung sicherlich Sinn.

---

[28] Dass Gerlach bei der Zusammenstellung der *Selectissimae cantiones* 1568 auf Gardanos 1566-7 zurückgegriffen hat, zeigt sich auch an anderen Stücken; vgl. GA² VII, LI mit Fußn. 58.

Lechner wird also nicht anhand einer „besseren Quelle" korrigiert, sondern selbständig emendiert haben. Die Edition des *Vexilla regis prodeunt* in der zweiten Auflage der Gesamtausgabe übernimmt deshalb die von Bonagiunta in 1565-4 abgedruckte Fassung, eine Entscheidung, die auch Peter Bergquist in seiner Edition der Motette in den *Complete Motets* getroffen hat.

Unabhängig davon, ob Lechners Fassung eine irrtümliche Emendation oder tatsächlich ein korrigierter Fehler ist, ist Lechners Leistung nicht hoch genug einzuschätzen, wie sich an zahlreichen anderen Beispielen seiner redaktionellen Arbeit zeigt. Und: Sollte Scottos Version in 1565-4 mit den Dissonanzen von Lasso so gemeint sein (wofür vieles spricht), dann hätten wir es sicherlich mit einem Extremfall an Textausdeutung zu tun, so extrem, dass selbst ein Schüler und genauer Kenner Lassos wie Leonhard Lechner sich hat irre machen lassen.

Abstract

In its first published version, from 1565, as well as in numerous of its reprints, Lasso's motet on the hymn *Vexilla regis prodeunt* (LV 225, GA² XI 333) shows striking dissonances in the three lower voices on the word 'patibulo' (bb. 28-29). When this passage is repeated almost literally by the three top voices (bb. 32-33), the dissonances have been eliminated. The dissonant passage appeared in the first edition of the *Selectissimae cantiones* (Nuremberg, 1568). In his revised edition of this latter print, from 1579, Leonhard Lechner removes the dissonances in bb. 28-29 by adapting the passage to the version in bb. 32-33. As Peter Bergquist has shown, Lechner's edition contains many editorial changes vis à vis the first edition. In the preface to the 1579 print, Lechner himself refers to the mistakes in the first edition, and claims that he corrected them after comparison with better sources.

In this article, I investigate whether the dissonant passage is a mistake or whether it can be interpreted as text expression of the word 'patibulo' (cross-beam). Furthermore, I discuss whether Lechner 'corrected' the dissonant version on the basis of an earlier, now lost source (maybe even having obtained material from Lasso himself), or whether he emended the dissonances autonomously. The evidence suggests that Lechner made the 'correction' on his own initiative. Both modern editions of the motet—in the Complete Motets vol. 5 (ed. Peter Bergquist) and the second edition of the relevant volume in the Lasso-Gesamtausgabe—keep the dissonant passage.

Research and Performance Practice Forum

■

Digital Scholarship for
the New Tinctoris Edition

■

D A V I D   L E W I S

In Spring 2011, the UK Arts and Humanities Research Council announced funding for a project to create a digital edition of all the surviving musical writings of Tinctoris, including Latin texts and English translations, as well as a wide range of commentary material. The edition (*The Complete Theoretical Works of Johannes Tinctoris: A New Digital Edition*) is being produced under the editorship of Ronald Woodley and Jeffrey Dean, and the edited treatise texts will be in place by the summer of 2014. The digital, and particularly the web-based, nature of the edition is central to the conception of the project, although it will also be possible for readers to print various versions of the texts.

There are substantial advantages to a digital, online approach, and these have been discussed elsewhere,[1] but many of these can be gathered under a single heading: *access*. A free online edition is *accessible* in ways that an equivalent printed volume could never be, not just in the number of potential users, but also by lowering barriers to use: all that is needed is an internet-connected device. A digital edition is also dynamic: it can be *transformed* in such a way as to enable a reader to access the information best suited to her current task in the most helpful way. Questions of access also affect contributors, who may find modifying or augmenting the edition's current content a more streamlined experience with a digital, rather than printed, resource. Finally, when the resource is completed or project funding ceases, and there is no longer staff or budget available for it, the continuing accessibility of the digital edition takes on extra significance and becomes a question of *sustainability*.

My role, as the researcher on the project responsible for the technological aspects of the edition, is in supporting the ambition to create an accessible scholarly resource and developing any software necessary to achieve this. In the process, some more general issues around digital editing and digital corpora for musicologists have crystallized. The issues discussed in this article are illustrated, where possible, by reference to the Tinctoris edition, but are deliberately selected to be general, in the hope that they are relevant and of interest to potential users of and contributors to our project, but also to others who are considering embarking on comparable endeavours.

This article is intended for a readership specializing in the humanities rather than in computer science or information technology, and so technological terms are defined in footnotes following their first significant mention: the term itself is shown in bold face to make referring back easier and to signal to those who are already comfortable with the term that they need not consult the attached footnote.

---

[1]   See, for example, Frans Wiering, 'Digital Critical Editions of Music: A Multidimensional Model', in *Modern Methods for Musicology*, ed. Tim Crawford and Lorna Gibson (Aldershot, 2009), 23-46; Theodor Dumitrescu, 'The Material Digital: Strategies of Making and Reading the Early Music Edition, Then and Now', in *Journal of the Alamire Foundation* 1 (2009), 125-47; and Jerome McGann, 'The Rationale of Hypertext', in *Electronic Text. Investigations in Method and Theory*, ed. Kathryn Sutherland (Oxford, 1997), 19-46.

I. Introduction

Given the comparative youth of musicology as a recognized academic discipline, digital musicology has a long history. Our new digital edition of the theoretical works of Tinctoris is therefore informed by fifty or more years of technological development and, at the same time, is alert to new ways to exploit more recent advances, especially where they allow us to make complex information more accessible to users. Despite its maturity, the field of digital musicology is still changing rapidly; it might even be argued that the speed of technological advance has had the paradoxical effect of slowing the development of the discipline, leading to risks of obsolescence and incompatibility. Nonetheless, as Dumitrescu observes, the 'database projects and online versions of earlier publications are indeed the true reference works of the twenty-first century, and these play an increasingly vital role in the working methods which our students are learning'.[2] Arguably, the situation is now becoming more stable, as key technologies and standards mature, whilst the increased capacity of storage and processing power of consumer electronics (not only computers, but also smart phones and tablets) makes digital editing projects less onerous and cheaper to create and maintain. Two broad questions must be confronted by anyone embarking on a new project: (i) the nature, quality, and form of the information stored to make up the edition; and (ii) how that information might be made accessible to all users.

The first question, which will be considered in section II, is—or should be—primarily a musicological question. Just as in print, editors must make decisions about policies of transcription, the granularity of transcribed detail, and the degree to which editorial interpretation is made available as a replacement or adjunct to a facsimile-like transfer of information. In print, these decisions may involve discussions with typesetters to agree approaches that might normally be rejected as poor typography.[3] There are similar practical questions for electronic deployment of an edition, but these too must be led by the requirements of the editors.

The second question, that of accessibility, will be considered in section III. This is only partly a matter of examining the potential users of a system and developing intuitive interfaces for them; to prescribe entirely how an edition shall be used would be undesirable even if it were possible: what is required is a combination of educated guesswork and inbuilt flexibility and extensibility. Accessibility goes beyond this: the advance of technology, the capricious nature of the **tools** that **software** is built on and with, and the evolving demands of users all mean that an application designed and developed during the course of a fixed-term project may inevitably lose some of its perceived usefulness with time.[4] If, however, all the *information* is made accessible in a

---

[2] Dumitrescu, 'The Material Digital', 125.

[3] The conflict between an editor's or a composer's desire for expressive precision and a typesetter's for conformity to rules of layout can require diplomatic handling. In his edition of Debussy's piano music, for example, Roy Howat was compelled to explain in his preface that departures from typographical norms were editorial decisions rather than engravers' errors (*Les Œuvres complètes de Claude Debussy*, Série I , vol. 1, ed. Roy Howat [Paris, 2000], xxv).

[4] **Software** is used here, synonymously with **program** and **application**, to refer to a sequence of instructions within a computer (or an equivalent device with a processor, such as a mobile phone). The instructions allow the performance of one or more specific tasks. The term software was introduced as a contrast with hardware—the physical components of a computer. Software is usually stored as files on a storage medium such as a hard disk or delivered through a network connection. Few pieces of software address computer hardware directly. They rely on an operating system, such as Windows or Mac OS, to perform basic tasks, but often also use software libraries, that is, software to perform

form that can be interpreted directly by a computer, without human intervention, others may be able to use the edition even if the software provided to support it fails. If this machine-accessible form includes aspects which can be interpreted by other software that already exists—whether that software takes the form of commercial applications or is the result of other research projects—the likelihood that the edition will remain accessible is further increased. This issue of *sustainability*, linked as it is with the nature and form of the information stored, is discussed towards the end of section II below.

II. Types of Information: Content and Structure

Editing a music treatise involves dealing with several types of information, of which the most prominent are likely to be a verbal text and notated music examples. The mixing of text and music in a single flowing document presents challenges of its own for the digital editor, as does the fact that examples of musical notation in treatises are not always syntactically complete as instances of music. Tinctoris's *Tractatus de notis et pausis*, for example, begins with a description of each of the symbols used for notes— *maxima*, *longa*, *brevis*, *semibrevis*, and *minima*—and in each case, the symbols are illustrated on a clefless staff (see Figure 1). Since pitch is irrelevant to the symbol being described and adding unnecessary elements to the examples might be considered confusing, omitting clefs makes good sense even though the result is not 'performable' music notation. Such examples sit on a continuum between typographical symbols on a page, graphical diagrams, and performable music, all of which may be encountered within the treatises to be edited.[5]

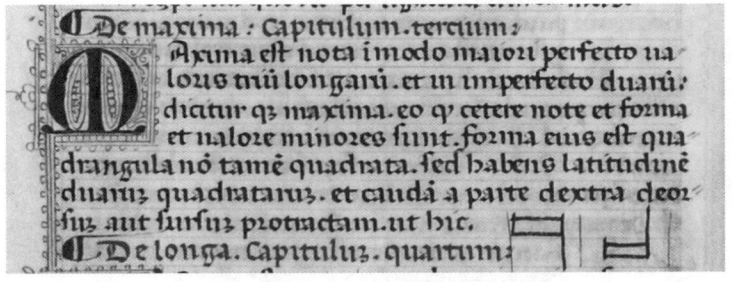

Figure 1. The first example of musical notation from Tinctoris's *Tractatus de notis et pausis*, showing two unpitched notes on a clefless staff (Bologna, Biblioteca Universitaria, Ms. 2573, fol. 47v, detail). Reproduced by permission

The decision of exactly what information is significant is an editorial one and the fine details cannot easily be predicted even by the editors: only a general policy can be specified in advance. Once an editor opts to include a piece of information in his transcription, there remains the decision of whether to record it in a fully structured,

commonly occurring tasks to save programmers from repeating themselves. Software will also be written in a programming language, which will have an interpreter and often a compiler. All of these components may, to varying degrees, be subject to changes that make older software fail. **Tool** is here used in the same way as it is in its physical form, as an item (in this case, an item of software), that may be used (often repeatedly) for a task.

5   Diagrams themselves will be considered later, as they pose rather different challenges.

'machine-readable' way, allowing the computer to interpret the information freely—so that, for example, the screen display can show a transcription in a choice of ways that more or less closely resemble the source—or as an annotation addressed to the reader. These decisions pervade the editorial process, and many examples could be chosen, but a simple, commonly encountered case is that of barlines. Barlines, structural dividers, or signals of the end of a work can be regarded as a single category of item and represented as such, perhaps as a structure in computer memory called 'barline'. Does it make a difference whether a barline runs from the top of the staff to the bottom or only cuts across a part of the staff (see Figure 2a)? Is a doubled barline to be distinguished from a single one? If so, what of more elaborate barlines, perhaps with added flourishes or scalloping (see Figure 2b)? We might expand the barline structure to be qualified with a description, perhaps: 'Solid line from the second staff line to the fourth' or 'Elaborate double black barline with red between the two lines and a scalloped line following'. In these cases, the information would be present in the edition, but not in a way that was comprehensible to the computer—it could display the description, but the barline could only be displayed on-screen in the normal way. Alternatively, the representation of barlines could be structured to allow more fine-grained information to be represented: from: 2; to: 6 or from: 0; to: 8; type: Vertical-Scallops. Here, the information content is the same, but it follows a pre-defined structure—it is now represented in computer memory as two numbers and a keyword chosen from a known list, rather than a block of text—that makes it readable by the computer and allows a more accurate display, along with the possibility of more detailed searching and analysis.

a. Partial-height barline from Ghent, Rijksuniversiteit, Centrale Bibliotheek, BHSL.HS.0070, fol. 163v, detail

b. Decorated barline from Brussels, Bibliothèque royale de Belgique,
Music Ms. II 4147 (Fétis 5274), fol. 29v, detail. Reproduced by permission

Figure 2. Forms of barline that might be represented in distinct ways

Verbal annotations, such as those given here, are generally easily accommodated through generic structures that can be simply defined in advance. On the other hand, the more detailed structure may require a special extension to or modification of the way in which information is represented internally. Generally, a more fine-grained and machine-readable transcription will demand software that is more sophisticated and may involve a more complex user interface or more laborious data entry;[6] the advantages for subsequent applications and flexibility of presentation must be weighed against this. A further factor to be considered may also be whether elevating a small presentational detail to this level risks giving it too much weight.

The example given above was illustrated with reference to an *internal representation*. When a piece of information, such as an edition, is being used by a computer program, a **structure** representing that information will be stored in memory.[7] The structure exists purely to allow the software to perform the tasks for which it was programmed efficiently and effectively, and there is no requirement that all the information available be represented or that it should be structured in a way that makes intuitive sense to a human. A common example of a reduced representation is used in tools for searching long texts, such as those of our treatise edition. In computing, as in print, this is very efficiently achieved using an index of words with pointers to the positions in the text at which they occur: this index in no way resembles the text itself, nor could prose be reconstructed from it.

Such simple internal representations are usually designed for a single, simple task: as the questions asked of the software become more complex and, in our case, more musical or musicological, then the internal representation needs to become more complete and more likely to reflect our intuitive ideas of how the information works and how parts of it are connected. This more complete view may require extra information that is not *primary* to the edition, and is not stored anywhere as part of the edition, but is calculated as or before it is needed—it might, for instance, be necessary to deduce note durations for playing sound examples or for automatic transcription to modern notation.

The sum of information of a digital edition can reside in many places: in database structures, in files, on local or remote disk drives, or, as we have seen, in a dynamic, in-memory representation that depends on the running of a specific application. In some online electronic corpora, information on the web site is not replicated in any separate data files, whilst in others, some 'knowledge' may only be present in software that interprets data files (as is the case for note duration in the example above). Meanwhile, what we often consider to be the main repository of information—perhaps a set of files or a database—must be considered incomplete unless accompanied with sufficient documentation explaining the nature, structure, and interpretation of that information.

---

[6] Since the editor must record information within a more complex structure, there is a tendency for the user interface to need more components, becoming more complex where a simple, less-structured annotation can be created using the same textual input box for all situations. This does not necessarily make the task more onerous—compare a 'double bar' button with a textual input for the same information—but the risk must be considered by the developer.

[7] **Structure**, and sometimes **data structure**, is used here simply to mean a way of organizing information in a computer, building on the more general sense of a structure as reflecting the arrangement of or relationship between entities. There is a more specialized use of the term in computer science to refer to generic types of space-efficient or fast information-organizing methods, usually provided as part of a programming language, but this sense is not intended here.

This last issue—the necessity for documentary explanation—is familiar in humanities scholarship in general, with the demand for citations of scholarly research, and all the apparatus surrounding a critical edition, whether distributed in print or online.

The distinction between formats and the information in an edition is crucial and was already recognized, for music, in the 1960s by Michael Kassler. At the time, Kassler was working at Princeton on a project initiated in 1963 by Arthur Mendel and Lewis Lockwood to encode what was then considered the complete works of Josquin, in all their variants, and many works of disputed authorship. The result was subjected to automated analysis intended to assist in tasks of filiation, author attribution, style analysis and modern transcription. For this purpose, Kassler devised a language, which he called MIR (Music Information Retrieval), that would allow him to perform the same analytical operations on music in several different encoding formats. This was necessary partly because of problems that he experienced when the university computer was changed, but also because he recognized that different encodings could facilitate different sorts of musicological tasks.[8] This was especially true in the days of limited computer memory and processing power, but still holds today for formats that are used by preference in a raw form rather than with large, complex programs—this might be by users editing them using a text editor, in which case optimization for a single task can make the text easier to read and edit, or directly by the computers themselves; this is an idea that will be discussed later when we consider computers as users.

This aspect of the information in a digital edition—encoding format—is often conflated with the editorial selection of content and the internal, digital representation of that content. An encoding format is a predefined way of specifying a data structure as a file or **data stream** and, broadly speaking, is one of two types.[9] The first type of encoding format is created by taking the software-specific internal representation described above and writing it directly to a file. The second type, the interchange or exchange format, requires a translation step from the internal representation used within the software into some standardized structure first. This confers the advantage of *portability*—that a file may be read by several different pieces of software—at the potential cost of the completeness and flexibility of the representation. This cost comes partly because the process of standardizing can be slow and bureaucratic, but also because the principles behind the format's definition may specifically exclude some of the information that individual users need to represent, leading to loss of information in the process of translation and exchange.

The issue of encoding formats for music is both old and well explored.[10] In over fifty years of music computing, no single dominant standard has emerged that satisfies

8 Michael Kassler, 'Toward Musical Information Retrieval', in *Perspectives of New Music* 4/2 (1966), 59-67.
9 A **data stream** delivers information over a network (from a server) rather than from a file on a local disk drive. Usually there is little difference in functionality between operating on a stream or a file, but where files are usually processed as complete structures, streams are often handled as they arrive, and may even be endless, as in online radio and television broadcasts.
10 The published proceedings of a 1965 symposium on 'Input Languages to Represent Music' runs to over 140 pages; see Barry S. Brook (ed.), *Musicology and the Computer; Musicology 1966-2000: A Practical Program* (New York, 1970), 48-189. Thirty years later, Eleanor Selfridge-Field (ed.), *Beyond Midi: The Handbook of Musical Codes* (Cambridge, MA and London, 1997) devotes more than 600 pages to the topic's discussion and analysis. Both texts do much more than simply discuss encoding formats, but their scope does give some indication of the scale of the topic.

the requirements of a 'universal' format for representing musical information.[11] The tension between completeness and portability is one that has counted strongly against past attempts.

MusicXML is one of the most prominent score-based interchange formats, and is supported by several popular music-typesetting applications. However, it explicitly rules out representing historical notation from before the eighteenth century,[12] as such a representation would unduly increase complexity and risk making compatibility between the various applications even harder. MusicXML is also incapable, by design, of the sort of text-critical information that plays a crucial role in scholarly editions such as ours.

For textual scholarship, the situation would appear to be simpler: text itself is easily stored in a file and, since the development and expansion of **Unicode**,[13] even quite esoteric characters can be written and read according to an accepted standard that, for the most part, is well supported. For more complex information, the Text Encoding Initiative (TEI)[14] has been working since the late 1980s to develop standard structures for describing formatting, layout, document structure, textual criticism, and so on. Whilst some details may be underspecified, and others perhaps overdone, the representational aspects of TEI have largely removed the need for other interchange formats in textual scholarship. The Music Encoding Initiative (MEI)[15] is an attempt to provide an analogue in music that is compatible with TEI and capable of being embedded within a TEI document, so that text and music can be combined in a single file. Begun in 2000, it now has support for mensural and plainchant notations, and is also being developed for the preparation of digital critical editions, including the *Carl-Maria-von-Weber-Gesamtausgabe*.[16]

Here, then, are two forces pulling in different directions: on the one hand, standards, defined and supported by others, are usually to be preferred to locally created ones, whilst on the other hand, it is difficult to predict the sum of information an edition will transcribe and so it is not obvious how to select an encoding format in advance of an edition's completion.[17] What is of primary importance for the Tinctoris edition, as for all editions, is that the encoding format must be complete enough to satisfy our

---

[11] This problem has been approached from a slightly different angle with an attempt to define a Dublin Core for music in Theodor Dumitrescu, Johannes Kepper, Andreas Kornstädt, Daniel Röwenstruck, Perry Roland, Craig Sapp, and Eleanor Selfridge-Field, 'The Dagstuhl Core', in *Knowledge Representation for Intelligent Music Processing*, ed. Eleanor Selfridge-Field, Frans Wiering, and Geraint Wiggins (Dagstuhl, 2009), <http://drops.dagstuhl.de/opus/volltexte/2009/1971>.

[12] Michael Good, 'MusicXML for Notation and Analysis', in *The Virtual Score: Representation, Retrieval, Restoration*, ed. Walter B. Hewlett and Eleanor Selfridge-Field (Cambridge, MA, 2001), 113-24.

[13] **Unicode** and **Unicode Transformation Formats (UTF)** provide a consistent, standardized way to store, communicate, and handle information about (primarily) textual characters. Restrictions to the memory allocation for each character of previous methods tended to mean that language regions used different ways of encoding text to make the necessary alphabetical or accented characters available. Unicode defines a large character set (including some musical symbols) and several ways of encoding it.

[14] See <http://www.tei-c.org>. An example of how TEI can be used to generate a clear and helpful edition of a music treatise can be seen in [Anon.], *Omni desideranti notitiam*, ed. Karen Desmond, <http://www.arsmusicae.org>.

[15] For an overview, see Andrew Hankinson, Perry Roland, and Ichiro Fujinaga, 'The Music Encoding Initiative as a Document-Encoding Framework', in *Proceedings of the Conference of the International Society for Music Information Retrieval* (Miami, 2011), 293-98.

[16] See <http://www.weber-gesamtausgabe.de>.

[17] It is for similar reasons that Dumitrescu prefers not to commit to MEI himself (Dumitrescu, 'The Material Digital', 144 n. 32).

editors. Only some aspects of this information can currently be translated into any existing single format, although most of it can be accommodated by combining several.[18] Ultimately, we plan to provide the content of the edition in TEI/MEI—which has the advantage of handling all the types of information we use—and the XML format of the Computerized Mensural Music Editing project (CMME)—which has been successfully used in previous editions.[19] We expect that these formats will need to be extended to support our needs; we will not wait, however, for such extensions to materialize, and we are developing our tools to be independent of these formats. Our approach to this will be described in more detail in section III below.

Sustainability

An undertaking that is based on technology must always be considered fragile in the long term: too much can change too quickly for the sustainability of the resources involved to be taken for granted. The increasing awareness of these challenges is reflected in the appearance of several infrastructure projects for supporting the sustainability, or future viability, of software resources.[20] From a technical perspective, the sustainability of software is usually seen as a combination of writing clear, well-documented **source code**,[21] supporting open, published technical standards and, ideally, distributing all materials publicly and under a **license**[22] that permits others to use, extend, and fix it.

Although important, this explicitly collaborative model—which is fundamental to much computer science research—is no panacea for digital humanities projects. The reasoning behind it is that, even if the original developer is no longer available for maintenance tasks, someone else will be, and that it is best if the task for that person is made as simple and clear as possible. In the general case, that developer might be a programmer hired for the purpose or a local computing student, but in the **open-source**

---

[18] An important potential 'glue' for relating the various types of information and encodings is the Resource Description Framework (RDF), which offers the possibility of a much less constrained way of providing information. Developing existing RDF models for use in the Tinctoris edition is well beyond the scope of the current project, but this is an avenue that will repay further exploration.

[19] See <http://www.cmme.org>.

[20] Relevant here are the Software Sustainability Institute (<http://www.software.ac.uk>), at the Universities of Edinburgh, Manchester, and Southampton; also *Sound Software: Sustainable software for Audio and Music Research* (<http://www.soundsoftware.ac.uk>) at Queen Mary's, University of London; and the *Integra Live* project at Birmingham Conservatoire, Birmingham City University (<http://www.integralive.org>).

[21] **Source code** is (usually) textual instructions, written in one or more programming languages, for executing a set of operations. Whilst most commercial computer applications are distributed in the form of compiled machine-specific code, this renders them difficult or impossible to modify usefully, whereas source code should be no harder for others to edit than for the original programmer.

[22] In printed volumes, it is usually sufficient for the author to assert ownership of the contents to bring into play well-established copyright legislation that provides legal protection from unauthorized reuse of their work. The same is true for software, but additional agreements may be demanded by the vendors, most commonly through an End-User Licence Agreements (EULA), which adds restrictions—the legal enforceability of which is often dependent on the presiding court. Conversely— and this is far more common in software than it is in physical publishing—the copyright owner can issue a licence that grants additional rights to the user, allowing them to modify and redistribute the work; such a work is usually termed 'free'. A more extreme form of licence, called a 'copyleft' licence, allowing modification and redistribution, but requiring all subsequent copies to be issued under the same licence conditions, which ensures that software released as free software remains so. There is some debate as to whether software issued with a non-copyleft license can be free.

model, the field is made open to anyone with both interest and time.[23] Highly successful software such as the Firefox web browser shows the power that the open-source model holds, but many such projects have significant corporate backing. Furthermore, the bulk of online communities that give substantially of their time for the development of open-source software have a limited range of interests.

The humanities in general, and musicology in particular, remain the object of highly specialized skills and limited outside interest, which reduces the likelihood of large online communities of programmers supporting our undertakings, whilst few academic music departments have ready access to computing expertise to provide internal support. Although this problem can be reduced by relying where possible on tools that do have large communities—for example by writing web-based software to take advantage of the huge communities around web browsers—it remains a serious concern.[24] Without technological contributors as well as musicological ones, the risk of software stagnation cannot be entirely avoided.[25] How we hope to attract such contributors for our Tinctoris project will be considered in section III below.

Thus far, modern digital editions have been described as similar to traditional web database projects. In such projects, a database is created and dedicated software developed to allow users to search and view aspects of the information. The most obvious examples of that approach might be journal archives such as JSTOR (<www.jstor.org>) or Oxford Journals (<www.oxfordjournals.org>), but more focused, project-based databases have been extremely common.[26] Such an approach presents, whether deliberately or not, a barrier between users and the information itself. This barrier causes no difficulty for as long as the web site and its servers work, or the relevant software is still supported, but when anything fails, there is an absolute need for on-site maintenance, which in turn demands ongoing recurrent cost and long-term commitment.

The alternative—to provide the data itself as well as applications designed to use it, rather than the applications acting as the sole point of access for the data—has been successfully applied by the Centre for Computer Assisted Research in the Humanities (CCARH: <www.ccarh.org>) and, of more direct relevance to Tinctoris, the CMME project (<www.cmme.org>). Writing software to read a music-encoding format is often easier than modifying complicated unmaintained software, especially if the format is well documented, and it may be the only option if the original applications are no longer available or were never released as source code. By providing our edition in several established and developing formats, and by releasing all the source code for our software tools, we hope to secure a degree of sustainability that would be impossible unless we

---

[23] **Open-source** software is distributed as source code (see n. 21), allowing others to see the programs and contribute to them. Open-source software is commonly distributed under some form of free licence (see n. 22) to make community development easier; this combination, free and open-source software, is commonly abbreviated to 'FOSS'.

[24] For sustainability, another important advantage of relying on web browsers is that their developers tend to work hard to support all older web pages; and so, for example, <http://www.archive.org/web/web.php> can present versions of sites from seventeen years' worth of archive and expect the modern browser to display them correctly.

[25] For example, with touch-screen devices rapidly becoming the dominant way in which users interact with online resources—including humanities archives (David Nicholas, David Clark, and Ian Rowlands, *Europeana. Culture on the Go* [Newbury, 2011], <http://www.e2.ma/click/vwkf/j7w2wb/fsqsf> [accessed 30 May, 2012])—resources written for desktop computers with keyboard and mouse, although unlikely to fail completely on these devices, may become awkward to interact with, and some functionality may even be totally inaccessible.

[26] See, for instance, the *Monastic Archives* database hosted by University College London (<http://www.ucl.ac.uk/history/research_projects/monasticarchives/> accessed 30 May 2012) for a typical example of a web-based user interface with a database on the server providing the information.

were to commit to providing software support for the full period for which we expect the edition to be useful; this is clearly impractical.

III. Types of User: Usability and Accessibility

People will be involved with the electronic material of the edition in two ways—as contributors and as consumers—although these two roles are by no means mutually exclusive. Contributions themselves also come in two forms: editions, in our case exclusively provided by project staff; and commentary, for which we intend to accept wider input.

An aspect of our Tinctoris edition that was not foreseen in the original description is our decision to elicit input from on-line communities, to help us develop tools that are genuinely of benefit to them and that can form a basis for further evolutionary stages after the current project is completed. Through an open, collaborative attitude towards code sharing and an appropriate policy on intellectual property, we hope to encourage a community of users and contributors that together can ensure sustainability in the long term.

Contributors: Creating an Edition

Initial plans for the technical side of the Tinctoris edition focussed on developing a graphical application for producing high-quality music examples. We initially chose to extend Gsharp, a relatively basic open-source score editor for Macintosh and Linux,[27] to accommodate the range of notational vocabulary used by Tinctoris. The early developers of Gsharp, Robert Strandh and Christophe Rhodes, have both been very supportive of the project, and the decision to proceed was based partly on the latter's experimental addition of Solesmes-style plainchant notation to the software. The user interface of Gsharp at the time had a minimalist feel, and for almost all tasks the editor was expected to employ combinations of keystrokes, based on those of Emacs, a powerful text editor developed in the 1970s and used primarily by programmers.[28] The use of these keystrokes gave a certain subset of users instantly recognizable access to a large number of commands, and also copied the **recordable keyboard macros**[29] that give Emacs its name, which allow complex, repetitive tasks to be rendered quick and easy. For the vast

---

[27] Gsharp is, in principle, platform-independent, but a variety of the tools on which it relies perform inconsistently under Microsoft Windows, and so enabling it to run under Windows would require more developer time than we have available. Should the tools, which are all free and open-source, be improved by others to support Microsoft operating systems, then Gsharp will automatically follow.

[28] See Christophe Rhodes and Robert Strandh, 'Gsharp, un éditeur de partitions de musique interactif et personnalisable', in *Document Numérique* 11 (2008), 9-28.

[29] A **keyboard macro** is a sequence of key presses that is stored in a program and may be recalled for subsequent reuse; a **recordable keyboard macro** stores these commands based on an example given by the user. To illustrate the use of this in a music editor, consider a sequence of alternating note values, say semibreve-minim-semibreve-minim, running to many dozens of notes. In a conventional editor, this might require the user typing the piece in to use a duration setting command at every note, slowing the process down significantly. In Gsharp, the notes can be entered in a uniform duration and then the act of moving one step forward and then halving the next note's duration can be recorded and then, on command, repeated any number of times.

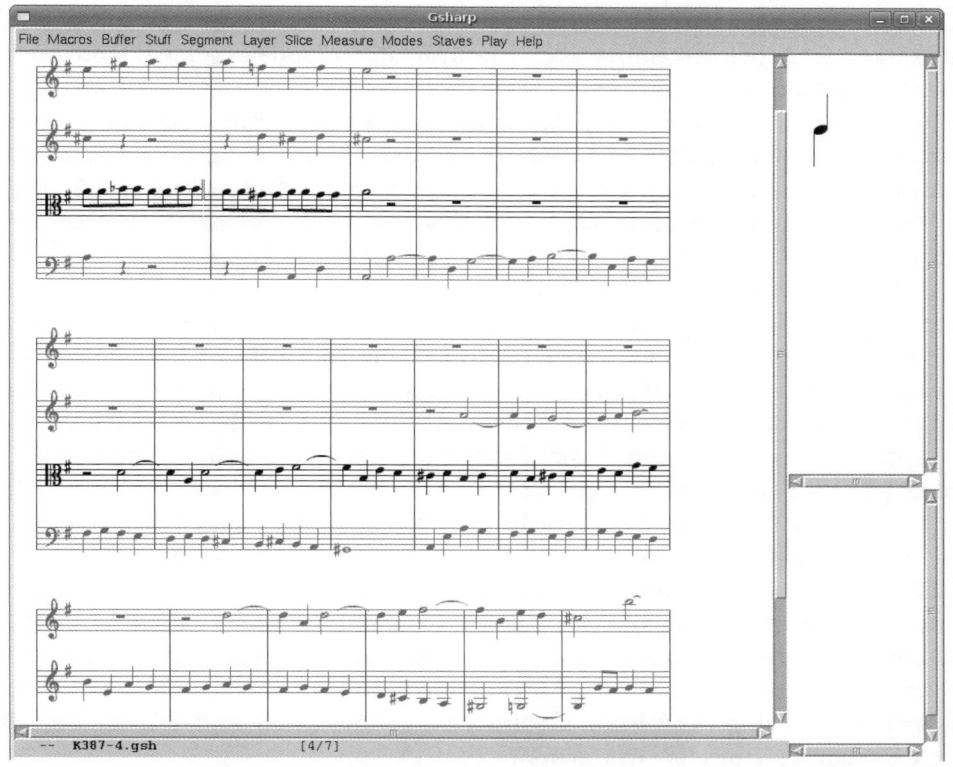

Figure 3. Screenshot of Gsharp's editing screen from before the start of development for the Tinctoris edition

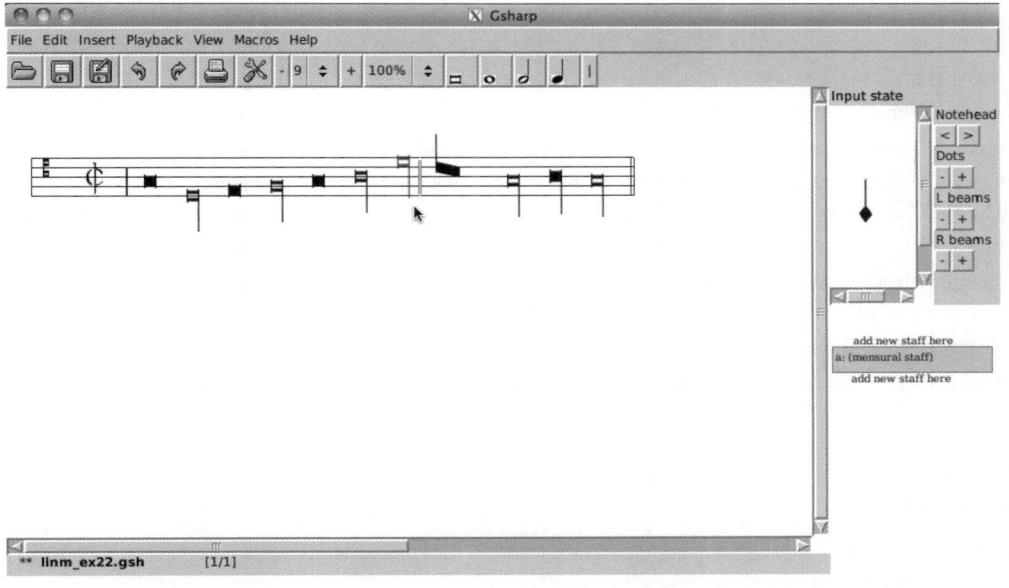

Figure 4. Screenshot of Gsharp's editing screen while a music example from Tinctoris's
Liber imperfectionum notarum musicalium is being entered

majority of musicologists who do not have Emacs experience, however, this powerful but esoteric mode of interaction was clearly unsuitable. Our development therefore had to strike a balance between supporting the necessary historical notations and adding more intuitive buttons, menus, and dialogues. Figures 3 and 4 give an illustration of how the software has developed from its original purpose within common-practice notation. Input of notes is still based on keying in a pitch name (something which can be problematic for unpitched examples), but other operations can now be carried out by either mouse or keyboard, depending on the preferences of the user.

Using a typesetting style modelled on the existing Woodley editions of *Liber imperfectionum notarum musicalium* and *Expositio manus*,[30] Gsharp supports mensural and, to a lesser extent, plainchant notations, with some degree of user-friendliness. Notes can be repositioned with the mouse to correct automatic placement, and ligature elements can be stretched or shrunk as desired. Gsharp can, with limitations, read and write files encoded in MEI and MusicXML file formats; it also has its own file format—a simple textual encoding of its internal data structure.

This software development actually preceded the launch of the Tinctoris project,[31] and so, although it was developed and tested by entering examples from existing editions, it had not been used in the actual process of edition preparation. Once we started transcribing new material, it quickly became apparent that a stand-alone music editor was not necessarily ideal as a user interface model: Tinctoris's use of music examples in his texts is often so frequent that any separation of the editing process into two distinct applications—having two pieces of software, one for editing text and the other for music—becomes a tiresome distraction.

A further problem lay in the development process. Once an editor has started work, the discovery of a feature unsupported by the current version of the editing software is a significant impediment. In most such situations, the editor must either continue, omitting the feature and returning to the examples once the software modifications have been made, or the process must halt while the programmer does his work. In a scenario where an expert editor's time is highly valued, especially in a project with a fixed end-date, finding an alternative to this may prove vital.

We made the decision to set Gsharp aside for the present purpose[32] and to consider a different approach. Jeffrey Dean, the first to start new editorial work on the project, devised his own way of typing in the verbal and the musical content of a treatise as a single, linear text, with speed and ease of entry prioritized. The programmer's task was to develop a tool that could display the edition so far—both verbal and musical text—as it was typed, skipping any unrecognized aspects of the input.[33] The tool takes the form of a web page with a text box on one side and a graphical display of the edition on the other

---

[30] Both editions are available at <http://www.earlymusictheory.org/tinctoris>, though they will ultimately be superseded by enhanced versions with a new interface. Archive copies of the original versions will remain at <http://www.earlymusictheory.org/tinctoris/archive/liber_imperfectionum/liber_imperfectionum.html> and <http://www.earlymusictheory.org/tinctoris/archive/expositio_manus/expositio_manus.html>.

[31] Funding of the development of Gsharp for the editing of early notations was provided by the Birmingham Conservatoire (2009-11).

[32] The intention to continue to use Gsharp for automated analysis and searching remains, and we do not rule out its use for typesetting more extended works.

[33] This last point is important for two reasons: firstly because as a text is typed, incomplete elements will appear to be errors until they are fully input; and secondly because this allows new codes to be invented as needed by the editor.

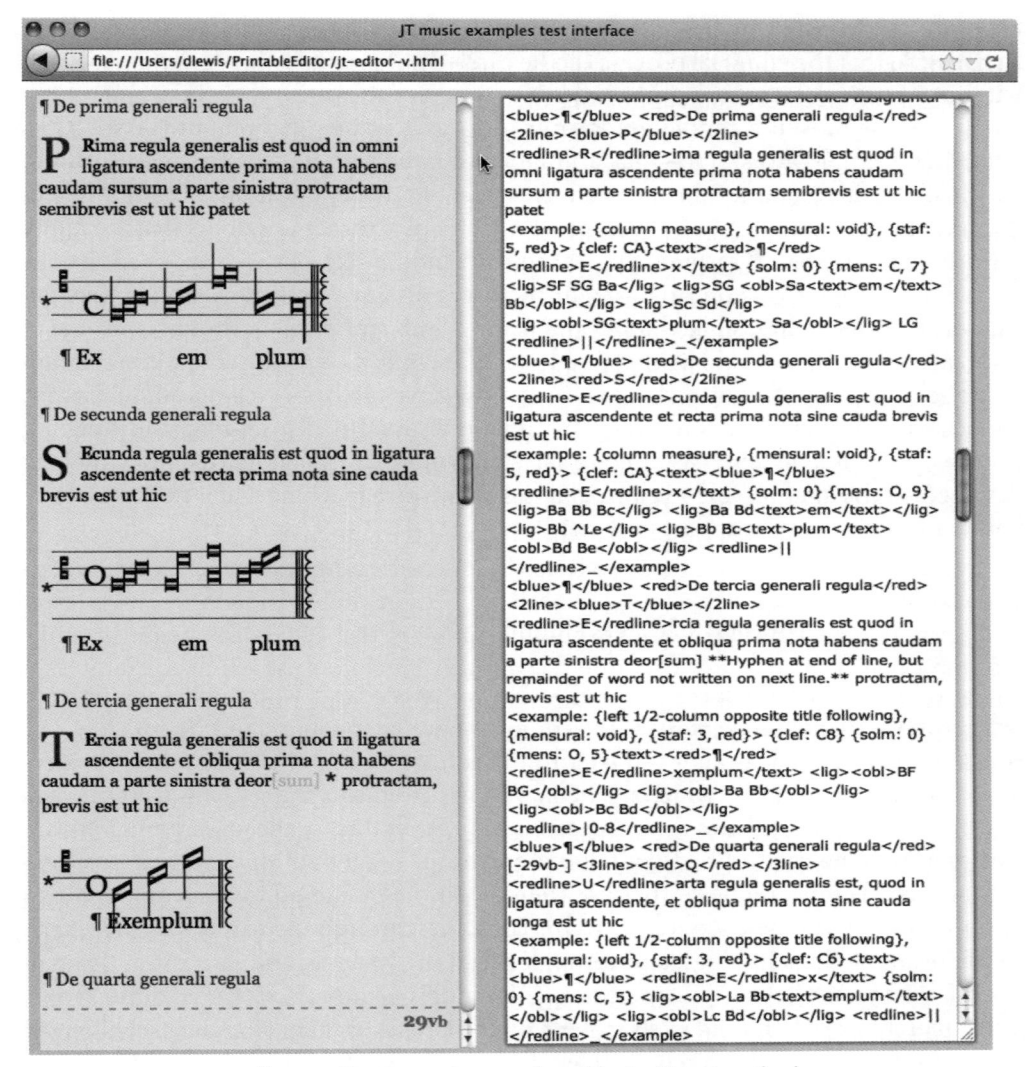

Figure 5. The current browser-based textual input method

(see Figure 5). It can interpret formatting descriptions, such as red text or large initials, as well as text-critical information.[34] (It should be emphasized that Figure 5 is not a representation of the end-result of the edition, but simply an in-house working interface.)

The input format that we use is to some extent both personalized and specialized—it is intended to permit fast entry of a particular sort of material by a particular scholar. It is also, by design, somewhat *ad hoc*. We will be making the tool available on our website and are happy to work with those who wish to try it, but we do not currently intend to develop a complete new format, nor is it our aim that others use the tool for textual input as we do. We chose this method so as not to constrain the editing process itself by the limitations of existing software or encoding formats. Our longer-term goal

---

[34] The internal representation for the software is actually slightly closer to the TEI/MEI data model, despite the less-structured textual form that acts as input.

is to provide the tool with graphical methods for entry, buttons, and menus (just as for Gsharp), so that the editorial process can be carried out primarily using the mouse, and without resorting to esoteric input codes.[35]

The use of web technologies for our tool—it is written entirely in HTML, CSS, and ECMAScript (Javascript)—has a number of important advantages over software which, like Gsharp, stands separate from browsers or other applications. Firstly, whereas the successful running of Gsharp relies on a series of libraries and tools that currently limits it to UNIX-based systems (i.e., Macintosh and Linux), our web application runs on the most recent version of all major browsers on any almost any device that can support a browser, and, since it uses only defined **web standards**,[36] should continue to do so even if further development were to stop. Secondly, since the actual distribution of the edition was always intended to be web-based, we can re-use a large amount of the application's display functionality in the final edition. Thirdly, sharing and tracking changes to documents amongst an editorial team is more easily handled using technology designed for the internet (the software can still be run on a machine that is not connected, but it also has network support built in).

Beyond Editing: Communities of Contributors

So far, three sorts of direct contributors—that is, contributors who themselves provide or alter the content and delivery of the edition—have been mentioned. The bulk of our consideration here has been given over to the editors, but there are also the providers of commentary material—which may come from the editors themselves or from users of the edition[37]—and, thirdly, there are technical contributors for the underlying software and its functionality. Indirect contributors, who provide opinions, corrections, bug reports, and feature requests that are then acted on by the editorial team, are also important; they can be encouraged technologically, through the use of issue trackers, commenting options in blogs, and through social networking, and in person, through workshops and conference presentations. This model of editorship is the traditional one, little different from that used by its paper counterparts. Although it has been challenged for more general, encyclopedic knowledge sources such as Wikipedia, the model dominates scholarship because of the guarantee of expertise and of the clear provenance that it can provide for any editorial decision.

The specialized nature of a resource, along with the skill and time required to build it, is usually taken as a reason against a **crowdsourcing** model.[38] For certain sorts of scholarly tasks, however, hybrid models are emerging that take advantage of this very

---

[35] Experience shows that textual codes permit users to enter information at far higher speeds than graphical interfaces can, but they do present usability barriers and can lose their advantages as their range and complexity of expression increases or as tasks become more graphical in nature.

[36] Because the World Wide Web connects devices with very different software and hardware, specifying standardized behaviours and protocols has been a central aspect of the web's development. **Web standards** embrace various programming languages, behaviours for communication, and data formats, coordinated by the World-Wide-Web Consortium (W3C: <http://www.w3.org>).

[37] See, for example, the support for user-contributed annotations in the Online Chopin Variorum Edition (OCVE: <http://www.ocve.org.uk>).

[38] **Crowdsourcing** is useful, though variously defined, term for the accumulation of information by the actions of large numbers of users rather than through contributors who are internal to an organsiaization or hired for the purpose.

specialism. The focussed nature of certain resources can mean that the audience itself will also be suitably expert, and this distributed expertise has several consequences: firstly, material supplied is likely to be reasonably authoritative; secondly, the probability of a user correctly identifying an error is high; and thirdly, the focus of the research community itself can potentially be reflected in the resource.

One approach to harnessing this free labour is taken by the Electronic Corpus of Lute Music (ECOLM: <www.ecolm.org>) for its most recent digitization effort. Here, automated Optical Character Recognition[39] software is used to generate transcriptions of images from the British Library's collection of lute tablature and vocal prints.[40] These editions are generated quickly but with errors, the correction of which, since the pieces number in the thousands, is beyond the capability of a small editorial team. A web-based editor was devised to allow users to register and, correcting small chunks of tablature at a time, to help in the transcription process.[41] The corrected transcriptions will then be viewed by a panel for final editing and incorporation into the corpus.

The ECOLM approach limits the involvement of the user community to a preparation phase, and they do not subsequently have any means of direct contribution to the corpus.[42] A more complete model has been used for the Duke Databank of Documentary Papyri (DDbDP: <www.papyrus.info>). This website allows registered users—unlike ECOLM's registration, DDbDP's registration is automated and not checked by the editorial team—to make transcriptions or provide corrections for any material in the database. The editorial team sees all proposed emendations before they are confirmed or rejected, and summaries of updates are generated regularly.

For the current Tinctoris edition, we could not consider direct contributions of this sort for several reasons: firstly, it would require open online access to all facsimiles of relevant sources, something not currently available; secondly, there is a lack of currently available tools for online entry of mixed music and text, something that we hope to remedy, but only as we prepare the edition;[43] thirdly, it is hard to predict the extent and rate of such crowdsourcing, and this is not compatible with the need to complete our edition in a fixed time; and, finally, the time required for verifying contributions could easily become too great. We do intend, however, to explore ways of incorporating user-contributed annotations and commentary, allowing the edition to act as a research hub; the Early Music Theory website itself is intended eventually to expand beyond the Tinctoris project, to encompass other relevant scholarly contributions from beyond the project team.

---

[39] Christoph Dalitz and Thomas Karsten, 'Using the Gamera Framework for Building a Lute Tablature Recognition System', in *6th International Conference on Music Information Retrieval*, ed. Joshua D. Reiss and Geraint A. Wiggins (London, 2005), 478-81.

[40] *Early Music Online* (<http://www.earlymusiconline.org>).

[41] A similar, but less-specialized project, transcribing the manuscripts of Jeremy Bentham, the founder of UCL, provides a dual-pane view with the user typing TEI-encoded text into one pane, whilst viewing a manuscript image in the other. It is described in Martin Moyle, Justin Tonra, and Valerie Wallace, 'Manuscript Transcription by Crowdsourcing: Transcribe Bentham', in *Liber Quarterly* 20 (2011), 347-56 (<http://liber.library.uu.nl/index.php/lq/article/view/7999>); at the time of writing, over three thousand manuscripts have been transcribed through the site.

[42] Certain registered users can contribute directly to the information about the pieces, such as titles, links between works, and so on, but contributions to the musical content of the corpus are more restricted.

[43] Clearly, were we to adapt our current strategy and allow contributors to devise extensions to a textual input format as they typed, maintaining consistency and coherence would become a significant challenge.

The largest contribution to our edition from the external community will, we hope, be through indirect methods: alerting us to errors or providing extra material or feedback through our website or blog, by Twitter (@earlymustheory) or by personal contact. If there are enough users who are interested in the project and its outcomes, we expect this to be a valuable source of additional expertise.

Consumers: Using the Edition

Although it looks like the more complicated task, building software for contributors is comparatively constrained and well defined when compared with catering for researchers as consumers of the edition. In a given editorial undertaking, it is possible to specify the workflow, to develop tools with the editors, and to cater for the finite range of tasks that they are expected to carry out. But what are the tasks being carried out by those who consult an edition of Tinctoris? What kinds of editorial decision will they anticipate having been made? Will they want to read linearly or by topic? In what language will they consult the treatises? Will they require modern-notation transcriptions of the examples? Will they be interested in spelling or punctuation deviations between sources? What might motivate a user to consult a diplomatic transcription of a manuscript the facsimile of which is also available online? In what ways might they wish to search a complete corpus of treatises?

The shortest answer to these questions is that we don't know. Through discussions online[44] and at conferences, along with consultations with the editors of similar works,[45] we hope to develop our understanding of the nature and needs of interested parties and communities. We start, however, from two fundamental assumptions: firstly, that the needs of users will change and their demands become greater and more sophisticated as the resource itself grows and develops; and secondly, that all parts of the user's interaction with the edition should be flexible and adaptable to suit the specifics of their particular task.

It was with this in mind that we started work on our preliminary designs for the edition website. One reason for carefully considering different users and presentation styles is the limitation of what can be shown on a computer screen. Although scholars have different methods of visually inspecting information, using an entire desk to compare different texts is common, and the amount of space used by a scholar laying out paper photocopies greatly exceeds the resources available on a computer. A normal print edition, when opened, is usually slightly smaller than a computer monitor, and editors can struggle even in print to make the layout of complex information intelligible. These constraints become even greater when we consider that the monitor is read from a much larger distance than a book, and so needs to use larger font sizes.[46] This limitation makes the flexibility of the layout and the ability of the user to choose how to display the edition even more important. In the simple case of a user reading through a text

---

[44] See http://earlymusictheory.org/blog/ and Twitter @earlymustheory.

[45] Most important amongst these are the *Thesaurus Musicarum Italicarum* (TMI: <euromusicology.cs.uu.nl>) and *Thesaurus Musicarum Latinarum* (TML: <http://www.chmtl.indiana.edu/tml/start.html>).

[46] A growing consideration must also be given to users of smart phones and tablets, which may have very high resolutions, but are, especially in the case of phones, too small to show many different aspects of an edition at once.

from start to finish with no interest in commentaries, apparatus, and so on, it seems desirable to present her or him with as close to a full-screen display as is practical. Activities that are more complicated may require compound pane layouts, but often a user will wish to switch between layouts or focus on a single pane, hiding some or all of the others; our new edition will therefore endeavour to cater for the most likely permutations of presentation that we can envisage.

One might expect that tools for the elegant handling of a critical apparatus would have been developed in Text Encoding Initiative projects long ago, but, beyond a crude level, this has not proved to be the case: few TEI projects have developed easily usable, general-purpose applications for text encoding, a problem that is generally acknowledged and which MEI is actively attempting to avoid. For our project, then, we must create our own tools for this task.

Computers as Users

There is another type of user that is a significant consumer of online information—the computer itself. Computers index sites for generic search engines, or harvest published data for re-imagining or re-analysis ('mash-ups'). They can also be used for the automation of more traditional music analysis tasks (presumably this was what Babbitt meant when he spoke of tasks that were 'sub-statistical').[47] Early music has led the development of such tasks since the sixties, and continues to do so today.

At this point, decisions about the granularity of the information available in the edition (discussed in section II above) become important. The more information recorded in a form that is accessible to computers for searching, counting, and analysing, the more potential there is for detailed investigation and unanticipated uses. Transcribing details of textual abbreviations, ornaments, and initials, for example, can allow the large-scale analysis of scribal practices, and providing musical examples in a structured way rather than as simple images permits the computer-supported exploration of the relationship between the music of the treatises and the repertoire of the time, by using Music Information Retrieval tools on this and other encoded collections.

Thus far, the discussion has focused on verbal text and musical illustrations. There are, of course, other forms of information that are essential components of an edition of a music treatise: most importantly the many figures that neither employ musical notation nor are purely textual—either because they have a graphical component or because information is conveyed by the layout of the text itself. Diagrams present several options to editors: they may wish to reproduce the item in facsimile (Figure 6a), or to use more modern image-drawing or photographic technologies (e.g., Figure 6b) to produce a rendition that can sometimes illustrate, in a purely visual sense, the points more clearly than even the original.

---

[47] Milton Babbitt, 'The Use of Computers in Musicological Research', in *Perspectives of New Music* 3/2 (1965), 74-83 at 74.

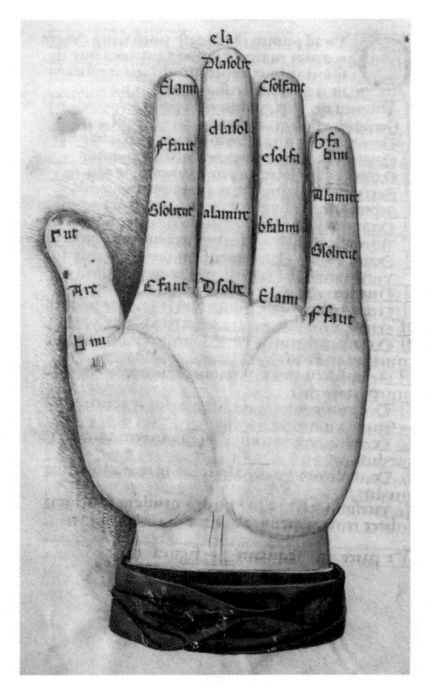

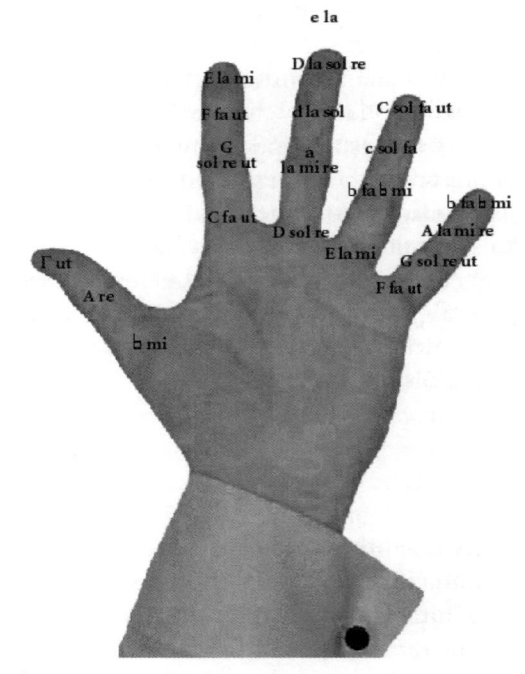

a. Facsimile image from Bologna,
Biblioteca Universitaria,
Ms. 2573, fol. 4v. Reproduced by permission

b. Image assembled using a graphics editor

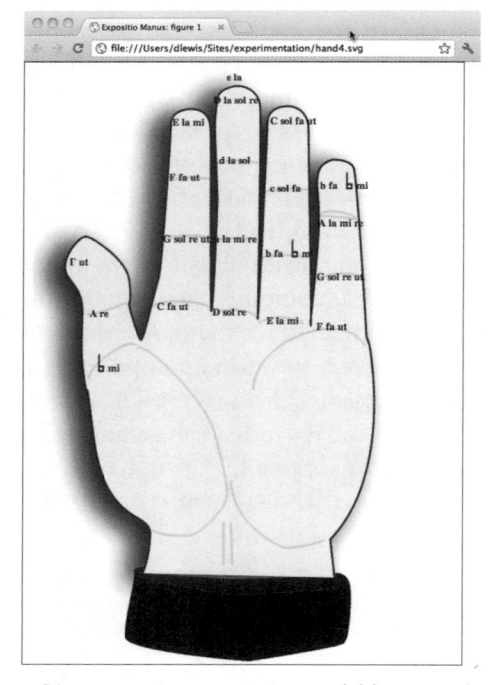

c. Diagrammatic transcription available to search engines as structured data

d. Extract of the file containing the transcription shown in (c)

Figure 6. Three ways of reproducing the Guidonian hand of Tinctoris's *Expositio manus*

Neither of these particular options is helpful to a user that is a computer, since neither provides much if any directly searchable information. Whilst Figure 6b conveys the intended information very clearly to us, a search engine would struggle to recognize the hand, to identify the text, and to apprehend the significance of its position. If one is taking this second option of redrawing the figure, then one could store the information contained within it in some structured way. It can then be made available to human users as an image, but to machines in a more appropriate form. There are many ways to approach this, but the most direct is to use a searchable graphic format such SVG (see Figures 6c and 6d). SVG is an XML-based image format, which can be embedded in (X)HTML or TEI XML, and is fully indexed by search engines such as Google images.

There is generally less homogeneity amongst diagrams in music treatises and the quantities are much smaller than that of verbal and musical content, so it is unlikely that large-scale automated analyses will immediately reveal very much, but even the ability to locate, through a simple textual search, diagrams with related content—different forms of the Guidonian hand, for example—could be useful to researchers.

The potential for direct computer assistance to musicological enquiry remains under-explored, despite half a century of work in the area. One of the greatest factors limiting this development has been the comparative lack of coherent musical materials in a suitable digital form; where information has been available, interesting results can follow rapidly, something that makes the development of new corpora all the more pressing.[48]

IV. Discussion and Conclusions

My primary aim in this article has been to describe some of the considerations involved in planning and executing a digital music edition. It is vital to emphasize the central role played by the musicologist: not only is it important that all the responsibilities of an editor of a print edition are preserved, but the additional opportunities provided by a digital edition entail extra decisions that must also be musicologically, not technologically, motivated.

If the editors are key to the process of devising an edition, then in the more dynamic world of digital editing, a community of users is central to its development and exploration. Dumitrescu, for example, writes of the 'responsibility' of the musicians who use digital editions, showing how with greater power to shape an edition to their needs, users gain an enhanced relationship with the materials, participating in what he calls a 'communal act'.[49] Beyond this, we have seen how the role of users in such an act becomes even more crucial where issues of an edition's long-term sustainability are concerned.

---

[48] See, for example, the work of musicologist Frauke Jürgensen and computer scientist Ian Knopke, which has ranged from the automatic recognition of compositional clichés in Palestrina to an investigation of double-leading-note cadences in the Buxheim organ book: Ian Knopke and Frauke Jürgensen, 'A System for Identifying Common Melodic Phrases in the Masses of Palestrina', in *Journal of New Music Research* 38 (2009), 171-81; and Frauke Jürgensen and Ian Knopke, 'A Comparison of Automated Methods for the Analysis of Style in Fifteenth-Century Song Intabulations', in *Musicae Scientiae* 10 (2006), 139-60.

[49] Dumitrescu, 'The Material Digital', 144-46.

The responsibility of the programmer in all this—to return to the theme with which we began—is the provision of access: editors must have accessible, intuitive tools, and they must also be given access to technological and user-interface options of which they may not yet be aware. Thus, whilst musicological considerations remain central for the digital edition, the design process works most effectively as a collaborative venture.[50] For the users, the programmer provides tools that respond to their needs and that support and encourage the creation of a community that can, through its engagement with the edition, secure it a successful future.

Abstract

A project to create a new complete digital edition of Tinctoris's theoretical works, funded by the UK Arts and Humanities Research Council, represents one of the most technically ambitious music theory editing projects of recent years. Multiple views of each treatise will be available, including translations and commentary, through an interactive webpage, printable documents and through open, standardized, machine-accessible formats. This article describes some of the considerations involved in planning and executing such a digital music edition, emphasizing the need to place musicologists at the centre of each step of this process. Whilst this is predominantly the role of the editors of the project, the wider community of scholars has an essential part to play, and one that is facilitated by Web technologies. To maximize the access to, and use of, the edition, technical and visual design decisions must be based on a sound understanding of the various roles users will take and the rich nature of the information sources being edited. Only through this fundamentally musicological approach to the technology can a sustainable resource be created.

---

[50] The research aspect of this role is often underestimated in digital humanities, an issue explored in John Bradley, 'No Job for Techies: Technical Contributions to Research in the Digital Humanities', paper delivered at the *Digital Humanities Conference*, College Park, Maryland, 22-25 June 2009, a 'draft version' of this paper is available at <http://staff.cch.kcl.ac.uk/~jbradley/docs/techies-maryland.pdf> (accessed 30 May 2012).

Contributors to this Issue

■

Jeffrey J. Dean is a Senior Researcher at Birmingham Conservatoire in England, employed on the UK Arts and Humanities Research Council-funded project 'The Complete Theoretical Works of Johannes Tinctoris: A New Digital Edition'. He is also a Distinguished Visiting Scholar at the University of Manchester and Executive Officer of the Royal Musical Association. He has worked since 1989 chiefly as a free-lance editor, book designer, and typesetter of academic books in the humanities; during the 1990s he was a Senior In-House Editor of the *New Grove Dictionary of Music and Musicians*.

David Lewis trained as a historical musicologist at King's College, London. He has since specialized in developing computer tools for musicologists or musicians. He is currently based at the Birmingham Conservatoire, where he is developing the technical infrastructure for a new complete edition and translation of the theoretical works of Johannes Tinctoris, and at the Department of Computing at Goldsmiths', University of London, where he works on an electronic corpus of lute music (www.ecolm.org), teaches, and is currently completing his doctorate.

Evan A. MacCarthy is the 2012-13 CRIA (Committee to Rescue Italian Art) Fellow at Villa I Tatti, the Harvard University Center for Italian Renaissance Studies. He studied Classics at the College of the Holy Cross and historical musicology at Harvard University (Ph.D., 2010) with a dissertation on music and intellectual life in fifteenth-century Ferrara. He has published and presented on Ugolino of Orvieto and Johannes Tinctoris as well as on late medieval chant and liturgy. Together with Edward Roesner and Greta-Mary Hair, he edited the seventh and final volume of *Le Magnus liber organi de Notre-Dame de Paris* (2009). He has served on the faculties of Harvard, MIT, and Boston University.

Bernhold Schmid studied musicology at the University of Munich, submitting his dissertation there in 1985 on the Gloria trope *Spiritus et alme* (published in 1988). Since 1985 he has been a researcher affiliated with the Music-Historical Commission of the Bavarian Academy of Sciences. Since 1996 he has worked on the edition of the collected works of Orlando di Lasso. He has published on music of the middle ages, the Renaissance, and the early twentieth century.

Ronald Woodley is Research Professor of Music at Birmingham Conservatoire, Birmingham City University, having previously held posts at the Royal Northern College of Music, the universities of Lancaster, Newcastle, Liverpool, and at Christ Church, Oxford. His research specializes in late-medieval music theory, as well as performance studies in the nineteenth and twentieth centuries. He is also active professionally as a clarinettist and chamber pianist.